PRAISE FOR *FUTUREFACE*

"Smart, searching . . . [Alex Wagner's] stinging criticism of the 'flossy statistics' set out in ancestry composition results is some of the best I've seen on the subject. . . . It's the concreteness of Wagner's own search, in all its messy detail and lingering uncertainties, that underscores our interconnectedness. . . . Meditating on our ancestors, as Wagner's own story shows, can suggest better ways of being ourselves."
—Maud Newton, *The New York Times Book Review*

"A thoughtful, beautiful meditation on what makes us who we are—the search for harmony between our own individual identities and the values and ideals that bind us together as Americans."
—Barack Obama

"A rich and revealing memoir . . . *Futureface* raises urgent questions having to do with history and complicity."
—*The New York Times*

"Motivated by basic questions of identity: who are my people, what makes me *me*, the author embarks on a long journey in search of family history and the certainty of belonging. . . . Along the way, she ponders the devastating racial history of America, the impact of colonialism on world history, and the jarring realization that her forebears may not have been benign. . . . Sincere and instructive, . . . this timely reflection on American identity, with a bonus exposé of DNA ancestry testing, deserves a wide audience."
—*Library Journal*

"A cultural commentator turns her acute observational skills and journalistic skills to the mystery of her own heritage. When Wagner started pulling the threads of history between her Burmese mother and her American father, it didn't take long for the perceptive journalist to see that things could get messy. Her thinking about American identity harkens back to a 1993 *Time* cover story that heralded a multicultural woman as 'The New Face of America,' which explained 'how immigrants are shaping the world's first multicultural society'—hence her concept of 'Futureface.' The narrative is part Mary Roach–style, participation-heavy research, part family history, and part exploration of existential loneliness. . . . Regardless of whether Wagner solved her mystery, the journey is worth taking; it serves as a welcome reminder that tribalism and xenophobia are dangerous but ultimately futile threats. As the author writes, the search for ancestry is 'a reminder that ultimately, we are all in this together—still.' . . . A timely investigation."

—*Kirkus Reviews*

"Alex Wagner is brilliant and hilarious. *Futureface* is a magic trick: She starts with the humble story of a third-culture kid's existential loneliness and ends with a smart, timely, and moving exploration of family lies, exile and immigration, genetics, and the mystery of human belonging."

—Eddie Huang, bestselling author of *Fresh Off the Boat* and *Double Cup Love*

"*Futureface* is an important contribution to the American conversation—Alex Wagner's story is insightful, moving, informative, and searing. I have deeply admired Alex for a long time as an original thinker, keenly observant journalist, and funny, empathetic human being. Read this book and you'll understand why."

—Wes Moore, bestselling author of *The Other Wes Moore* and *The Work*

FUTUREFACE

A Family Mystery, an Epic Quest,

and the Secret to Belonging

Alex Wagner

ONE WORLD

NEW YORK

2018 One World Trade Paperback Edition

Published in the United States by One World, an imprint of Random House, a division of Penguin Random House LLC, New York.

ONE WORLD and colophon are registered trademarks of Penguin Random House LLC.

Originally published in hardcover in the United States by One World, an imprint of Random House, a division of Penguin Random House LLC, in 2018.

Library of Congress Cataloging-in-Publication Data
Names: Wagner, Alex, author.
Title: Futureface: a family mystery, an epic quest, and the secret to belonging / by Alex Wagner.
Description: | New York, NY: One World, [2017]
Identifiers: LCCN 2017038006 | ISBN 9780812987508 (trade paperback) | ISBN 9780812997958 (ebook)
Subjects: LCSH: Wagner, Alex. | Journalists—United States—Biography. | Women journalists—United States—Biography. | Burmese Americans—Biography. | Wagner, Alex—Family. | Wagner, Alex—Travel. | Identity (Psychology) | Belonging (Social psychology)
Classification: LCC PN4874.W254 A3 2017 | DDC 070.92 [B]—dc23
LC record available at https://lccn.loc.gov/2017038006

Printed in the United States of America on acid-free paper

oneworldlit.com
randomhousebooks.com

987654321

Book design by Caroline Cunningham

For Cy, of course

He is part of an assembling crowd, anonymous thousands off the buses and trains, people in narrow columns tramping over the swing bridge above the river, and even if they are not a migration or a revolution, some vast shaking of the soul, they bring with them the body heat of a great city and their own small reveries and desperations, the unseen something that haunts the day.

—Don DeLillo, *Underworld*

INTRODUCTION

———*//*———

There is a line between Us and Them, and I've seen it. Or at least part of it. Along the Arizona-Mexico border—in the American town of Nogales and the county of Santa Cruz—is a cloud-scraping thirty-foot fence made of vertical steel rods lodged in concrete. In theory, border fences like this are built to keep citizens from both countries on their respective sides of the border. In truth, the fence, erected by Americans, is intended to keep Mexicans in Mexico. And to keep America... American. Safe from invasion and confusion, strong in its defenses, discerning in its welcome.

It's only mildly effective.

Back when I visited the border, I was the anchor of a cable news show, and the border had become a fairly obsessive focus of mine. I wasn't alone. The border had become an obsession for a lot of people, not least the men and women assigned to police it, the American border patrol. Our country was spending billions of dollars guarding that border with agents, drones, cameras, and exotic military hardware. The fence was only the most visible sign of our extravagant vigilance—and I went to Nogales to see it up close.

We took a break from shooting to eat lunch, and I noticed that the border patrol had stationed a sentry further down along the barrier. We, meanwhile, had cameras with us, lights, makeup artists—a whole crew. But neither law enforcement nor the media presence did anything to stop a pair of fruit sellers on the Mexican side of the wall from lassoing a rope to the top of a border fence post, climbing up, and rappelling down to the American side of the border. All in broad daylight, in under five minutes. Those two fruit sellers made a mockery of that wall—and it was mesmerizing. Here was an act of alchemy: The two of them, in an instant, transformed themselves from Mexicans—in the land of their ancestors, feet planted on a patch of earth to which they unquestionably belonged—to intruders.

All of a sudden, they were part of a different story, one that they would in some way change, if only by adding to its supply of readily available and delicious fruit. And they weren't just crossing a visible wall marking an invisible border. They were crossing a line inside themselves: between the native and the immigrant, the one who belonged and the uninvited stranger. They had become something new. That sprint over the wall was, in microcosm, the adventure story that has defined and threatened human existence from the beginning—a movement from one land to another. But was it flight or invasion or just an act of survival? Those fruit sellers hit the ground, composed themselves in a blink, and embarked, with quick steps, on the day's business. And nobody said a word.

Stories like this—about immigrants, refugees, exiles, and

internal migrants—have always had a hold on me, perhaps because of my own family's history of migrations, escapes, settlement, assimilation, and, um, amnesia. But these are universal struggles, too, and they have reappeared again and again in my professional life: when I was the editor of a music magazine, the director of a global nonprofit, a political journalist. Usually, we understand them as human rights concerns or battles over resources like land or jobs or government assistance. But I, at least, also see them as complicated romances.

For a few months in 2013, I spent a not-insignificant amount of time researching Maricopa County, Arizona, intrigued by the twisted drama unfolding in a community of retirees; descendants of homesteaders; Latinos whose families had been there for centuries; Native Americans whose families had been there for millennia; and new immigrants who had only just crossed deserts or oceans of paperwork to get there from Mexico and Central America. In all of that longing and violence, possessiveness and anger—in the battles between these waves of immigrants and exiles, refugees and natives—what did it mean to belong? Just as crucially: Who got to decide? Each answer gave rise to new questions.

In reality, immigration isn't just outside versus inside, the lawful versus the illegal. It's a story about the messy, sad, terrifying, and occasionally beautiful experience of leaving one place and starting over in another. I realized that my interest in the subject wasn't simply about the politics, but in immigration as an interior act—becoming something new—and as the social act of losing one home and making another. Immigration raises into relief some of our most basic existential questions: Who am I? Where do I belong? And in that way, it's inextricably tied to an exploration of American identity. Here we are, in a nation of immigrants, exiles, captives, refugees, and displaced natives, staring together into that existential void.

These are the questions many of us either devote our lives to answering or spend our lives evading. They are questions I've asked myself—without much in the way of conclusion—when I thought about my Burmese mother and American father, when I thought about the country that pushed and pulled me, when I thought about friendship and loneliness and the possibility of having my own child and attempting to guide that child to some inextricable truth about Our People. All this contemplation made me identity hungry and identity fatigued—it made me want a simple answer, an easy story about who we are and why we're here together. I started to see my preoccupation with immigrants, exiles, and refugees—and the attendant concerns about home and identity and belonging—as the edge of a longer, more complex puzzle. Turns out, the mystery I was really trying to solve was my own.

PART I

———— // ————

SOLITAIRE

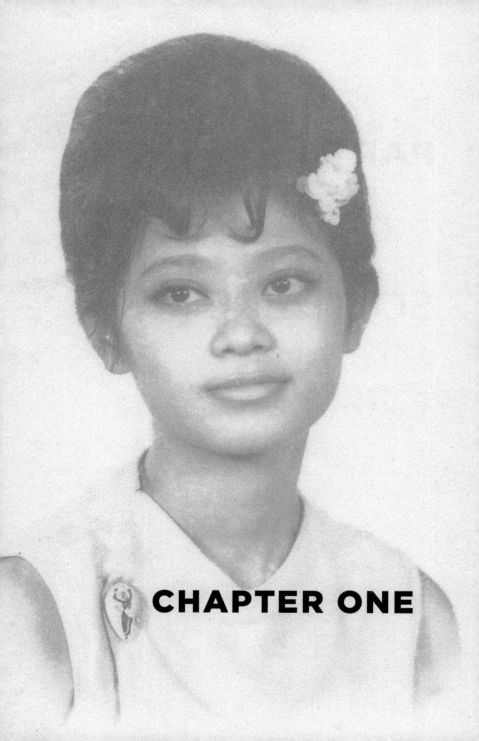

CHAPTER ONE

—— // ——

I played a lot of solitaire growing up. I was an only child and a nerd and thus alone a lot of the time, and when I wasn't, I was asked to mind my manners and keep quiet around the adults.* For most of my adolescence, I used a weathered pack of dark blue playing cards that had the logo of the International Brotherhood of Teamsters embossed in gold on the back: a pair of horse's heads atop a wagon wheel. Adults would see the horse head next to the Teamsters name and laugh in disbelief that a union with alleged mafia ties would have a horse's head anywhere near its logo. I hadn't yet seen *The Godfather*, and so I didn't understand the irony, but I often pretended I did. "I know!" I would say, laughing along without understanding. I was alone, on the outside of the joke, wishing (rather pathetically) to be on the inside—where everyone else was.

The Teamsters union was where my mother worked, at the tail end of the heyday of American labor organizing, circa 1971.

---

* Don't feel bad for me. I never had to fight for dessert!

She had immigrated to America from Rangoon, Burma,[*] in 1965, escaping a military dictatorship. From her initial landing pad in Washington, D.C., she went on to attend Swarthmore College, became enamored of leftist politics, and moved to Philadelphia after graduation to live in a commune with her French boyfriend and print up copies of what she described as a "socialist daily."

The French boyfriend fell out of favor, and my mother moved back to Washington, D.C., where she found a job at the Teamsters union. That led to an interview for a job at the Alliance for Labor Action. The man who interviewed her there was my father, and from the moment they met, she couldn't stand him. Perhaps that should have been a warning, but instead it became their meet-cute: They hated each other! And then they got married.

My father's ancestral path to that game-changing interview began on the opposite side of the world. He was the fourth child of a rural mail carrier in northeast Iowa, the son of an Irish American mother and a father who claimed roots in Lux-

---

[*] Burma is now officially known as Myanmar. This dates back to 1989, when the ruling military junta changed the name of the country in what many considered a bid to deflect international attention away from the gross human rights violations it was carrying out across the country. My family—and all the Burmese exiles I have known—continued to call the country Burma, as an act of defiance—a refusal to acknowledge an illegitimate junta and its decrees. (As a matter of fact, referring to the country as Burma was official U.S. policy through much of the Obama administration.) At any rate, throughout this book I refer to the country and its people as Burma and Burmese. Despite its unfortunate colonial nomenclature, it remains the way in which my family has identified itself and separated itself from a regime that has persecuted and killed its own citizens—and continues to.

embourg. My dad showed an early interest in politics and, like my mother, came to Washington to do the work of liberal causes. There were no socialist dailies or French girlfriends, but he had longish hair and worked on George McGovern's presidential campaign and knew Hunter S. Thompson. My mother and father's remote histories intersected on a bridge of progressive bona fides and casual early seventies bohemianism. Only a few generations back, their families had been separated by oceans and mountain ranges and steppes. But in Washington, their shared values were enough to draw them close.

They were married in 1975 and several years later had their only child—me, a daughter born of an unlikely set of Burmese-Luxembourg-Irish bloodlines. Of this weird heritage, I knew little. Our Burmese story was relayed to me by my mother and grandmother, in occasional fits and starts, usually with food as the catalyst. A pot of chicken curry would summon some certain memory, which would in turn beget a snippet of family history. But only a snippet—the stories were carefully constructed, well-worn vignettes that never risked genuine revelation. Burma was kept at a safe distance from our American lives.

My father's people were from Europe. His grandfather left the Old World sometime during the late nineteenth century, motivation unclear. I didn't know much about his departure and why he'd made it, or even much about the place where he began: Luxembourg, a strange country about which little was discussed in my family. The one detail that slipped through was the name of his exotic-sounding hometown: Esch. And all we knew about Esch was that it sounded like the sort of place you'd want to get away from.

Luxembourg itself was largely irrelevant. For most of my adolescence, I confused it with Liechtenstein, an ant-sized country buried between Austria and Switzerland. Most everyone else also confused Liechtenstein and Luxembourg, and when forced to identify either country, would offer that it was "The smallest country in the world?" It wasn't.* My father's mother and her family were from Ireland, but as far as American family histories went, Ireland didn't interest me much. The good parts of being Irish had become common property, as familiar as Saint Patrick's Day. Everyone knew Irish daughters were redheaded and pale and the boys drank too much and were always in fistfights. I was none of those things. So Luxembourg was the ancestral provenance I most frequently cited, but that was a little like being from the dark side of the moon or an island in the center of an ocean: It was like being from nowhere.

As a child I didn't think much about the improbability of these family histories, or that I was in some way charged with their inheritance. And no one told me much about it anyway. I was mostly taught that my ancestors, whoever they were—the people thrust upon me by the random genetic alignments in the universe—should in no way affect my destiny. Anyway, wasn't that the whole point of America? Dynasties were for the Old World. Tradition was something held aloft by Queen Elizabeth and her Easter egg–colored suits, and bloodlines were for horses and pharaohs.

America, as we had been taught, was about forward move-

---

* Not even close. Liechtenstein is the sixth smallest country in the world. Vatican City is the smallest.

ment, not backward. Such was the proposition written in the American Gospel of Expansion and intoned to us by countless self-made politicians of every political stripe: "Go west, young man!" And by "Go west," we really meant "Look forward— don't worry about all that shit you're leaving behind."

I understood that at Christmastime my father's side of the family enjoyed drinking a sludgy and highly alcoholic concoction known as a Tom and Jerry, that there were nuns who'd rapped his knuckles in middle school, and that in his hometown, large families were not an exception, but a given. These were my main cultural reference points for "Irish Catholic." And they represented the extent to which my life was informed by this heritage: not in the least. They were stories recounted as asides, reminders of my father's storybook beginning before he came east.

Elsewhere in our house, Asia was present but not entirely accounted for. When my mother went to bed each night, she knelt in prayer toward a small gold statue of the Buddha as she recited her prayers, softly and quickly. She'd touch my knee as we drove past cemeteries, and whenever I mentioned death, she would mutter in Burmese under her breath. She made me spit on my fingernails every time I trimmed them. Practically speaking, this is what it meant to be half-Burmese: a series of traditions and voodoo-like practices I didn't really understand but nonetheless accepted.

Every April, when it was time for the annual Burmese New Year's water festival of Thingyan, the immigrant community in and around suburban Silver Spring, Maryland, would traditionally gather in someone's backyard. On the streets of Rangoon, men and women and children threw water at one another in celebration of the new year—and to cool off in the middle of the excruciatingly hot dry season.

But in the mid-Atlantic United States, sloshing water around on 54-degree early spring weekends was an annual torture, a trauma visited upon me and my white tights by boys, usually aged ten to twelve. Armed with plastic buckets brimming with cold water from the garden hose, the boys would unceremoniously hurl water at me, with very little mirth for the coming year. I hated it, and would have much preferred to celebrate the New Year—everybody *else's* new year—with Dick Clark and the Times Square ball and a glittery, feathered tiara (for me, not Dick Clark). Each April, as I beelined back to the circle of adults giggling and clucking at my soaked clothing, I felt annoyed and angry that I had to suffer through these stupid indignities, these annual pretend celebrations of heritage and calendar.

I thought of myself as generically American, both in cultural preference (Chips Ahoy, *Murder, She Wrote*) and appearance (Esprit and Sebagos), but occasionally, I was reminded that how I saw myself wasn't necessarily how everyone else saw me. As on the day when I sat at the counter of the American City Diner and the white line cook turned to ask me, while my father was in the bathroom, if I was adopted. I brushed it off, as if this were something I was asked all the time (it most certainly wasn't), laughing to relieve him of the burden of such an awkward question, and responding, "Oh no, my mother's just Asian!"

Moments like this were reminders that, to some people, I was *not* generically American. I had invested fully in the story my parents told me. I considered most everyone—white line cooks, black flight attendants, Puerto Rican teachers, whatever—American, just like me, never minding that we didn't look alike or come from the same places. We were here! And yet the feeling was not always mutual: In the eyes of certain folks, who were universally certain *white* folks, I was not generically American; I was something else. If my "we" included them, theirs did not include me.

Even then, as a twelve-year-old in the diner drinking a vanilla malted, I recognized the power of this exclusivity. I was deferential to it, offering a grinning explanation as to why I didn't look the way some line cook thought the daughter of an average white American should look, a statement that verged on an apology. The cook's certainty over what was generically American and what was not generically American seemed to be deeply entwined with something—blood or DNA or place—that was far more definitive than the casual connections I'd forged in my life thus far. Esprit tops and Nabisco cookies were American products, but for the cook, they weren't sufficient identifiers. I envied this sense of ownership over who was (or must be) a Typical American—his specificity regarding who *belonged*—even if it made me feel fairly terrible to have an identity I'd casually assumed and embodied suddenly . . . denied.

If I wanted to belong, to circumscribe my identity in some similarly definitive way, I eventually realized that the answer was not in trying to retrofit myself into the world of generically white Americana (where I would never be at home), nor did it mean full accession to the suburban Burmese exile community in Silver Spring (which seemed even more alien and had a significant language barrier to boot).

After all, neither my maternal nor paternal lines had held

much sway over my life thus far—Luxembourg and Burma were about as resonant as Narnia and the North Pole. But when I considered my heritage as a single thing, rather than an either-or proposition where one was forced to toggle between Rangoon and Esch, these two poles—Burmese and Irish-German—taken *together* offered something entirely, definitively new. And this category of Broadly Mixed Race Heritage, this was a place I could belong!

To a certain degree, the halves themselves no longer mattered; it was almost as if they canceled each other out, and in the vacuum that created there was something new and unburdened by expectation and history. I wouldn't be bound by stale, atavistic ideas about identity, some hokey old timer's notion of what "regular" America looked like. That was the past! The signifiers of my tribe would be as rigorous in their inclusion as that line cook was in his exclusion: The less you fit into any one category, the more you belonged.

My thinking about this brave new identity crystalized on November 18, 1993, when the cover of *Time* heralded "The New Face of America," which, kind of (if you squinted or were legally blind), looked like me.[1]

"Take a good look at this woman," the headline dared the reader. "She was created by a computer from a mix of several races. What you see is a remarkable preview of . . . THE NEW FACE OF AMERICA." The thrill!

Inside was a story that promised to explain "how immigrants are shaping the world's first multicultural society."

I was a sophomore in high school and the cover was a revelation: *I* was the new face of America! Somehow I was a precursor, sent from the future to show the people of America what they would all look like a few generations hence. Just as *Time* promised, these parents of mine—one immigrant plus the child of some immigrants—had unknowingly created the *futureface*.

When I found a box, in late high school, filled with my mother's old clothes from the seventies, there was a tiny bright green T-shirt emblazoned with orange iron-on letters that spelled out RANGOON RAMONA. It was something my father had made for my mother, based on a nickname that had been retired several anniversaries ago, but here was the perfect shirt for me, futureface. Rangoon Ramona. Who was she? It was like Clark Kent finding the *S* logo.

"Rangoon" was the capital of Burma, far away on the other side of the world. "Ramona" was continental, the Old World. The old European world, that is. It dawned on me—sitting on the linoleum floor of a basement redolent of wet wood and cat litter—that there was *something* here. I felt lucky. To be Burmese without the Irish-German half was to just be *Asian*. To be merely a descendant of Irish Germans was just to be white. Oh, but to be both! To be both was to be the space between them, the whole world that their stories traversed. It was to be the future.

And so here I was, in my mother's hand-me-down RANGOON RAMONA T-shirt, defending not one particular culture but swimming around—gloating, even—in the new thing created from the mixture of two. It seemed almost greedy. On a trip to Hawaii right before college, a local called me a "hapa." What exactly was a hapa? "It means you're mixed!" he said to me, and the revelation was akin to having lived your whole life thinking you were a pigeon only to find out you were a toucan. Tropical, ambiguous, exotic. Hapa.

Shortly after college, on a visit to New York, I was wearing a single feather earring and ordering a coffee when a man with a deeply cleft chin came up and asked me, with the hushed incredulity of an actor on *The Bold and the Beautiful,* "What's your blood?" I responded, "O negative," because he deserved a ridiculous answer for an absurd question . . . and then I promptly recounted the story throughout the day to anyone who would listen. "Can you believe that douchebag?" I asked my friends. They could not believe that douchebag.

The idea that I could name my "blood" was a reductive and outmoded concept. Instead, I had enrolled myself into a polyglot Tribe of All with great gusto—just as America herself, in the third quarter of the twentieth century, had also found new purpose in celebrating multiculturalism. For this country, the leap toward diversity came after years of official cultural monotheism: an institutional allegiance to white patriarchy that started at America's inception and began to shift only with the 1960s flowering of cultural studies programs born of protest, starting with the establishment of African American studies in the late 1960s. Even white Judeo-Christian scholars started to question whether a rigorously monochromatic, Judeo-Christian canon best represented our dynamic and increasingly polychromatic society: Didn't women and brown folks play pivotal roles in the building of our democracy, our economy, our history—often in opposition to the very same white patriarchy? If there was a common American story, how could it be told without them?

By the 1970s, scholars and activists and authors were doing

what I had done: They were wearing the proverbial feather earring; they were donning the seed-bead necklace. This was the Dawn of the Age of Hapa. In 1980, historian and activist Howard Zinn released his alternative chronicle of our national project, called *A People's History of the United States*. This was a history that accounted for the labor of slaves, the work of women, the struggles of the native people; the nation making and destiny shaping that happened at the grassroots, rather than the constitutional conventions—but was no less pivotal. Zinn's text could be taught in classrooms as an alternative to the dusty, one-sided histories of yore, and American liberals were now taking their turn at reframing a story that had been told since time immemorial.

In my own high school during the early nineties, a steady diet of dead white men—Chaucer, Hawthorne, Donne—began to change. Now we would read Chinua Achebe's *Things Fall Apart*, and Alex Haley's *Roots*. Now we would study Ghana, Mali, the Songhai Empire, and Benin. We would know Africa, because Africa, not just Europe, had birthed America. Knowing this not only made us wiser, it made us stronger: truer to our values, our people, our histories. America was not simply the Stars and Stripes; it was a mosaic, a quilt, a rainbow. There was power in being mixed.

Or at least that was the idea. Because as soon as *The Canterbury Tales* was sidelined for Langston Hughes's "I, Too," the backlash began. And, boy, was it swift. Who knew that so many folks were fans of "The Knight's Tale"?

Conservatives started to attack this new hybridized American canon as a threat to national identity: All of a sudden there was Dinesh D'Souza and his book *Illiberal Education*, railing against multiculturalism as a balkanizing force on American campuses. All of a sudden there was Pat Buchanan, running on a platform of cultural nationalism, blaming immigrants for America's troubles, drawing a firm line in the sand between Us and Them. The nineties were wild!

But the criticism of Age of the Hapa was not limited to the right wing: Liberals recognized that the "melting pot" idea necessarily eliminated the differences between cultures, breaking them down into one mushy brown stew—and wasn't this, too, a sort of surrender in the culture wars? I remember vaguely toward the end of my high school career being cautioned not to refer to America as a "melting pot" but instead as a "salad bowl"—the idea being that the ingredients in a salad bowl better kept their integrity, even though they were mixed. A tomato was still a tomato—even if it was surrounded by iceberg lettuce.

Things got even more complicated by the time I went to Brown—which was, incidentally, the *only* school my parents requested I not apply to. "Political correctness has run amok over there!" my mother declared one autumn Sunday after reading a less-than-flattering story about the school in *The New York Times*. My father didn't really know what precisely constituted political correctness, but concurred anyway. Naturally, I decided to apply early and chose to attend as soon as the mailman had delivered my acceptance letter. (I had never even seen the campus.)

At my future alma mater, I attempted to navigate the choppy waters of multiculturalism: engaging in private hand-wringing over whether I should join the South Asian Students Association, or whether the very existence of this group reinforced the marginalization that it aimed to combat. (Answer: I joined, but never attended any of the meetings.) I took post-colonial literature classes, and I read Edward Said.

The generic mantle of "mixed" felt empowering but also weightless, in a way that race, as I understood it, was not supposed to be. I knew there was no such thing as a racial history without baggage, but I had no conception of how to assign that weight, how to reconcile the pasts of my futureface or the price paid for the privileges that I was now so eagerly adopting. So I didn't. Somehow, I reasoned that because I was a new thing, a Burmese-Luxembourgian, my role in the American story of blood and plunder was unwritten. Ultimately, I chose not to think about the backstories of the European and Asian cultures whose blending had created my Broadly Mixed Race Heritage. I opted for that most American of paths: forward, to the future, with complete disregard for the shit that had been left behind. I wasn't ready to relinquish my new power. There was a war going on, and, having seen the future, I knew who'd win.

Even as I spread my toucan's wings, I still struggled with the more quotidian problems of being alive, or being me, the kid who still played solitaire, if metaphorically. As I grew older, I became better at making friends and finding companions, but these relationships were always partially instrumental: I was trying to stave off loneliness.

"We are born alone, and we will die alone" my father used to intone, in case I had any suspicions that my best friends and favorite pets would be escorting me to eternal damnation or heavenly salvation. It wasn't what an only child needed to hear over a Saturday morning bowl of Kix, but this is what he thought of as wisdom, a thing to remember in good times and bad, and so he repeated it often and I came to believe it. When my parents finally divorced, some twenty years after they got married, this koan took on even more meaning: My parents' unlikely and exotic partnership had ended, and I was truly alone, like an astronaut on a distant planet. Other people had families to guide them through the Milky Way galaxy of life. I had only two separate satellites and no base station.

Friendships created connection and rituals, but those friendships, as delightful and anchoring as they were, were born from circumstantial origins. My friends were my friends for the same reasons two strangers got married and became my parents: We bonded over shared schools or professional worlds or political causes or tastes in music, not because we were tied together by blood and tradition. And, just like my parents, as conveniently as we had come together, we could be broken apart.

This sense of existential unrootedness, of transience, followed me into adulthood. Leaving college meant losing rituals and friends; changing jobs (relatively frequently—thanks, twenty-first-century economy!) meant losing associates—and sometimes even identities. Each one of these changes felt seismic, if quietly so. How did other people adapt so easily?

A few years ago, after the umpteenth job change and millionth fizzled attempt at casually rewarding friendship, it occurred to me that all these efforts were external ones, dependent on the tricky and unreliable chemistry of interpersonal relations. And the problem I was trying to solve was an inherently interior one, something no amount of shared ricotta pancakes or emailed correspondence could truly resolve. I was asking my bosses and my friends and my semi-friends to account for something that was very nearly impossible to resolve. I didn't have a people. I didn't know where I could find home.

Not incidentally, this is something that we are also grappling with as a country—at various volumes and with various degrees of indignation: Who are our people? What makes them so? White Americans, once the country's comfortable majority, used to tell themselves golden stories about the past—a time when everyone knew who they were and where they belonged. They didn't know what DNA was, but that didn't matter; American communal identity was in the land and the blood. This, of course, was never quite the truth; even when segregation was the law of the land, aggressive cultural mixture was what set America apart from other countries. But for most Americans, tucked into neatly segregated corners, even if they listened to rock 'n' roll and put nacho cheese on their chips and watched Bruce Lee at the drive-in, this aggressive cultural mixture happened . . . somewhere else. Not in their hometowns. Not in their homes. Not in the canon. Especially not in the White House.

Our blood is changing. White men and women may have voted monolithically to install the forty-fifth president, but they are unlikely to be able to do so again: Their numbers are shrinking. America is browner, richer, poorer, angrier, lonelier. The constants—to the degree that they ever existed—are gone. We have tried to replace the old ideas of how we belong with other forms of connection based on pastimes and politics, a casual tribalism born of geography or Instagram likes. This was my parents' story, a union formed by chemistry and liberalism, novelty and interests. But the question of belonging can't simply be answered by a collection of habits and jobs and addresses or even by a political platform. It requires something deeper and undeniable. A story that draws a circle: Inside the circle, you find (okay, yes) yourself . . . but not just you. You're not alone in that circle—you also find your people. And this is what it means to belong, in the truest sense.

America is fracturing because its citizens are losing the ability to find that larger story. On both sides of the political spectrum, a movement is growing based on that craving to find a narrative that accounts for us, that tells us who we are. There's a creeping sense that multiculturalism might not be the answer to, but the seed of, our discontent. That we've forsaken specific ancestry for something fashionably exotic, and this has made us disconnected and isolated, or angry and confused. In response, we've seen the growth of benign forms of reconnection to the old ideas of blood and land: the sudden preponderance of genealogy websites and genetic tests designed to find every lost ancestor floating in your DNA. We've seen immigrants holding on to old identities, or trying to forge new ones—but not assimilating into white America, a place that's lived in but not understood to be home.

We've seen African American quarterbacks taking knees at football games and brown-skinned superstars building their performance art around the iconography of New Orleans and the West Indies and Africa. Some of the responses have been less benign: the rise of explicit white ethnic nationalism as a political force; a passion for building walls; the demonizing of Mexicans and Muslims and anyone who looks like a Mexican or a Muslim; and a return to an "America first" mentality, where "American" means exactly what it meant to that line cook all those years ago, which is to say, not black or brown or mixed. Not me.

And yet, I can't be angry that so many others crave that same sense of belonging I longed for, so many years ago, sitting on the living room floor, playing solitaire and listening to Starship on the actual radio—the indelible feeling of self-recognition and camaraderie that might endure beyond transient affiliations. I have long recognized the absence of belonging, a questioning loneliness, in myself. And now it's split the country around me. We've divided ourselves, segregated our communities into Us and Them in an attempt to feel whole, to better affirm who *we* are. In the process, we've ended up even more alienated and more confused about who we *actually* are: After all, the undeniable existence (and encroachment!) of Them is a challenge to the very concept of Us. How can America actually be our own, if so much of it is made up of people who live and act and think in opposition to us? And if divisions aren't the way to draw an irrefutable, satisfactory line around identity, what circle to draw? And how?

Might I ever find, for myself, that grounding, sustaining thing?

After so much time, so many years, spent looking outward to answer this question, I wondered if what I was looking for wasn't within me already. If instead of trying to be the lonely avatar of the mixed-race utopia to come, I could go back. I could search my own blood to find my people in the here and now. Was there some part of my story, in its improbable combination of DNA double helixes and far-flung genetics, that might offer connection to that elusive Camaraderie Supernova for which I'd been searching? One's personal story is constant and irreversible, after all, something that will be with all of us from the next lunch hour until the last glimmers of light pass over our eyelids. If you could find a way to carry it (and all the people from it), then you'd never really be alone again.

I began contemplating this and how I'd go about it. I'd never dug into the family archives with any degree of rigor (or interest, if I was being honest) and knew so little about, well, everything that had come before my parents and me, the prehistories that ultimately determined my own story. I was going to have to learn. I was going to have to get serious about the past. I began to steel myself. And then, just as I was beginning my search, edging into the darkness of the family past, something impossibly serendipitous occurred. An event that snapped me once and for all out of my futureface fantasies, and offered this curious loner something impossibly seductive: a family mystery. It was a lifeline to another way of being, a hidden tribe of elders who might claim me as their own—and (more urgently, perhaps) whom I might claim as *my* own. A chance, at long last, to know myself and where I truly—really, for real this time—belonged.

CHAPTER TWO

---//---

We talk about our identities—our race, our nation, our tribe of like-minded souls—as if they are something inevitable, inextricably tied to who we are, a trait formed in utero. I've always known that's not really true. My own particularly elusive tribal membership was proof that identity is not, in fact, written in our cells: It's something we learn, something we choose, something we have to cultivate—or lose along the way. Someone's identity might be a stolen birthright, it might be imprinted in the crib by Mom and Pop, it might be learned (the hard way) on the junior high school blacktop or (most awkwardly) at the office water cooler.

Or it might just rest inside a Pandora's box, opened against one's better instincts because, for some people, the answer to the question "Who am I, really?" is pressing and intoxicating enough for a spelunking into the unknown.

I'd missed out on the crib-side branding and the birthright—and to me, for a while at least, not being part of any particular group freed me of race and tribe, the powerful and destructive ideas that were the source of so much of the world's misery. Let the other kids roam in feral gangs across the schoolyard blacktop, let the high-functioning professionals gossip among the hair dryers after SoulCycle class—Alexandra Swe Wagner could glide through life without a herd. Or at least I thought I could. Because when I was presented with that potentially hazardous Pandora's box of heritage and identity, it turned out to be too tempting not to open. Taboos, heartbreak, familial fallouts be damned—I was gonna open that thing and peer inside, embracing all the wild shit that flew out of it.

Of course, it wasn't an actual box (if only it had been that easy!), but a spur on an otherwise fairly humdrum anecdote, a casual aside that turned into a saga all its own. And it came from my father, as he spun a honeyed story about his heritage, having no idea that he was about to steer his own narrative insanely off course.

On the day of my First Holy Communion, I got a nosebleed. I already felt like I didn't belong at the church in the first place, given the fact that I'd only sporadically attended the required religious education classes. Accordingly, I didn't really know any of the Bible passages or the lyrics and hand movements to the happy Catholic songs that all the other kids in my communion class seemed to know by heart. But there, sitting in one of the front pews of Holy Trinity Church, on a chilly May morning, wearing the required white dress, my nose started running bright red. Only my father was with me (my mother the Buddhist did not attend the ceremony), which made it even worse:

the white frills, the blood, the sheer lunacy of this proceeding, my entrance into Catholicism.

It was by dint of my father that I was even doing this. The rest of our neighborhood was off celebrating May Day with a group of honey-making, suspender-clad beardos who brought in an actual Maypole every year to celebrate the pagan rites of spring. The juxtaposition between that folksy seasonal hedonism and the stiff, very godly Catholic ritual could not have been more obvious. Here I was in a marble hall, eating the body and blood of Christ for the first time, mopping up nose blood with a roll of toilet paper from the church bathroom. I would so much rather have been on Brandywine Street, running down the block in an azalea crown and celebrating the rites of spring with the rest of my agnostic, liberal neighbors. I was young but in some vague and unarticulated way, I understood my implicit right as an American to bastardize, sample, create, and forget traditions as the mood struck me. Frolicking in the dappled sunlight of the Slatterys' front yard seemed more worthwhile than trying to remember Catholic prayers in a chilly marble apse. Why wasn't I out there, twirling around the Maypole?

I was angry with my father for making me take part in this event, which was gussied up as an ostensible entry into my Catholic heritage. It was a sham aimed at connecting me to his family traditions, but it was all happening without context, like reading the middle chapter of a very long history book without knowing what came before and what might follow. I hadn't gone to religion classes—okay, fine, I had been conned into attendance once or twice with the lure of free doughnuts in the church basement, but I had no real connection to whatever was supposed to be taking place at the altar. If this was my heritage, it was woefully incomplete. My father had made his own mix-and-match choices about Catholic tradition, passing down to me Catholic values but ignoring Catholic liturgy. Secular manifestations of Catholic social justice were part of my education; Isaiah 12:2 was not. (Is it any surprise that I never received the sacrament of Confirmation?)

Being from Iowa, growing up without great resources, knowing the value of a dollar and the importance of a handshake—these were all central to my father's identity. But being raised Catholic was more than just important to him. It was foundational. Catholic values, as defined by the progressive, anti-poverty wing of the church (rather than the Vatican), were the foundation for my father's political beliefs. He referred often to Catholic ministries to the poor as a reason why he'd come to Washington in the first place: He'd wanted to solve the problem of hunger in America. My dad's home-brewed sermons about forgiveness, empathy, and charity were often fairly convincing. And I had to admit, as I grew older, that this strain of Catholicism evolved into a benevolent and guiding force in my own political orientation.

But while my father shaped his life with his religion's most progressive political values, the pomp and circumstance (and nosebleeds) of Catholic ritual were not as resonant. Maybe this was because he had left the circumscribed life in small-town Iowa where the church—its rituals and community, more than its words and ideas—was necessarily the center of family life. By the time he was a young man, he'd moved to the swingin', polytheistic Washington of the 1970s, where many of those same words and ideas were reinforced and applied in the political work that obsessed him, but the rituals and community of small-town Iowa grew further and further away.

And when I came along, he didn't have the room in his schedule—or the desire to make room in it—to indoctrinate his only child to the ways of the institutional church. He figured a Catholic political education, taught in a series of kitchen table homilies—rather than pre-scheduled religion classes—might suffice. I was steeped in my father's own secular translation of the New Testament, but set adrift from the richness of his familial past, except on the rare occasions when I rested on the unfamiliar oak of a church pew, a stranger in a strange land.

This was no small loss in the transmission of the Wagner legacy. The church *was* the legacy, in large part. And, outside of the realm of political ideals—a realm both airily untouchable in its intellectualism and boringly earthbound in its pragmatic intent—it was a legacy denied to me. The institution of the church was the basis upon which nearly all of my father's childhood memories had been built: Religion was the bark wrapped 'round his family tree. My father, Carl Robert Wagner, Jr., attended Catholic schools with all of his sisters and brother, and went to a small Catholic college after that. The nuns and priests were his surrogate parents, his disciplinarians, his spiritual guides. His father, Carl Wagner, Sr., made sure his clan prayed each night and attended mass every Sunday. It was in the sharing of these rituals that they also found their people.

According to my dad, the tiny town of Lansing, Iowa, had five churches, which were organized mostly around ethnicity. The biggest among them was the Church of the Immaculate Conception, where everyone was reportedly of Luxembourger, German, or Irish Catholic stock. The same held true for my father's Catholic high school—Saint Thomas Aquinas. "It was all Connors and Murphys or Wagners and Schwarzkopfs," he said. The Lutheran church was virtually all Norwegians; no one had any idea who went to the Seventh-Day Adventist church; Saint Luke's Episcopal (or maybe Methodist?) Church was where all the "highbrow" Protestants went; and as far as the First Presbyterian churchgoers were concerned, my dad "wasn't sure."

"There was an incredible awareness of who was and who wasn't Catholic," he told me. "The Gaunitz brothers"—the owners of the meat market where he worked—"used to constantly make fun of Catholics and call them 'mackerel snappers,' because they ate fish on Friday."

Ironically, that mackerel was sold by the one Jewish family in town: Jacob and Rose Erlich, who ran the Lansing fish market. Every Thursday, Jacob and his sister Rose would drive to all the Catholic houses and ring their bells. "Mom would answer the door to see what fish was fresh. Jacob would weigh the fish right there and give them to her," he remembered, with no small amount of nostalgia. "Eating fish on Friday, it was the way things were done in the Catholic church when I was a kid."

Jacob Erlich was the one to urge my father to go to college: "When I was a senior in high school, he must have asked me twenty-five times where I was gonna go to college," my dad recalled. "He encouraged me to do it." I had never heard of Jacob Erlich before; it seemed strange to me that someone who'd played such a pivotal role in his life would appear only now, in such a late chapter.

I asked my dad whether the Erlichs might have faced bigotry as the only Jewish family in a one-horse/five-church

Christian town. He dismissed the thought entirely: "No, not at all." He was sure. "Jacob and Rose were Jewish . . . but it was irrelevant really," he proclaimed, as if its lack of relevance to him was definitive.

But the theoretical irrelevance of other people's cultural backgrounds was part of what defined the culture of my father's childhood. When my dad was a junior in high school, he entered the Iowa Oratorical Declamation contest and memorized the essay "I Speak for Democracy" by a young woman named Elizabeth Ellen Evans—and with it, he won the state contest. Fresh off that success, he was asked to reprise the performance in front of the local Kiwanis Club, whose members were made up, in large part, by the town businesspeople—among them, Jacob Erlich.

The speech itself is an earnest bit of mid-century patriotism (ancestors giving their blood for freedom on "the sands of Okinawa," ancestors bequeathing "the sweet, delicious coldness of the first bite of peppermint ice cream on the Fourth of July"), but it isn't particularly jingoistic.

As my dad stood in front of that crowd of clerks and grocers and fishmongers, intoning a rudimentary but nonetheless heartfelt homily about religious tolerance and American identity, Jacob Erlich began to cry. By way of an explanation, my father offered: "I think it was the first time in his lifetime in Lansing—the first time in an honorific way—that Judaism had been referred to." The negative space of that positive emotion seemed pretty evident: If Mr. Erlich was moved by this moment of explicit inclusion, it might be because he'd felt excluded for so long from this community that my father took as his birthright. But when I pressed my father further on whether this single Jewish family might have somehow been marginalized—or if their exclusion from the parish was lonesome, or even possibly miserable—his answer was a firm no.

Instead my father was insistent that the Erlichs were simply interesting secondary characters in the larger tableau of Hunky-Dory Lansing, people who didn't know compromise or adversity. If anything, Jacob Erlich was a grateful prop—at least in my father's retelling of his declamation performance—his tears illustrative of the magnificence of our country, where difference was accepted without question, and indeed was often a source of pride. The "I Am an American" anecdote was less about Jacob Erlich than it was about my father and his town and their mutual largesse. It was an affirmation of his tribe's centrality to the life of this town and country, but also of the graceful way they wielded that power. They were white and Christian; they were American—so powerful as to appear invisible, at least to themselves.

And then, out of the blue, that entire narrative was thrown upside down.

"Your aunt Susan thinks we were Jewish," my father mentioned one day in passing, as if everyone had someone in their family who *secretly believed they were Jewish*, "because we had Mogen David wine at Thanksgiving."

That day, my dad's friend Larry Kirk was over at the house, and it was Larry who clarified: "It's a kosher wine."

My father seemed unconcerned.

"I didn't know that," he said. "Wine was—no one knew any-thing about it. Beer was the drink of choice in the Midwest."

For those readers who did not grow up in Jewish house-holds—or devout Irish Catholic households where tradition-ally Jewish beverages were apparently served at the dinner table—Mogen David wine, like its cousin Manischewitz, is a syrupy concoction consumed mostly at Passover seder, and by young teens who have not yet reached legal age and wish to get blitzed on alcoholic grape drink. At the turn of the nineteenth century, Jewish immigrants from the Old World soaked raisins in water and then boiled down the liquid to make their version of bootleg wine for Passover dinner. It sounds undrinkable, but it was surprisingly popular.

By 1890, the six top kosher vendors in New York alone sold forty thousand gallons of the stuff.[1] Once the native Concord grape was discovered for winemaking purposes (and extended shelf life!), the first commercial kosher wineries began opening up across the country. In Chicago—a hub for recent arrivals from Luxembourg, as it happened—there was headquartered the hilariously misnamed California Wine Company, which eventually became the Wine Corporation of America. One of its top sellers was Mogen David wine.

My father explained away the consumption of kosher wine at the dinner table of his semi-rural Iowa childhood home as some kind of dalliance with high class, a failed attempt at cos-mopolitanism. This seemed fishy to me: There was no other evidence that he could point to that revealed an interest in met-ropolitan custom or experimental dinner table foodstuffs. In his house, there was fish on Fridays, doughnuts on Sunday, and corn in between.

If one delved deeper, our family patriarch seemed to be oriented in quite the opposite direction of homeschooled oenophile. "My dad was almost a socialist," my father explained. "He wouldn't let me join the Boy Scouts—he called it a 'paramilitary organization.' He'd turn on the radio every night at six to listen to Lowell Thomas with the news, and he would always say something to the extent of 'General Motors, General Electric, General Eisenhower!' He was skeptical of power."

To be clear: Carl Wagner, Sr., was no Bolshevik Upper West Sider with a taste for NPR and Oregon pinot noir. This was a man who delivered the mail each day, went to church, and lived a decidedly modest life. It was impossible to imagine someone so resolutely proletarian purchasing bottles of what was then a pretty exotic quaff, especially if hops and barley were the standard. Unless, in fact, Aunt Susan was right—and we were Jewish.

So my father's casual remark didn't pass, not for me. The possibility of Wagnerian membership in the wandering tribe of Jews was very nearly impossible to imagine. Actually, it was more than that: It was pull-out-the-tablecloth-in-the-middle-of-a-fifteeen-course-dinner disruptive. My father's family story had been so charmingly anodyne, so painfully white-bread, that the very suggestion of mystery, of lost roots, of secret Jewish ancestry, challenged our conception of the Wagner clan's "traditional" Irish Catholic roots.

My ancestral bragging rights had till now centered on my far-flung Burmese family on my mother's side—what was more exotic than Burma?!—but here was a whole new chapter of intrigue. About me. Yes—it was grossly narcissistic. My first thought upon hearing what I will refer to as the Jewish Theory was to reflexively imagine how much more intriguing "Burmese Jewish" sounded than "Burmese American." Sure, Judaism was passed down through the maternal line, so, technically speaking, I was not on-the-official-books Jewish, but that didn't negate my theoretical lineage. And, hey, if someone was offering a ticket, I was taking it.

But really, what excited me most about this development was the sense of belonging that being Jewish conferred. At dinner with my agent Ari, I mentioned this news to him, and he was legitimately happy for me. "I always knew you were part of the Tribe, Alex," he said, grinning. (It was very difficult to please Ari unless you were offering him a lucrative deal, preferably in the Chinese market—and so this felt particularly rewarding.) I understood "Our Jewish Heritage" to mean something powerful—far more powerful than "Our Iowan Irish Heritage." To be Jewish was to decisively answer the question of identity and community. The notion of identity that had been forbidden to me—denied to me even as I denied it!—the idea that I could belong somewhere and find myself in that belonging, suddenly became, I realized with some surprise, a thing that I dearly wanted.

I casually discussed the Jewish Theory with my second cousin Karl, a student in New York City and fifteen years younger, which meant he was possessed of a millennial's matter-of-factness born presumably out of a footloose attitude toward mortality and bloodlines and procreation thanks to his generation's dependence on social media (or so I hypothesized). Karl didn't seem tied to any particular part of our family story, and that made him a reliable narrator. Nor did he find it awkward or uncomfortable that I hadn't eaten bratwurst with the family lately (which is to say, anytime in the last decade) and suddenly exhibited newfound interest in our family tree.

Immediately, I wanted to know what he knew about the man who first brought the Wagner bloodline to America, our great-grandfather Henry Wagner. All biographical information had been left out of my father's wistful recollection of Iowa life. What kind of man was Henry? What kind of woman was his wife, our great-grandmother Anna? What was hidden in the treasure trove of family anecdotes that might betray a lost religion, membership in a forgotten society? I wanted information—as much of it as Karl could spill out over dinner. We met at a restaurant downtown. I paid (it was only right!), the first and possibly the smallest of the many expenses I'd have to cover for the pleasure of being told my own family story.

I tried to control my brimming mania as I peppered him with questions. I'd brought a pad and pen with me and wrote down everything he said, all the while trying to act nonchalant, as if by nature I always transcribed dinner with friends. I felt like I had to obscure the sudden ardor of my quest to expose a family, lest my father and his sisters stage some sort of Catholic uprising and issue a Certificate of Deniability Regarding the Jewish Theory. I felt like a private eye, hot on the trail, desperate not to give away any of my leads. I was greedy for details, biographical sketches, whatever Karl could produce. At some point in the interrogation, in the middle of all the familiar stories of aunts and uncles and Iowa, Karl let slip another tantalizing clue.

Apparently, Great-Grandfather Henry was an avid fisherman, content to drop lines on the banks of the Mississippi River. Some years into his life, on one of his countless trips out on the water, Henry got himself into some kind of trouble. There was an accident of some sort, Karl recounted, and suddenly Henry was heard screaming for help. In Yiddish. As in the High German language of the Ashkenazi Jews.

This knowledge of Yiddish—a language I now discovered was spoken "informally" by my great-grandfather—was obviously unbeknownst to me, but it was apparently accepted if largely undiscussed among later generations. My father certainly never made mention of it. But for me, this was all the evidence I needed. We were Jewish. Or at least it was *a pretty good bet* that we were Jewish. And yet my father, distressingly, clung to the idea that this was instead some sort of kooky ethnic happenstance, simply evidence of Henry's skill at foreign languages. Such delusional logic was akin to saying you lit a menorah in December because the candles lent a lovely, midwinter glow and not at all because you were, say, *celebrating Hanukkah*.

And so: I decided to contact my aunt Susan, my father's sister. As the youngest of six Wagner children, Susan had spent a lot of time alone with adults growing up, since many of her brothers and sisters had already left the house or were too old to play with baby Susan, making hers an unusual solo act in a family as big as theirs. Like me, she grew up as a silent presence, surrounded by adults who didn't always take notice of her. This gave her lots of opportunities to overhear things.

While she had only the dimmest recollections of my great-grandfather Henry and his wife, Anna, this was understandable, given the fact that they both passed away several decades before she was born. But Susan had spent time with my great-uncles and -aunts in a way that the other children hadn't. I asked her what she might recall about any possible Jewish clues—she was, after all, the one my dad had said "believed we were Jewish" because of the kosher wine—and she emailed me a few weeks later:

> When I was in high school I often visited my uncle Leo. He was the youngest and last living of [Henry Wagner's] children. Our conversations were centered on news of my siblings, what I was learning in school, and politics, and were accompanied with doughnuts and a small jelly glass of Mogen David wine. Uncle Leo, like Dad, was deeply religious, but did not hold the parish priests in high esteem. During one of our less-than-positive conversations about the local clergy, Leo said, "Well, I'm just an old Jew." Unfortunately, the conversation went no further, and I didn't press for details. Certainly one of those I-wish-I-could-go-back-in-time moments.

It was staggering that Susan could remember—explicitly!—an admission by someone in the family that we were Jewish. Here was seemingly irrefutable proof that there was some specific Judaism that coursed through our veins. But, unbelievably, no one had followed up! I didn't understand how you could hear something like this and remain unfazed. Here was a family that said Christian prayers every evening after dinner. A family that went to mass each Sunday without fail. A clan of children for whom Catholic parochial school was the only existence they'd ever known in a town with a single Jewish family—a group of teary semi-strangers—and yet a table-side revelation regarding their own Judaic roots was met unblinkingly, as if it had been an observation about the weather. As Aunt Susan sat at the table with her uncle Leo, he announced his Judaism, and that was . . . the end of the conversation. Pass the doughnuts and the Mogen David wine.

I tried to imagine myself in a similar position: If, say, over cocktails one evening with my grandmother, she had announced, "Well, I'm just an old lesbian." I imagine that there'd be some follow-up on that—say, a *Wait, what?* Or, *You were a lesbian when, again?*—though one never does truly know what one would do in a moment like that. Maybe the allusion to Judaism registered confusion . . . or embarrassment? Maybe it was just too absurd to follow up on. Maybe both my father and aunt had heard this before, but in their minds it was too outlandish to be considered seriously.

Or was there a more sinister reason my father had resisted following up about his allegedly Jewish heritage? He might have gone on at length about the Erlich family to me and what wonderful people they were . . . but they were clearly outsiders. And perhaps my father's fond recollections about how "well" the lone Jewish family was integrated into Christian Lansing society masked the fact that everyone in town, including my father, was acutely aware that they *were* different. I wondered if the suggestion that he was different, too, didn't strike him as a revelation (as I understood it) but, rather, as a threat. It would challenge what my father thought of as his heritage, the true north to which he could point as the origin for his political leanings and his value system. In fact, it would make his legacy as flimsy and poorly understood as mine.

For me—someone who had no particular link to the institutional church, who could barely name the twelve apostles, who went to Reform Jewish nursery school (by mistake, mostly—my mother had missed the application deadlines for all the other schools in town, or so she says) and believed herself to actually be a practicing Jew for the entirety of age four, Jewish roots were not a disruptive, panic-inducing proposition, by a long shot.

What did it mean for the Wagners not to be Catholic? Not recent-covert-convert Catholic, not Catholic by way of Judaism, but Catholic going all the way back to Saint Patrick's conversion of the Celts. That kind of Catholic. It was hard to fathom, given the magnificently large shadow the church had cast over my father's home life and his cultural orientation. It was therefore cause for quiet, private panic. And the most efficient way to deal with the possibility of panic was to do everything in your power to avoid it. So my father brushed the theory aside, willed it away, and clung to a series of questionable hypotheses instead.

But I was ready to get at the truth. Not simply because I had a natural inclination toward detective work in general (thank you, Cam Jansen), but because it had awakened something in me. I was newly woke to the possibility that after all this time adrift I might now connect to something deeper and solve that longstanding and existentially unnerving question: Where the hell did I belong and who the hell did I belong to?

Ari my agent had even opened the door to his clan—the tribe!—and wasn't this what I had been looking for all along? To be Jewish was to possess an identity rooted in the earliest stories recorded by the human hand! To be part of its traditions and practices, partner in an unseen bond that united people across the globe. To understand the mysteries of gefilte fish, to commune in seder dinners, to be part of a heritage that had always seemed indelible, especially compared to my hazy, dotted line of lineage. How could I not care about this? I was consumed by a need to know.

This need to know is what fuels other people, too, in the global search for identity. Even for those of us who believe we've escaped the confines of heritage, we *Homo sapiens* still very much desire to know where we came from—a truth that would seem to be wholly at odds with both red-state American exceptionalism and blue-state ethnic transcendence. Thus the explosion in genealogy services and genetic testing to determine ancestry, which is now a billion-dollar industry.[2] Maybe it's symptomatic of our sense of entitlement—that we are all due an Ancestor Quest of our very own. I sensed this keenly when interviewing my cousin Karl and peppering my father with questions about his boyhood: I needed to know the answers, but I also *deserved* to know them. That entitlement is itself a symptom of everybody's basic desire to find themselves again in a world that seems so utterly, inescapably lonely—gauzed in story but not fact, muddled by hypothesis without conclusion.

As I plotted the next stages of my investigation, the need to know started to blossom inside of me. I started to wonder: Why did I care so much about my paternal relatives' history— and seem so dispassionate about the no-less-stark unknowns of my Burmese roots? On my father's side, the mystery was intriguing and necessitated an epic wander through the mists of time, where I could interrogate the dead (or at least look for clues about their lives). But on my mother's side, it was my own damn fault that I was in the dark. I had withheld these stories from myself! Everyone who could and would tell them was still living; they just needed to be asked.

My family and its mysteries represented two approaches to the existential mystery of identity and belonging. Both were fundamentally American tales, concerned with the future, not the past. (My mother and father, in their recollections, had equally emphasized the ways in which their respective clans proved that America was a place of inexorable momentum forward—after all, look what they had made for themselves in cosmopolitan Washington, coming all the way from where they had.)

But there were clear differences, too. My father's history was the story of American assimilation: a family that crossed the Atlantic and landed right in the heart of America, white and Christian and ready to belly up to the counter for their scoop of that patriotic peppermint ice cream. But in this transaction—in the trading up of some specific, thorny European story for a broader American version—who knows what was lost?

My mother's story was also an immigrant tale, but not so clearly one of assimilation. She didn't look like the "average American," and she possessed traditions and language and re-flexive mannerisms that placed her, clearly, as someone who had departed someplace else to come here. She and her mother had fled their Eden when it met its ruin, but they remained, even in their welcome American exile, nationalists of a sort. If you had asked her what was really wrong with life in Burma, there was not much of a list. Growing up in Rangoon had been a series of endless halcyon days. There were no poisonous seeds of discord I could find in her wistful recollections, except for the emergencies that had pushed our family out at the very end.

As I started reflecting on my Burmese heritage through the lens of my newly-embarked-upon Ancestor Quest, it occurred to me that in my mother there was a Burmeseness rooted in blood and land that might equally be thought of as an identity, a tribe, like the one I sought. I had been intrigued by the Jewish Theory (which I was now greedy to categorize as the Jewish Reveal). It suggested, most profoundly, that in the Wagner family's American assimilation, something—very important, I now realized—might have been lost. And I wanted badly to recover it. The Jewish Theory forced a revelation that the very thing I had first treated with indifference and rejection—the actual components of my identity—was something I now needed (and aimed to grasp firmly). I would find the things that had been lost in our dive into the American Salad Bowl!

In other words, the formerly blasé futureface hapa— generally happy to be mistaken as a Sioux Indian or Egyptian Coptic—was suddenly fixated firmly on specific identity and genealogy. How easily the landscape had shifted! From pan-multiculturalism to a tribe where I belonged, whether Hebrew in origin or Bamah Burmese. I wanted definitive proof that I was not alone, that I belonged. But where and with whom? It was a mystery to be solved—several mysteries, to be honest— and, oh, did I love mysteries. I was on the case: telephone, magnifying glass, library card, passport in hand.

CHAPTER THREE

———— // ————

I began this adventure where most everyone begins any adventure: at home. My parents divorced long enough ago that they could once again share holiday dinners and gossip about their only child, but I decided to approach them separately, so as to keep things simple, or at least simple-ish. On my father's side, there were numerous family sources I could speak with, but not many who would remember very much about times past. In November 1967, my father's father, Carl N. Wagner, Sr., died in Lansing, Iowa. His wife, Mary, joined him in the Great Beyond twenty-six years later. Their daughter Dorothy died of cancer several years before that. And the family archivist, their son Jim, left this world after a heart attack a few months before Dorothy. In other words, it was a large family, and all of the surviving relatives were (relatively) young, so getting to the root of who we were was going to require work beyond Facebook missives and clarifying emoticons.

Complicating this was the fact that my father was decidedly crappy at staying in touch with his family. It seemed ironic, or just plain sad, that America's boom in Ancestor Quest-ing was happening at precisely the same time when our estrangement—from one another, from our families—was skyrocketing. Here I was, looking to better know the ghosts in our family, while my father and I were out of touch with the flesh-and-blood relatives who could offer camaraderie in real time.

How had we let things atrophy to this point? I had no siblings and as such was never tasked with the upkeep of familial relations. I was probably (definitely) a bad friend because of this. Calling aunts and uncles and cousins—with whom I hadn't spoken in years—with pesky questions about what they remembered about our family made me uncomfortable. I suppose that reconnecting to community (that is, family) lay at the root of this entire project, but when faced (literally) with the prospect of corresponding with my father's people, I felt queasy. I was not yet ready to call Aunt Kathy and (possibly) hear the displeasure in her voice if she brought up the fact that it had been a decade since we'd last eaten bratwurst together.

So I began with my mother's family on the Burmese side: Relations here were not as distant as those on my father's side—due in large part to the fact that my grandmother had mostly raised me, and we were therefore in regular communication. The branches on this side of the family tree were still very much tangled up together. Time and circumstance had not (yet?) alienated us from one another, perhaps a matter of recent immigration versus long-ago immigration, perhaps a function of Asian tradition (my mother's mother lived with us for several years, something that did not happen with my father's mother, who eventually moved into a retirement home), perhaps a result, simply, of geography. My mother's immediate family moved to America and settled on the East Coast (we were only in sporadic communication with the family that had gone west), and so we saw one another frequently. Thus there was not the same self-directed shame in play when it came to my ancestral detective work.

I went first to the oldest person in our family, the one whose memory could stretch the farthest back in time: my grandmother. She was not like other grandmothers, insofar as most grandmothers did not play poker through the night. Nor did they evade the disposal of their precious (but stinking) durian fruits by hiding them under the kitchen sink . . . and then deny to the owners of the sink that they had hidden (stinking) durian fruits near the kitchen plumbing. Most grandmothers did not covet diamonds and forget birthdays. Most grandmothers did not try to get arrested while protesting in front of the Burmese embassy.

Before the Internet and Twitter, before hashtags and streaming video, she was the member of our family most fully briefed on all the developments out of Burma. When the military junta shot and killed thousands of peaceful protesters following a massive protest on August 8, 1988—a turning point in contemporary Burmese politics—the person to phone our house with the news was my grandmother. "There's been a coup!" she declared, ordering me to relay this message to my mother. "There's been a coup!" I shouted. (I wasn't entirely sure what a coup was, but it sounded dramatic.) It was she who met with and supported exiled Burmese pro-democracy activists, well into her eighties.

When a group of increasingly aged but nonetheless highly focused Burmese men—uncles, as they were known—gathered to form an exile government known as the National Coalition Government of the Union of Burma, my grandmother was their treasurer. She was a righteous matriarch of the fledgling pro-democracy movement—a position she'd adopted from her American perch—once shit back home really began to hit the fan in the 1980s.

I imagine that she was able to reconcile this Burmese activism with her status as an American citizen because while my grandmother considered herself a fully integrated member of American society—buying sweaters at Lord and Taylor, opining on members of Congress as if she knew them—she didn't really consider herself "an American." She would often begin sentences with "We Burmese . . ." (and, occasionally, "We Orientals . . .") as if to demarcate the line between where she lived—and was indeed fully invested—and who she actually was.

Since embarking on my Ancestor Quest, I now viewed this connection to Burma in a new way—she, no less than my father and his idyllic stories of Iowa Catholicism, had that thing I wanted so much: a stake in a single, clear identity, one that clarified and strengthened her beliefs and stirred her to action through nearly a full century of life. Jewish or not, her certainty in her beliefs, her effortless navigation between worlds, appeared to me a possible route to finding that same committed sense of myself.

Anyway, for nearly all of her ninety-eight years, my grandmother had been keenly, fully *alive*. She was selfish (she felt no embarrassment in being waited on by my mother, or me, or really anyone who was interested in the job), but she was also intermittently benevolent, not necessarily when expected, but as dictated by whim.

As it concerned our relationship, her benevolence mostly took the form of food (breakfasts of Burmese yellow peas and rice) and jewelry (gold bangles)—though it wasn't merely the act of proffering some edible or material good that was the gift, per se; it was her communication of confidence in who I was, who I had grown up to be. She made clear that if she hadn't approved of my life, I would not have gotten her emerald rings. I knew this because of the gifts *not* given to other children with questionable career paths or controversial political beliefs. No emeralds for them! Instead, they got smiles—and expedited conversation.

While she was undeniably picky, she didn't worry about unpleasant things—instead, each day, she rolled her Buddhist prayer beads through her gnarled, tiny hands, drank what we roughly estimate to be four glasses of wine, and slept soundly for eleven hours a night. She watched the news religiously, and she couldn't stand Republicans.

And she was an excellent source. In the twilight hours, when most nonagenarians had a hard time recognizing the faces of those immediately in front of them, she could still answer questions about events that had taken place decades ago. Her recollection of the faintest details—the name of a principal who had shown her father kindness *at the turn of the twentieth century*, or the piping hot chicken noodle soup she tasted on her very first trip to America *in 1951*—was so effortless that we took it for granted. Born in 1917, she had seen most of the twentieth century, and indeed her biography was a chronicle of its spectacles and miseries, its cruelties and opportunities.

When we discussed our grandmother's impossible life, my cousin Geoff recalled Salman Rushdie's *Midnight's Children*— not because Rushdie was Indian and we were half-Burmese and our parents had lived under the same British Raj—but because Rushdie's narrator seemed to have fully understood the impossibility of summarizing her particular type of twentieth-century life, one that had survived colonial rule and dictatorial regimes to emerge, finally, into the beginnings of a democracy. "To understand just one life," wrote Rushdie, "you have to swallow the world."

Mya Mya Gyi was born in Pakokku on February 16 in the year that was colloquially known as the Year of the Great Fire, which by all outside accounts was 1917. In that year, Europe was still charting the course for much of the globe even as it was being shattered by a war that would reshape that very same world. From Camp Dodge in Johnston, Iowa, my paternal grandfather was shipping off to Europe to fight in World War I as part of the 163rd Depot Brigade. My maternal grandmother, meanwhile, was born under the British flag. Burma— along with India, Pakistan, and Bangladesh—was part of the British Raj and referred to in those days as "India." And yet to suggest to my grandmother that they were Indians—or Brits—would seem laughably absurd. We were Burmese, of course! she'd protest. But the soil beneath their feet was not their own. The land belonged to someone else.

My grandmother was ethnically Bamah, and there's a reason the country was (kind of) named after her people: They were at the top of the socioeconomic ladder. With more than 135 ethnic groups within its borders, Burma from the beginning was a diverse and cosmopolitan culture, and that wasn't even counting the Baghdadi Jews who set up Rangoon's shops or the Italian traders who came to King Mindon's court in the mid-1800s. There were the Chin, Kachin, Shan, and Karen people—each with their own dress and cuisine, and often their own armies.

If anything united Burma's disparate tribes, it was the ruling military junta that took power in the early 1960s and engaged in a brutal campaign of oppression against the country's ethnic minorities—a battle so bloody and violent that it would keep Burma at war with itself for nearly half a century. But beyond this common enemy, you'd be hard pressed to find common cause among the various ethnic groups.

The main difference between our family in Burma and other families from other tribes was class. My grandmother was the daughter of a Burmese civil servant named U Myint Kaung— a man who bought three pairs of Saxon shoes with his first sizable paycheck and introduced the family to Christmas stockings and whiskey cake from Rowe & Co., the luxury department store in downtown Rangoon.

When my grandmother informed me of this, it went a long way in explaining why she directed her ire toward the Indians, not the British: It was the British who proffered luxury items (that her family could afford) and indoctrinated young Mya Mya to a glittering world beyond the Burmese shores—while the Indians were simply continental neighbors who had triumphed in the war of colonial favoritism, an ignoble victory if ever there was one. U Myint Kaung had decidedly European tastes, but he wore those English Saxon shoes with a traditional Burmese aingyi and gaungbaung, sartorial declarations of independence.

He was raised in the Wesleyan Methodist mission schools and spoke fluent English, but remained a devout Buddhist, one who had no issue giving up his worldly possessions near the end of life to become a monk (much to his wife's chagrin). Nevertheless, he spoiled his youngest daughter, my grandmother, awfully.

She was the youngest of the family, the last daughter in a house of six children. Daw Tin Pu and Daw Tin U were the eldest daughters, and when it came time for a third, their mother very badly wanted a son. She was instead gifted another daughter, whom she unapologetically and somewhat unbelievably named Kyi Kyi Thein, which means (roughly) "No more"—as in "Please: No more girls." The heavens either didn't hear the request or opted to teach our family a lesson, and another daughter, Kyi Kyi Nyein, was born. Apparently, her name was an even firmer exhortation to whoever might be listening: According to my grandmother, her name was best translated as "Seriously, stop—no more after this."

Maybe the distress calls had their intended effect, or maybe it was just time, but, finally, a son was born, and he was named Aung Myo. Aung meant "successful," and Myo was for the town in which he was born: Maymyo, a picturesque little hill town in northern Shan State. After all the desperate and demeaning nomenclature, "Successful one from Maymyo" seemed downright platitudinous, but I suppose it was better than "Thank God, finally one with a penis!"

By the time my grandmother was born, the gender war seemed to have come to a close, and she was named Mya, the Emerald, a stone of "calm contentment." She was lucky not just in her name, but in everything else, too.

"I was introduced at a young age to Cadbury chocolate," she recounted, in the way that other children had been introduced to arithmetic or *Aesop's Fables*, as if the elementary indoctrination into chocolate would somehow prepare her well for life and its unknown twists and turns. "And we had bananas at tea time," she boasted, suggesting these tropical fruits were somehow a sign of superiority. At the age of sixteen, my grandmother begged her father for a car, a relatively newfangled machine in 1931. "Whenever I spelled the letters D-o-d-g-e," she added, "my father had to spell Y-e-s. I was quite spoiled! Quite spoiled. I was the youngest. The first one I saw in a catalogue, my father directed [my mother] to go buy it in the capital city. With cash"—as if credit would cast doubt on the family solvency.

If doling out Cadbury and bananas and motorcars at a young age did anything, it imparted upon Mya Mya a sense of entitlement and of high-class taste. This became more than a hallmark; it evolved into some sort of secret badge that my grandmother wore—always—to distinguish herself from everyone else. In fact it did, in some ways, prepare her for the future. When she fled Burma nearly forty years later with nothing, and had to start over in the West, knowing the taste of milk chocolate and the thrum of an American motor was like currency. She could return to these tastes, these experiences, these objects, as if they were proof that yes, her life had been extraordinary and uncommon. They were her security when she had no money, a cultural savings that would never be drawn down, come what might.

And indeed, even for me, these objects and acquisitions were reassuring proof that we were somebody. My grandmother's charmed life in Burma—as she recounted it to me—was evidence that the blessings we would accrue later on, here in America, were not a function of circumstance or otherwise arbitrary largesse, but the continuation of a blessed existence that we had somehow earned, one that had followed my family from the life they left behind on the humid deltas of Rangoon . . . all the way to the Atlantic coast of the United States. I believed, with her stories as my proof, that the inevitable accrual of good things was in a way my inheritance—and that nothing could ever take that away.

Mya Mya's mother, Daw Thet Kywe, was described to me as "not a giggling type of Burmese woman." You could probably divine that fact based on her hardcore naming preferences for girl children, but irrespective of that, the decidedly un-giggly type of Burmese women in my family saw giggliness as an indicator of vapid personalities and/or moral turpitude. Our un-giggling matriarch was adventurous and ambitious, captivated by metropolitan life. It was she who requested that the British transfer her husband, a man of "country" tendencies, from dusty Pakokku in Upper Burma to the leafy delta city of Rangoon, where she traveled several times a year on shopping trips to buy diamonds (love of diamonds was apparently a genetic trait). Their first city residence in the capital was a luxury two-bedroom apartment on Fifty-second Street, one with running water and what was known then as an English toilet.

While her three eldest sisters were educated in English missionary schools only until the fourth standard, my grandmother Mya Mya and her sister Nyein went unusually far in their schooling, given the fact that in Burmese society (as in the United States in the 1920s and '30s) female students did not tend to advance into higher education, let alone graduate school. My grandmother began college at the age of sixteen, when she entered Rangoon University. Nyein graduated second in her class at Rangoon Law School and forevermore would be quoted in family lore as saying that her ambition in life was to be "the first Portia of Burma" after Shakespeare's cross-dressing lawyer in *The Merchant of Venice*. Such were the highbrow feminist reference points in our family, which, despite the strangely misogynistic names of my great-aunts, offered no further indication that women were to be treated as any less than full, voting members of the household . . . if not outright dictators.

"My sisters smoked—and they liked English food," my grandmother told me. "They rolled their own cheroots when our father was away on business, and they kept them in big lacquer boxes to hide from him." He may not have liked his daughters sucking on the small green cigarillos made with uncured tobacco—but in Burmese society, women were often the primary tobacconists, and they remain so today.* "My oldest sister in Mandalay smoked cigarettes. She read the newspaper every day, cover to cover. And she could talk about anything."

According to my grandmother, Nyein's reference points were so specific and timely that when she disliked a particular

---

* The cheroots are fairly noxious, though.

shirt Mya Mya was wearing, she one day announced—with disgust—"You look just like the wife of Patrice Lumumba!"*

My grandmother and her sisters quarreled with one another in the catty, upper-crusty fashion of characters in a Brontë novel. Instead of empire-waist dresses, there were longyis. In place of tea and scones, it was bananas and biscuits. These genteel, prosperous scenes, as described in my grandmother's oral histories, gave the impression that life in those days was charmed and charming, and maybe just a little bit shallow. My mother also recounted impossibly romantic stories about her own adolescence in Burma: games of lawn tennis and croquet, swishy embassy parties under twinkling lights, the fragrance of frangipani blossoms wafting in the air as she walked to school. My own walk to school was punctuated with the smell of car exhaust and the cattish breath of the crossing guard who stood at the intersection of Davenport Street and Reno Road. My mother, meanwhile, could still smell the soil after the monsoons, remembering vividly how she would use a giant palm leaf as an umbrella when the rains arrived.

My grandmother eventually left home and settled down. Never one to be plagued by self-doubt, she announced to me that she was "quite popular," and by that she meant "I had a whole lot of boyfriends."† She added, by way of explanation, "They used to visit my house. As friends!" Her older sister was no fan of these

---

* I'm not exactly sure what kind of shirts Pauline Lumumba—wife of the Congolese independence leader—was preferential to.

† Not a bad metric, all things considered.

platonic visits, and scolded my grandmother to behave. "You should be prim and proper like a Buddhist girl brought up by a decent family. Don't spoil our name. You should behave yourself. Don't flirt with all these people!"

One lowly student (a history major, Mya Mya specified) tried his hand at courtship, about which her sister was "quite nosy and observant," pointing out "there was only half a thumb on one of his hands." Said lover's chances from then on, naturally, were doomed. Ultimately, she married a man named U Thant Gyi, a family friend and (scandalously) a widower ten years her senior, patriarch to his own clan of four children. Unfailingly gentle and good-natured, he was as much a father as a husband to his young bride—friends joked that when they wed, U Thant Gyi had five children: his four, plus my grandmother, Mya Mya.

U Thant Gyi was a relatively powerful government bureaucrat in the Burmese education department, happy to indulge his wife's whims, never fighting and preferring to run away from home for days at a time rather than deal with her nagging—at least according to my mother. But his marriage to my grandmother was a successful one, in that they had two children together and stayed married until the end.

Here was the place where our stories—my grandmother's and my own—finally intersected. I knew U Thant Gyi firsthand, though our time together was brief: Mostly what I remembered were his last days on terra firma, when he was dying of esophageal cancer and had been brought home to gaze at his garden through a set of sliding glass doors. I was nearly three years old and carried around with me a bottle of childrens' pink Tinkerbell nail polish, which he graciously allowed me to paint on his fine, dark Burmese hands. Even as a child, I remember being struck by the generosity of this gesture (my father would never have indulged the same), and this quiet benevolence remains, in my mind, the most marked (and, to be honest, the only) trait that I remember about him. That and a predilection for Brach's butterscotch candies, which turned out to be genetic. But still: I did touch him—and therefore my connection to all that history was tangible, tactile.

Despite all the granular details my grandmother could recount about life back then, her memories still felt weightless. They were intoxicating and pleasant, like perfumed vapors from an old armoire, but they were decidedly incomplete and very nearly transient, offering little to hold on to. That is to say, I had certain information—but what did I really know?

And so I began my own research to fill in the blanks, to better understand what was happening outside of the plush interior of the family's Dodge motorcar. After all, the things happening elsewhere—which was to say, in the streets immediately outside their happy compound—were terrible enough to force my family out of Burma . . . forever. Somehow, this sweet story went rancid, and the good ole days became a voyage of flight and exile. I realized that as much as I delighted in the stories of newly purchased Saxon shoes, as vividly as I could imagine the Cadbury chocolate softened by Rangoon's tropical heat, these stories carried as much heft as the tales my parents told at Christmas about sleigh rides and chestnuts. U Myint Kaung was Drosselmeyer in *The Nutcracker*, a benevolent character filled with seasonal largesse; our sugar plums were bananas.

I knew that my grandmother had a cunning way of curving

reality to fit her needs, of seeing what was worthy and lustrous rather than what might have been impoverished and painful. This was equally a result of privilege (comfortable people enjoy comfort, after all) and deprivation (better to focus on the good ole days when living in the mean present).

Perhaps this was why Burma still felt so distant to me—I was romanced by the elided storytelling, but it had simultaneously kept me at arm's distance from the country itself. It was impossible to make a connection to Burma when Burma might have been the Sugar Plum Fairy's backyard. I lived in the age of Trumpism and dating apps, ISIS and Soylent meal substitutes, dystopian realities that seemed wholly at odds with my blissful Burmese heritage. If I really was going to dig in and determine whether these were my people, I needed some sort of corroboration about what, exactly, was really happening.

I realized that apart from Mya Mya's recollections of the halcyon days of banana-noshing Rangoon Society, I didn't really know what else had been going on in the country, especially at a time when so much was changing. Burmese independence from the British was right around the corner, and the beginning of modern Burma's slide into oblivion was about to commence. What was happening while the cheroots were being rolled and the newspapers thumbed through?

All I knew about Burma in that period was that the military began to flex its muscle, and that the place where George Orwell lived for several years somehow morphed—rather quickly—into a reasonable facsimile of *Animal Farm* itself. But what, exactly, happened to refashion what had been a nascent but well-regarded independence movement, complete with a booming economy and an educated population, into a place of nearly unrecognizable hope and despair—in just a few short years? What could have caused a generation of Burmese, including my family, to abandon the frangipani blossoms and night markets, the bustling shopping centers and fragrant curries from home—for a cold, unknown place on the other side of the world . . . and to never look back?

My mother and grandmother never expressed a single sentence of regret about leaving Burma behind, and yet they remembered the place with near-mystical reverence. I couldn't square these two notions and realized I had only the most embarrassingly vague understanding of the circumstances in Burma when they left. Who exactly was in power? How restive was the population? What did the rest of the world know about what was going on? When did the poison start coursing through Burma's veins? No one in my family seemed to know, or if they did, they must not have been paying close attention. But I would have to. At this point in my career as a journalist, I understood that few old timey narratives were purely uncomplicated, happy ones. It always rang alarm bells when anyone got misty-eyed about the good times, because, in reality, those were often the actually pretty bad times for quite a few other people, especially the characters outside of the immediate story line. One man might want to make America great again (actually, a few men) but a boatload of people were plenty happy with how far America had come since then.

The stories that I'd been presented about home, or at least the heartwarming edits from my father's and mother's sides, had been remarkably free of complication: Could that really be?

I already knew the answer. After all, they weren't in those places anymore—they'd left them! Why the flight—and what happened in departure? It was one thing for my elders to hold these polished narratives close to their hearts, well-worn keepsakes that reminded them of home, but if this was going to be my story, I needed to understand it truthfully. And apparently, that began with some very basic information.

I started scouring the Internet, ordering out-of-print books and obscure volumes of history that could provide a window onto Burma in the great period of our family heyday. I looked for clues, hooks into the past that might shed some light on the circumstances beyond the house on Shan Road, trying to unwind the relationship between the Brits and the Burmese, as well as (and perhaps even more important) the Burmese and the Burmese.

My cousin Geoff had been a Fulbright scholar in Burma and immersed himself in all manner of historical research as part of his fancy-pants Columbia University doctoral work. We were discussing our family history one afternoon when he mentioned in passing that U Myint Kaung had worked as a director of Burma's cooperative societies. I had no idea what these "cooperative societies" were, but I didn't let on to that fact, lest Geoff grasp how woefully unprepared I was to embark upon this research. I nodded, and he kept talking.

"I think the co-ops were kind of a failure?" he offered, as if he also wasn't quite sure what they were.

Geoff looked at me and I looked at him, blankly. While I couldn't offer my cousin anything in the way of confirmation or denial, I remember thinking this was strange: Failure was not something that had ever been mentioned in conjunction with our halcyon days of triumph and cheroots. Nor was it something associated with our family on the whole, because we were naturally successful and inclined toward unprecedented achievement. I'd found a snag in the carefully woven story. So I pulled it.

PART II

BULLET HOLES AND ASHES

CHAPTER FOUR

———— // ————

"Ko Po Kyin," she said, "you have done very much evil in your life."

U Po Kyin waved his hand. "What does it matter? My pagodas will atone for everything. There is plenty of time."

—George Orwell, *Burmese Days*

As it turns out, I would unravel the story of my maternal great-grandfather's homeland—and discover that it was not some sort of mist-covered Brigadoon-style utopia, but a place that was saddled with every society's ongoing crisis since the birth of modernity: a crisis of identity. Who are we? Who belongs here? These were familiar questions to me, after all: Determining who my own people were was a problem that had plagued me since I was a kid, unsuccessfully avoiding cold buckets of water at the suburban Thingyan festival in early April.

But now these queries had taken on an epic scope, thanks to my ancestral search. The seemingly benign personal quest that sent me back to Burma—my newfound avid interest in understanding my heritage—was, in fact, the core of the crisis that had splintered Burma, had indeed broken the world apart and spun my family halfway across the globe to the place I was born. But I didn't know all of this yet. To understand it, I had to first find my great-grandfather, a person filled with passions and fears and convictions and doubts, and not the sepia-toned patriarch of the mystical good ole days.

Burma's natural world was the lush, blooming backdrop in U Myint Kaung's biography. I could imagine the papery white flowers of the teaks that began to bloom when the rains arrived in June, until the downpours receded in August. I knew that for much of the twentieth and early twenty-first century, the ruling military junta had exploited these tall hardwoods, which account for half of the world's teak forests. The trees were destined at some point or another to become outdoor furniture or boat decking—timber from the East to make playthings for the West; money from the West to empower dictators in the East.

And then there was the jade—that green aluminum silicate believed by the Chinese to be the bridge between heaven and hell that streaks the rock formations of Burma's jungles.[1] My grandmother and mother had bangles made of the stuff, and I could still hear the way they made soft clinking sounds when rubbed together. Burma's jade accounts for nearly three-quarters of the global supply, and continues to be extracted in brutal conditions that more resemble a squalid underworld than the celestial beyond.[2]

But back in the late nineteenth century, before U Myint Kaung had purchased his first pair of Saxon shoes, and when the British were just beginning their takeover of the Bamah and the Kachin and the Shan and the Chin, the export that put his country on the map had its humble origins in the fertile deltas of the Irrawaddy River, a place both unassuming and bloodless. Rice—Asia's staple crop and Burma's mainstay—brought this corner of Southeast Asia international acclaim.

With the opening of the Suez Canal in 1869, several years after U Myint Kaung was born, Burma became an agricultural powerhouse. Ships traveling from the port of Rangoon no longer had to circumnavigate Africa to reach the markets (and mouths) of Europe. A vessel could depart the warm waters of the Bay of Bengal and arrive in the chilly North Atlantic in five weeks, a voyage that had previously taken six months.[3]

Rapidly industrializing Europe and its cities of Amsterdam and Paris and Brussels needed food. Rice entered the Old World through the port cities of Hamburg and Rotterdam, Gdańsk, and Bremen[4]—not far from landlocked Luxembourg, where Henry Wagner would soon depart for the New World. The markets in Western and Northern Europe spurred rice production elsewhere—including the Carolinas, American states where backbreaking labor was very nearly a component of the soil. But in this moment, it was Burma under the British that became the world's "rice bowl"—a claim that my mother's mother and my mother (and even I, on occasion) never let anyone forget, lest they think our motherland some lazy-ass backwater with no real industry to speak of.

Where Burmese kings had restricted the export of rice, the British saw opportunity and dollar signs and set about conquering the rice bowl.[5] Their first incursion began shortly after the Burmese made inroads toward British India, conquering the kingdoms of Manipur and Assam in 1821. In response, the Brits declared the kingdoms of Cachar (in Assam) and Jaintia (in northeast India) to be under their protection, setting the stage for confrontation: The First Anglo-Burmese War began in 1824.

There would be three wars between the British (assisted by the Indians, over whom they had established dominion) and the Burmese monarchy, culminating on November 27, 1887 (precisely ninety years to the day before my birth), when the British deposed the last Burmese king, lowered the country's flag, and raised the Union Jack over the teak roofs of the palace compound. Thanks to Sa'id Pasha, the tens of thousands of Egyptians who died slicing open that waterway from the Red Sea to the Mediterranean, and the tens of thousands of dark-skinned laborers forced into a permanent hunch at harvest time, the port of Rangoon became a major shipping outpost.

From 1885 until 1910, rice production in Burma went from a few hundred thousand tons to 1.5 million tons.[6] The British Empire was further enriched, and Burmese like my great-grandfather were now educated in British schools, taught to speak their language, and otherwise encouraged to adapt to the colonial powers.

Burma the British colony may have seemed a willing cele-brant in the pageantry of global trade, but behind the curtain a steep price was being paid by the Burmese themselves. Rice was its own kind of hell. The seeding and sowing, the thresh-ing and harvesting by hand—it was labor so tough that in later years the Burmese military would forcibly conscript citizens to harvest.[7] (It is a system that largely remains in place today, al-beit with deteriorating transportation infrastructure and worse crop yields.) Seeds and fertilizer, irrigation equipment: These all cost money, and Burmese farmers—even in the middle of a rice boom—struggled to find capital to cover the costs of growing the crop on their land. The cash outlay was over-whelming.

With no real banking structure to support the loans, the farmers turned to Chettiars, moneylenders from southern India who had decamped for Burma, seeing an open market for their trade.[8] They'd lend money out to farmers, but should the farmer default, the land became property of the Chettiar. Rice productivity fluctuated with the seasons, harvests were unpredictable, and interest rates were high. Property titles began to default into the hands of the moneylenders, and farmers who had owned land for generations became tenants, subjects of absentee landowners who had neither the interest nor the inclination to be rice farmers. It was a bad deal for the moneylenders and their depositors back home; it was a bad deal for the farmers of Burma. It was not a very fine balance. The British rulers and their Burmese subjects understood this, particularly my great-grandfather U Myint Kaung. It was the cause to which he would devote much of his adult life.

To be clear: I had never, ever been interested in agricultural economics. Nor did I concern myself previously with Burmese crop yields or agrarian policy. I was confused enough about the 2007 mortgage crisis here in the States; it never dawned on me that one day I would find the subject of nineteenth-century Indo-Burmese moneylending something worth pursuing, let alone something that I'd actually find interesting. But it was interesting! Because it was mine.

This heretofore arcane data—the crop yields and agrarian policies and economics of rice—this was part of my family story. And for the first time, I could see how the titanic forces of global history (plus the more regional history of the Burmese almanac) was part of my ancestral tale. The opening of the Suez Canal, the colonization of Upper Burma, the appetite for rice in the lowlands of Europe—these massive, abstract forces that shaped the world were no longer nebulous, no longer something that just affected an unseen population in generally sweeping fashion. These seismic developments hit my backyard. Trace your ancestry and you end up charting the course of global struggle.

Maybe this was why so many people were so intoxicated by the practice: *Who we are* is a product of battles fought long before us. The winners and losers from centuries ago determine our very existence, as well as a not-incidental part of our day-to-day fate. Genealogy forces the realization that the "beginning" of any story—the uppermost branches of a family tree, the origin tale passed down through the generations—is no beginning at all. Go far back enough, and you'll realize that your ancestors and their lives were inevitably part of a much grander narrative: the history of the world itself. No family story flows from nothing, after all.

So I had a stake in all of it—colonialism, war, the British Empire, the succession of Burmese monarchs, the rain in Rangoon—and within those epic forces was the thread of our story, in the form of a certain person named U Myint Kaung, a man who made decisions, chose certain paths, and came to be a certain way thanks to the chaos of history and the unpredictability of human nature. To seek answers in reference books would not be enough. I had to get down to the personal, to understand what specifically he'd done (or tried to do).

Without doubt, this would be the hardest part of the search. Though it may feel satisfying to couch your own family story among the great movements of time, you inevitably realize that history, as cruel as it is, has winners and losers. Because of this, one's people may be (yes) champions or (gasp) villains. Of course, everyone wants to believe that their ancestors were the winners, the day savers and unsung heroes—or that if they were the losers, they were the valiant innocents, the ones fighting to keep the world from falling apart. But who were they really? Were they innocents, or were they criminals? Did they do the right thing or the very wrong one? I'd have to ask: What role did my people play in our newly discovered Burmese drama?

"Chettiar banks are fiery dragons that parch every land that has the misfortune of coming under their wicked creeping. They are a hard-hearted lot that will ring out every drop of blood from the victims without compunction for the sake of their own land."[9]

This was the testimony from one Karen member of the legislative council before the government of Burma in 1929. The Great Depression had pushed tensions between the farmers and the lenders to an all-time high. In 1930, Chettiars occupied 6 percent of total land in Burma. Eight years later, they owned a quarter of the country.[10] It was putting it mildly to say that this chafed at the national identity of the Burmese.

Before things reached this point, there had been a plan for another way. The British, seeing the writing on the wall with the Chettiars, had a lightbulb moment: a way to finance rice production without Indian interlopers and, in the bargain, school the Burmese in the ways of thrift and Christian responsibility. They called this lightbulb the cooperative credit societies, a three-tiered Rube Goldberg machine designed to produce virtue, credit, and rice.

The co-ops fell into three tiers: At the bottom were credit societies (made up of individuals and households). Managing them were the credit unions, composed of several credit societies, who were supposed to vet community members for loans. At the very top were the banks (chief among them the provincial bank) controlled by the British—and which, when necessary, lent to the credit unions. The banks were able to do so thanks to their deposits from the well-to-do public, of which a fair share were European.[11] My great-grandfather worked at the essential pivot of the whole system: the credit union. U Myint Kaung's job was to make sure money was going to the right people: Burmese with that elusive "money sense."

It was a pyramid structure—one that was supposed to be rooted in trust and community responsibility—but the word "pyramid" was an unfortunate indicator about how successful this particular financial strategy would end up being. You could already see where there were problems with this plan: If the credit societies lent to wayward Burmese with no real money sense, or if the credit union did a crappy audit about the financial solvency of the individuals it was lending to, well, then . . . someone was gonna pay for it.

The societies proliferated in the early 1920s across Burma. But by 1925, the "cooperative movement was clogged with bad Societies" and loans were being made "too easily."[12] Something called the Calvert Committee was convened to assess exactly how this happened and it recommended the provincial bank be "wound up forthwith." (British English didn't allow for much alarmism, but this signaled the proverbial hand hitting the proverbial red button.) By 1932, the all-important provincial bank had been liquidated.

What happened, exactly? The Calvert Committee pinpointed "an inherent weakness . . . characteristic of the Burmans." That flaw was "a certain delicacy in dealing with the faults and misdemeanors of their neighbours. [The Burmans] prefer to put up with the administration [of] malpractices in the hope that . . . the Government may one day come and put things right."[13]

In other words, the Burmese, in the eyes of the committee, were simply too polite to turn down bad candidates for loans—too weak to say no to their neighbors and fellow farmers who were looking for capital. U Myint Kaung and the other supervisors at the credit unions had performed faulty audits (or none at all), and compensated for these bad decisions by papering over them. These supervisors were declared to be "untrained, uneducated in co-operative banking or co-operative principles and unfit to be let loose amongst any body of cooperators."[14]

Terms such as "untrained" and "let loose" should give you a sense of the respect accorded the Burmese supervisors, who by all (British) accounts ran their cooperatives with the competence of roving, wild (albeit occasionally benevolent) pigs. The bottom of the cooperative society pyramid was riddled with negligent assessments, crony capitalism, rotten apples, and financial obfuscation—in part due to that thing that the British wished so badly to improve upon—the Burmese character. A second, more far-reaching report again focused on Burmese competence: "In Burma, the character of the people is such that a system of official control cannot succeed."[15]

In trying to get a wider look at my family history, this is what I discovered: My people were weak and dishonest and stupid and corrupt. But if you asked anyone in our family if they thought that the patriarch U Myint Kaung had been a power-house government minister, some sort of proto–Ben Bernanke of agrarian finance, they'd have said yes without hesitation. My grandmother glossed over a lot of details in her retelling of our family history, but when I asked her about her father's position, she enunciated very clearly when she dropped that title: deputy commissioner for the Cooperative Societies of Upper Burma, a sort of bureaucratic humblebrag.

Did she not know that the cooperative societies were . . . a di-saster? That they were at the center of Burma's own little fi-nancial bailout? Did we not know our people were failures? Or did we just not care? I cared, in part because America was going through its own reconciliation of Financial Sins, and it pained me to think of my great-grandfather as an actor who'd brought so many Burmese to their knees, courtesy of a failed banking system. (I, unlike the British assessors, was not ready to pin the blame on a certain, unavoidable character flaw in the Burmese people. The system itself seemed pretty faulty and badly managed.) More than that, though, I was both incredu-lous that this history had been entirely hidden until now (it seemed painfully ignorant to crow about a title if you didn't understand the work), and also, in some strange way, relieved by the humiliation. It made U Myint Kaung real, in a way that all the other stories about him had not: He had tried and he had failed. Just like I had, just like everybody who populated the world in which I lived. Shame was hard, but it was also humanizing. Much more so than my grandmother's icky and ingratiating Legend of the Dodge, this family story, based in shame and disgrace, made U Myint Kaung a real person.

My grandmother may have been too busy to follow the specifics of her father's career flameout, given the fact that she was off studying and flirting with nine-fingered suitors at Rangoon University. But discovering the epic shitstorm that was the Co-operative Societies Experiment definitely illuminated U Myint Kaung's later decision to leave behind all of his worldly possessions and head up to the monastery to devote the remainder of his life to Buddhist meditation. This was a common practice in Burmese society—the pursuit of an existence devoid of materialism—but it was made all the more poignant after the cratering of his lifelong endeavor. He was done with the material world.

Maybe he was now convinced that the path to redemption lay in selflessness, in commitment to the community. Those British officers knew a lot about making shoes and whiskey cake, but they didn't understand his fellow countrymen, and they certainly weren't in any position to make pronouncements about the true nature of the Burmese.

My mother later told me that after the whole system of co-operatives came crashing down, U Myint Kaung's wife—who came from wealth and had invested all her money in the co-ops—lost all of her savings. Aghast and inconsolable, she confronted her husband: "Why didn't you warn me about what was to happen?" she demanded. According to my mother, he reasoned (quite phenomenally): "If the workers and the farmers did not know, then why should you?"

If he was not good at his job—if he was guilty of professional malpractice—U Myint Kaung appeared to have been an intensely moral person. For me, he exists only in anecdote, and therefore these stories—told mostly by my grandmother—are all I have to divine his motivations. But I think he must have been scarred by what happened to his country's economy and what he had done to precipitate its failure. I also believe that he held on to the ideals that brought him to this line of work in the first place, up until the end of his life. That became especially clear when I considered one particular story about him that I had known very well even *before* I embarked on the project to figure out who my people were. My grandmother had repeated it countless times—and each time she did, it gave me a sense of pride.

After having relinquished his ties to the family and spent some unspecified amount of time at the monastery, U Myint Kaung got word that his wife had begun the unsavory practice of moneylending—making small loans and then charging interest, the very thing he had worked to eradicate (or at least marginalize) in setting up the farmers' cooperatives in Upper Burma. She had, after all, lost most of the money she once had.

From my grandmother's recollection: "He marched down the hill to our home and said to my mother: 'Are you starving? Do you want for anything?' She protested—vaguely—and then begrudgingly admitted she did not want for anything, nor was she starving.

"Well, then," he said, "Don't bargain so much."

And he turned and went back up the hill. She never charged interest again.

While the British (and Burmese) worked to stabilize an economy that was on the precipice of financial collapse, the seams stitching together Burma's patchwork union had more than begun to strain. To be clear, Burma is one country in the same way that Iraq is one country, which is to say it's not. It—like Iraq—is a collection of contested land that's been fought over for decades, with some years bloodier than others. Burma's borders were drawn arbitrarily over time and in the aftermath of battle, by conquerors and colonialists alike. The tensions between the Chin and the Shan, the Karen and the Kachin—as well as the wealthy Bamah and the British ruling class—while already significant, were under remarkable strain in the waning years of colonialism, right as my grandmother came of age.

I knew this, growing up, mostly because Burma's war within a war—the ethnic tensions that had exacerbated the military campaign to subdue the country and harvest its riches, both human and environmental—was a part of discussions about the problems plaguing the country. And yet, for whatever reason, I had never seen this truth as a hindrance to my claim of being "Burmese" and the secret pride that my tribe, our tribe, was the one for whom the country was named.

For a few years in the late aughts, I ran a nonprofit organization focused on combating international human rights violations around the world. As part of this work, I went to the Thai-Burma border to visit refugee camps where entire generations of children were languishing: This was the cost of Burma's forever war with itself. Ethnic minorities had been uprooted and forced to the margins, whether because of intertribal conflict or (more usually) targeted campaigns of violence launched by the military regime. The camps were sprawling cities, without adequate resources for a population that would live in them for years on end. And yet, amid this heartbreak and turmoil, I couldn't forget the fact that these Burmese were not Bamah Burmese—they were Kachin or Chin or Shan or Karen or another tribe. And though I felt terrible for them, was angry at the deplorable situation and resolute about holding someone responsible for it, I couldn't help but notice a sneaking and unshakable sense of ethnic superiority within myself.

My people were not in these camps, after all. They were not forsaken into misery and squalor, but had instead escaped it when they could, because of their resources and education and class. This was evidence of the powerful narcotic of identity: how quickly, and easily, one could go from pride to superiority, from celebration of self to dismissal of others. Even as I recognized this, even as I grew older and more acutely aware of how vigilant one needed to be in pushing back against the dark impulse to separate Us from Them, there was still something in me that clutched at supremacy, however subconsciously, as I thought about Burma's miseries. The distinction was a refuge—and who didn't want a refuge?

I was trying to find meaning in connecting my family story to blood and land, but blood was precisely the thing dividing the land, carving it into subgroups and territories. Blood was the thing that would continue to fuel division, to speed the dissolution of society and break apart the Burma that my mother and grandmother could still dream so vividly about. It was the seed of our despair.

As it turned out, my grandmother's allegiance to Burma was tied not to the country, necessarily, but to her slice of it, her ethnic subgroup, her class. Even after the British lowered their Union Jack for the last time on January 4, 1948, Burma's tribal strife continued to escalate, but I'm getting ahead of myself. Our family wasn't in the hills of Shan State or pushing off the Karenni Christian army (far from it), but simmering race tension could be found right in our kitchen. Quite literally simmering.

"We had an Indian cook who made the most delicious curry," my grandmother wistfully recalled. By way of a coda, she offered—always—this caveat: "And he robbed us blind."

From these aromatic and lusty recollections, I could very nearly taste this curry. For most of my adolescence, when I was confronted by soggy grilled cheese sandwiches and limp tater tots in the school cafeteria, my mother offered impossible childhood stories of her own: the family driver dropping off stacked tiffin carriers during *her* school lunchtime, small aluminum containers filled with piping hot vindaloos and dals, all prepared by the same masterful-if-greedy hand. But the story always ended in the same refrain: He robbed the family blind! Oh, this cruel price we had to pay, unspecified rubies for untold biryanis. It was an impossible choice, but there was only one to make. The cook was dismissed, taking with him all those curries and vindaloos—and what a loss this was. Replacements were hired, but no one could replicate that harmony over the stove. That Indian cook! Who was he? No one ever mentioned his name, only the dishes he prepared.

From the outset of the Indian-Burmese commingling, many Burmans, including my grandmother, referred to Indians as *kala*. The word's origins may be from the Sanskrit word *kula*— meaning "caste man"—or *kala*, for "black man." Or it may be from the Burmese word *ka la*—the term for "coming from overseas." Even after half a century in the United States, my grandmother always referred to Indians as *kalas*, which we American-born offspring giggled at but didn't quite understand. As it turns out, she might have been calling them, basically, house negroes.

According to public health and humanitarian professional Nance Cunningham, a prominent scholar on the Burmese language, most explanations for the word that you hear nowadays "are colored by prejudice." Cunningham offered that *kala* might mean "coolie"—but then doubled back on that by noting that there already happens to be the word *ku li* in Burmese. Further, a chair in Burmese is often referred to as a "coolie sit"—so the word "coolie" was also already in play. In the end, we concluded that *kala* had something to do with blackness—a racist designation with assuredly classist suggestions.

By the late 1980s and '90s and the early aughts, my grandmother had officially lived in America for thirty, forty, fifty years. She had gay friends dating back to the 1970s—friends with whom she drank cocktails after work at the Library of Congress, friends who were hers for life (most of them died before she did). She spoke glowingly of the young black men who delivered groceries to her small one-bedroom on Capitol Hill in the 1960s, right after she had arrived in the States, and as she retold these stories, over time they went from being "young black men" to "young African American men." She fully grasped the implications of the language around identity, and she understood the social merits conferred by having gay male friends in the disco era, of engaging with young black men during Jim Crow.

So she knew well the power of identification, especially as it informed the American hierarchy of the enlightened, one in which educated white liberals were allegedly at the top of the pyramid, and, among the immigrant classes, Asians were often at the very bottom: reclusive, tribal, still clinging to the ways of the Old World. She was not going to be lumped in with any suspicious Korean shop owners of the Rodney King era, nor would she be confused with those country Chinese who didn't understand nappy hair. She went out of her way to promote her most Western acceptance of those two pilloried subsets: sexual and racial minorities. This, as much as her fluency in English and predilection for cosmopolitans, was hard evidence that she had assimilated, and was therefore somehow greater than the sum of her own parts. In her seeming tolerance, ironically, she moved closer to a certain white, liberal American ideal.

And yet, long after she received her American passport, she still called Indian associates, waiters, and friends *kalas* (mostly behind their backs). This term was usually dispatched with a smile, and because of this, her discreet bigotry had the veneer of a sort of delicate charm. The in-laws and cousins and grandchildren excused her use of it, in most cases pleading ignorance. Or we dismissed it as a vestige of home rather than indicative of some deep-seated racial animus. My mother, more acutely aware of how inappropriate it was, would shush my grandmother in Burmese after every utterance, while my uncle would scowl and let out a disapproving bark. But it never stopped her, really. In this I had found, whether I liked it or not, another catch in the family narrative.

I heard echoes of my grandmother's awkward behavior in a classic tale ritually recounted by urban liberal white folks every year: the trip back home for the holidays, where our enlightened white friend's beloved uncle or grandparent lets loose a racial epithet over dessert, poisoning the atmosphere. It was not easily laughed about, because that kind of racism—white racism against black people, immigrants, or Jews—was connected to the worst of American and Western history, to pogroms, to slavery and lynching, to genocide. For some reason my grandmother's vague slurring of Indians seemed more benign—embarrassing more than genuinely disturbing. Until I examined that snag a little more closely.

Her general predisposition toward Indians as untrustworthy outsiders, a race to be skeptical of, became less acceptable and certainly less charming once I looked at the blood-soaked history of our Burmese intolerance. In trying to better understand Burma and race, and just how offensive the word *kala* might have been, I picked up a small used library book from the University of California, Irvine. An out-of-print book, *The Indian Minority in Burma* by N. R. Chakravarti, is written with a highly critical eye toward the Burmese, as if to dispel my ideas about bigotry being discreet. In a rebuke to what I had always thought of as my grandmother's funny little cultural aversion, it outlines fifty years of subjugation and violent oppression of the Indians at the hand of the Burmese.

For context: There were a lot of Indians in Burma when my

family arrived in Rangoon in the 1930s. A whole lot more than I realized: Rangoon, in fact, had become a mostly Indian city. I didn't—couldn't—have known this, because in her recollections, my grandmother never once discussed the city or its inhabitants. She always spent much more time on her specific, cloistered world of teatime bananas and English-language newspapers.

For many years, it was assumed that Burma would become a Chinese state. According to the colonial historian Sir George Scott, "Unless some marvellous upheaval of energy took place in the Burman character, the Chinese were almost certainly destined to overrun the country to the exclusion of the native race."[16] Ah, but the lazy Burmese never did cede their country to their northern, ostensibly far more industrious neighbors (that would come approximately one hundred years later). In fact, it was the Indians who effectively colonized their fellow colonized:

In 1872, Indians were 16 percent of Rangoon residents.

By 1901, they were 50 percent. Burmans made up only 33 percent of the city.[17]

Indians were propelled by poverty back home, and encouraged to migrate east by an immigration policy that miraculously managed to infuriate the native-born Burmese population for its lack of protections for them *and* punish the newly arrived Indians, thanks to a lack of protections from the Burmese. The Indians migrated in vast numbers: In 1922, 360,000 of them migrated to Burma. By the 1930s, Indians owned the capital city: They built Rangoon; they ran its businesses and they conducted its trade. The Indian Chettiars already had a monopoly on moneylending, and by virtue of that played an

instrumental role in the agricultural sector, but they domi-
nated the trade and banking industries, too.

Still, in much larger numbers—perhaps as much as 99 percent of their country's immigrant population—Indians were
Burma's laboring class. They harvested crops; they mined silver and lead; they ran ships up and down the Irrawaddy; they
moved earth and pulled rickshaws. They tailored suits and
made dresses. In 1931, the second-largest occupation (not including semiskilled or unskilled workers) held by Indian migrants was domestic service. That year, census records tell us
that 11,242 male Indians were employed as house help—and at
least one of them worked for our family.

For their role in the engine room of the Burmese economy,
the Indian laboring class (unsurprisingly) got little in the way
of respect or security. Many were brought over the border by
unscrupulous labor contractors known as maistries—sort of
proto-coyotes of the nineteenth century who hauled their cargo
over the Bay of Bengal in subhuman conditions. Here's Gandhi's description of what seemed like an impossibly wretched
situation on the sea route to Burma, the so-called Golden Land:

> There are for the use of these 1,500 passengers two tiny
> bathrooms and twelve latrines. . . . This gives an average of
> one latrine to 75 passengers and one bathroom to 375 pas-
> sengers. There is only a sea-water tap in the bathrooms, but
> no fresh water tap. . . . There is a sort of a running corridor
> in front of each set of latrines. . . . Dirty water and urine from
> the latrines flow into this corridor. . . . Foul water continues
> to roll to and fro on the floor with the rolling of the ship. . . .
> The lowermost deck is nothing better than a black hole. It is

dark and dingy and stuffy and hot to the point of suffoca-
tion.[18]

Indians seeking promise in Burma paid hefty fees for this
scummy, sewage-filled experience. It didn't necessarily get a
whole hell of a lot better after landfall, either. Upon disembar-
kation, most immigrants entered the very bottom of the food
chain: They earned abysmally low wages and lived in hellish
setups, crammed as they were into squalid, disease-infested
lodging houses that were "perennially flooded with rain or
tidal waters or with stagnant pools of sullage waste."

They were shuttled into this dark misery by the scores: A
report of the Rangoon municipality noted one home where in-
spectors "found in one room 23 inmates—the dimension being
only 18 × 14 feet."[19] Opiate and alcohol addiction surrounded
by filth and open fornication: This all formed what was described (not necessarily hyperbolically) as "a tragic total complex of their slum life."[20]

So it was grim, and though the British took notice, they remained mostly bloodless in their assessments. Speaking at the
annual dinner of the Rangoon Trade Association in 1930, British governor Sir Charles Innes diagnosed the problem thusly:
"No one can read what the Rangoon Health Committee wrote
in its report about the lodging houses of Rangoon without a
feeling of shame, but also of apprehension, for these lodging
houses must be hotbeds of tuberculosis and other diseases."

Translation: These bottom dwellers might be carriers.
Shouldn't we do something to make sure they don't infect us
all?

I don't know about whether our family's gifted curry maker

lived in squalor, but the fact that many (if not most) of his countrymen and -women did adds context to his thievery. And
while the disappearance of baubles and gemstones was grounds
for dismissal from the family home, perhaps there were more
nefarious forces that cemented his fate. In other words, the
cook may have stolen those family jewels, but one doesn't imagine that his termination was hard to come by. Indians, after all,
were regarded as lower caste—my grandmother had no compunction referring to them as *kalas* for the rest of her life. It
was very clear that he wasn't deemed a valued part of the family, even if his dal was sublime.

The Indians in Burma were like Mexicans in America or the
Senegalese in France—marked with the scarlet *O* of "outsider,"
despite the fact that there existed webs of connections weav-
ing their homelands together with their destination countries.
This part of Burma's—and my family's—history surprised me
(though it shouldn't have): how very precisely history repeated
itself. My ancestral spelunking had not simply revealed a more
squalid story than I'd imagined, but—more jarring than that—
that story paralleled the moment that we were now living
through, and indeed *had* lived through.

I'd always presumed that that we, my Burmese folk, had been
the oppressed: forced to flee our homeland to reboot in America, a gang of brown exiles who created a new life on Western
shores. But as the tortured reality of Burma's history unfolded
in my research, I realized that we outsiders were once insiders,
perched atop a rickety system of class and caste. Turns out, we
the marginalized had once marginalized a whole class of our
own—we'd just done it on the other side of the globe and left it
out of the stories we told ourselves in later months and years.

Inevitably, this was true for families and their ancestors everywhere, but the real mistake everyone made was in pretending that these behaviors and sins and denials weren't a reliable pattern in our collective history, and in telling one another and our children that back then it was just great times and golden oldies, simmering curries and shiny new cars.

Even in Burma's halcyon days, the problems were the same as they were today: the powerful versus the powerless; tensions around immigration and labor and dark skin. How did a society react when forced to grapple with an influx of people from elsewhere, people who happened to be driving the economy of a country but were nonetheless relegated to its lower miseries? Shame and marginalization!

History has no real beginning or ending, we simply choose points that are most convenient for the narrative, especially as it concerns the stories about our success. In other words, a lot gets left out.

The legacy of the Indians in Burma spanned wars and marriages and dinner plates, but any public accounting of their number and density was (and remains) further complicated by class distinctions among the Indians and, of course, the divide-and-conquer manipulation that the British Empire perfected among its colonies. Upper-class Indians were the soldiers of the British during the Anglo-Burmese wars and therefore deemed forevermore the patsies of colonial rule in the eyes of the conquered Burmese. Up until Burma formally separated from India in 1937, Indians often took the high-ranking positions in the British government of Burma, and the country's army was composed largely of Indian soldiers.

In a 1938 pamphlet on Indo-Burman conflict, a young Communist leader named Thein Pe Myint put it bluntly: "When the British attacked and occupied Lower Burma as well as Upper Burma by unlawful force, their work was done mainly by the Indian Sepoys. For this reason, *we Burmese hate them*." (Emphasis mine.)[21]

Indian officials lived and drank and dined largely among themselves (or with the British), rather than with their brown brethren, and therefore the relationship of immigrants in Burma to the middle- and upper-class Burmans especially—my family, for example—was not one of Brown Solidarity, but of intrusion and of oppression. U Myint Kaung may have gone to British schools and worked for the British monarchy, but he was still a Burmese Buddhist. He knew exactly who had conquered his country and with what assistance.

My family was still living in Mandalay when the Rangoon riots of 1930 began at the docks as a fight between Burmese laborers and Indian dockworkers. Indian workers—pressing for higher wages from their employers—struck on May 8, 1930, and the largely British firms that hired them opted instead to break the picket lines with Burmese workers. Seventeen days later, the shipping masters cut a deal with their Indian dockworkers by agreeing to four pence extra per head in daily wages—and the Indians ended up paying for this paltry raise in blood.

The lately employed Burmese scabs didn't appreciate being replaced once contract negotiations had been completed and the strike was over—keep in mind this was the beginning of the Great Depression—and they took to the streets of Rangoon with swords and iron bars and anything else that could inflict maximum pain. For nearly three days, Indian workers and shops were targeted, and because the capital city was an Indian city, not much of Rangoon functioned during what was termed a riot, but was really a rampage: no sanitation systems, few public services, and no business activity to speak of.[22]

In the end, there was no full accounting of how many people died, but most estimates place the figure in the nebulous "hundreds" of deaths and "thousands" of injuries.[23] For these three days of terror, there was very nearly no response. Accounts vary, but only two arrests seem to have been made—neither one for murder or destruction of property.[24]

No compensation was doled out to the families of the slaughtered. Rangoon's Indians mostly just hid, then shut their mouths and went on about their business. They stayed in the city, a seemingly inextricable part of its fabric, until a formal separation between India and Burma was announced in 1937, and Burma was made a separate, autonomous colony under the British crown.

But this didn't stop the bloodletting. Burma remained under the British thumb, and nationalism was on the upswing. The Indian minority in Burma had few (if any) protections under the law, despite what had happened to them in the decade prior, and their complicated history fighting the Burmese on behalf of the British made them prime targets for a restive, angry citizenry. The burgeoning nationalist movement—led by Burmese Communists—played a not-insignificant role in this.

This is Thein Pe's assessment of the situation at that time:

The Indians never consider the interests of the Burmese. They are always seeking their own benefit. They never dream of working together with the Burmese for better or worse; instead they segregate themselves into a privileged minority. On many occasions in national politics as well as in district and urban administration, they make alliances with the Europeans just to oppose the Burmese.[25]

My grandmother was just finishing her studies at the university in 1938 when the tension came to a head—again. A small booklet, printed in 1931 by a Burmese Muslim named Shwe Hpi, was highly critical of the Buddhist priesthood. Almost no one had heard of Shwe Hpi or read his pamphlet, but seven years later, as Burmese nationalism was cresting, several nationalist papers picked up old excerpts and printed them for general consumption.[26]

If you didn't grow up in a predominantly Buddhist nation, or with a Buddhist parent (especially *my* Buddhist parent), it's hard to conceive of the role that monks play in society. In Burma, they are the very embodiment of piety and enlightenment, and as such are accorded the utmost respect. On my first visit to Rangoon in 2008, my mother would make me cross the street to avoid the monks who were strolling around the city in the early mornings, begging for alms. This was a sign of obeisance—a word that nobody used as often as my mother (in fact, apart from my mother, I've never even heard *anybody* use the word "obeisance").

The rest of the world came to understand the importance of Burma's monks during the Saffron Revolution of 2007—so named because of the saffron-colored robes worn by the thousands of monks who took to the streets to protest the oppressive military regime that had run their country into the ground and put their democratically elected leader under house arrest for more than a decade.

These monks weren't only wizened old vegetarians, or men with dusty bones accustomed to incense-filled prayer halls. Yes, the 2007 revolution featured a selection of wise old abbots, but most of the images beamed back to the West were of virile young men who looked more like freedom fighters than the elders of holy cloth common to the increasingly aged churches of America and Europe. These monks meant business; they were men of action. That the government summarily cut them down and drove them into hiding was not just an affront to democracy; it was a rebuke of Burmese values. For exiles and citizens alike, the image of a military officer wielding a baton against a monk was a sign that things—already pretty awful— had reached the very bottom of the dung heap.

But in 1938, Shwe Hpi's pamphlet decrying the previously unassailable monk took on outsized importance. Nationalist broadsheets such as *The New Light of Burma* and *New Burma* inflamed the situation by printing editorials targeting the Indian Muslim minority. This begat public apologies from Burma's Indian population, which seemed to do little to stem the tide of anti-Muslim anger.

Also in 1938, racial and religious hostilities reached a crisis point during a demonstration at the country's holiest Buddhist shrine: the Shwedagon Pagoda.

Amid the pagoda's gold-leafed spires and tinkling bells, violent anti-immigrant rhetoric fired up an unruly mob of protesters—who then descended the hill and launched an "indiscriminate attack on Indians . . . on a scale very much larger than that witnessed in 1930 and 1931, including cold-blooded murders, grievous hurts, looting, arson, etc."[27]

Once again, the government proved mostly useless, and once again, there was no full accounting of the lives taken or interrupted by injury, nor did anyone determine how much business was lost or destroyed. This period of marauding and aggression stretched from July to September 1938 and was described as "a long period of horror" for Rangoon's Indians—one that likely wounded and claimed lives into the thousands.

Little was done by almost anyone in the wake of this bloodshed. The government response—even in India—consisted mostly of unanimous and official public indignation, rather than any measurable action to protect the people who had built Rangoon and were being crushed in its racist rampages.

The Burmese account insisted that Indians had instigated the violence by stabbing a Buddhist monk—and later spearing a Burman to death. Thein Pe did, however, concede that "the Burmese being more hot-blooded, reckless and impetuous than the Indians can easily turn the tables against their aggressor." And so they did.

The Indian Legislative Assembly asserted that its government—as well as the British and Burmese—had been criminally negligent in protecting Indians' interests in Burma. But the Burmese had no interest in curbing the movement that gave rise to the chaos: nationalism. In fact, the outrage in India over the violence against Indians in Burma had the awful, circular effect of further inflaming *Burmese* tempers. Nationalists "considered it an uncalled-for interference in Burma's internal affairs and threatened to take retaliatory measures if the Indian agitation was not stopped."[28]

It was sickening, the rage and destruction, hell-bent nationalism run amok—but also familiar to anyone raised in the twentieth-century West. Why did we keep doing this to ourselves, over and over again? I'd thought, or hoped, that Burma before its fall had been somehow different, exempt from the cruelties of the masses, free from the bloody entitlements of power. It was not.

And as I learned about all of this from Mr. Chakravarti's little yellowed out-of-print library book, I began to wonder: Where was my family when Rangoon was being torn apart? How had no one ever mentioned this to me? Fine, the Indian curry was magnificent, but somehow the violent oppression of Indians in our own backyard never made it onto the family radar. The Burmese public was not in the dark: Fifty thousand copies of Thein Pe's pamphlet detailing what had happened were distributed to the Burmese public—the highest recorded circulation of that type of material *in Burmese history*.[29]

My grandmother graduated from Rangoon University in 1938 with honors in Pali and a minor in Sanskrit—the sacred language of Hinduism that formed the basis of the Indian language and Burmese holy texts. She understood well the fact that one culture had a very great deal in common with the other, especially in the realm of the devout—but in all her recollections about those golden years, she never made mention of this carnage.

It wasn't just Mya Mya Gyi, or the rest of our family, that conspicuously avoided this chapter. It was like amnesia, or maybe even a cultural lacuna: Burma had erased from its collective memory what had happened to these people, or, more specifically, what the country's most virulent strains had done in the name of body purification. So much so that my grandmother—nearly seventy-five years later—still felt free to refer to the race of the punished as caste men, black men, outsiders, the house negroes of the good old days, never once mentioning that they had been subject to abuses and assaults too numerous to catalogue. How weird this seemed in retrospect, and how strangely disgusting that she would focus on the loss of rubies and pearls and lamb vindaloo as the Seriously Traumatic Event Involving an Indian that befell her and our family, rather than this insane, terrifying chapter of violence that she had presumably borne witness to.

With this history in the near background, much of Burma's Indian population fled the country following Japanese occupation in World War II; those that remained were expelled in 1962—a not-surprising (though still foul and heartbreaking) decision on the part of the ruling military junta, which was intoxicated with nationalist fervor. For the most part, this forced exodus of Indians from Burma was better documented as a chapter of great shame. There were too many Indian exiles who remembered too much about all the things they had lost in departure—businesses, friends, lives. There was so much detritus in the wake of this expulsion that Rangoon was never the same again.

I began now to see the outlines of a noxious pattern in the accusations and amnesia. In Burma, it had been the targeting and expulsion of Indians—while here in the United States, it was Mexicans and Muslims and Guatemalans and Hondurans and Sudanese and Syrians (they were most certainly darker, whoever they were). It was the very same fracturing, along the very same lines—sad confirmation that animus and violence and expulsion always end up screwing everyone, even the people doing the expelling. (Ask the Burmese of today whether the expulsion of the Indian minority was a good thing for their economy, to say nothing of their reputations.)

This was an important development, in and of itself: I could point to this Burmese tragedy as evidence that the xenophobes here and elsewhere were on the wrong side of history, but what was perhaps more noteworthy—what all of this research revealed—was that *my* folks may have been the ones wearing the MAKE BURMA GREAT AGAIN trucker hats, with Shwe Hpi standing in as their Trump. At the very least, they were the ones turning a blind eye to the chaos, a blindness that carried over even into our new start in America, where the Indians remained *kalas*—even half a century later—just as the Mexicans will probably remain wetbacks to some other, privileged set of future Americans.

The self-loathing didn't end there. As it turns out, it wasn't very hard to find the truth, or at least the context behind all of my grandmother's lovely stories. Yes, it took reading a few books and a fair amount of Googling and the deployment of a (somewhat) fine-toothed bullshit comb, but not much else. As far as my great family project was concerned, this was merely scratching the surface, and yet how easily it gave way! How swiftly the picture dissolved from "bananas at teatime" to something much more complex and sad and violent. I felt like a sucker for having indulged in the old-timey elegance of her stories, for not having questioned what was really going down mere blocks from the light-filled house on Shan Road. I felt like a simpleton for having believed our family mythmaking—I, who prided myself on having some sort of magical, twenty-first-century gimlet eye. Was this any better than the tourist of the American South visiting the old plantation houses, marveling at the china and the gowns and the sweeping staircases, never once glancing past the big house to the slave quarters just beyond?

As all this historic information shook my conception of self and family in the here and now, so, too, did this research throw a mammoth-sized wrench in the narrative of repression and exile that my family had been spinning for much of the past few decades. I'd boasted throughout my adolescence about my grandmother's status as a pro-democracy activist, her zeal for the righteous cause of Aung San Suu Kyi, and her personal fight for democracy in Burma. But that fervent patriotism, it turned out, was born of a darker strain of ethnic nationalism.

In July 2013, *Time* magazine, arbiter of newsworthiness and chronicler of international trends, ran as its cover story a picture of the monk Ashin Wirathu, under the headline "The Face of Burmese Terror." Wirathu is headquartered in Mandalay, in central Burma, and some people refer to him as the "Burmese Bin Laden" (something he apparently accepts without compunction), the figurehead for a growing violent Buddhist movement that seeks to destroy the presence of Islam inside Burma's borders. But the language he uses is basically torn from the pages of the Burmese nationalist papers of the 1930s:

"We are being raped in every town, we are being sexually harassed in every town, being ganged up and bullied in every town," he announced to *The Guardian* in 2013. "In every town, there is a crude and savage Muslim majority."[30]

Never mind that Muslims account for only an estimated 5 percent of Burma's population. (Buddhists are the overwhelming majority at 90 percent.) Wirathu's followers have done their best to shrink that percentage through slaughter: One particularly gruesome rampage at a Muslim boarding school killed thirty-two students and four teachers. The most persecuted among them, the Muslim Rohingyas, have lived for decades as landless, stateless citizens in the southwest Rakhine State—where they languish in squalid camps, and are unable to vote in elections to perhaps choose representatives who might take into consideration their plight and lift them from this deplorable existence.

In 2012, after the rape of a Buddhist woman by an allegedly Muslim assailant, ethnic tensions exploded: The Rohingya became targets, and 140,000 of them ended up in camps for internally displaced persons.[31] By 2016, the Burmese military was in an all-out assault against the Muslim minority: In one particularly brutal incursion, 1,500 Rohingya homes were burned. An estimated 65,000 of them fled to Bangladesh at the end of the year, forced out by violence, systematic rape, and destruction.

And by 2017, the Burmese government was engaged in what one top UN official called "a textbook example of ethnic cleansing."[32] Rohingya villages were being burned, their residents raped, killed, and otherwise hunted. The depravity was not to be overstated: Babies were being thrown into fires, stabbed to death—as their mothers watched, gang-raped and left for dead. Whole families were being extinguished, live grenades thrown through the front door. As a result, more than 400,000 Rohingya fled Burma—desperate to survive.[33]

In the eyes of certain international observers, this systematic and sanctioned violence is often explained as Burma's (deeply troubled) effort to stave off Muslim jihad: The Burmese government—and indeed figures like Wirathu—are fighting against the encroachment of Islam in Southeast Asia (Indonesia, Malaysia, Sri Lanka), lands that were formerly Buddhist territories. This is their mission to secure ancestral lands, or at the very least act as a bulwark against a rising tide of violent extremism (never mind the twisted irony). But—as I discovered in my running of the bullshit comb through history —wasn't this Buddhist cleansing mostly a contemporary expression of long-held bigotry against Indian Muslims?

Most uncomfortably, I began to rethink my family's very own brand of Burmese nationalism—which, okay, had nothing to do with rioting or marauding or any bloodlust that I could pinpoint, but was firmly rooted in the same nationalism championed by the heroes of the movement who overthrew the British. My grandmother had long been a vocal advocate for Burmese democracy. She attended monthly protests and organizational meetings, regularly taking minutes for a group of exiled elders who were intent on one day regaining power, once the military had been ousted or had surrendered in a bloodless coup. She read news from the home front fanatically and held strong opinions about what was happening back home, reserving her most pronounced disgust for the military leaders who had destroyed her country beyond recognition. The actual battlefront may have been on the other side of the world, but she considered herself a soldier nonetheless.

The leader of this de facto movement, the spiritual guide in both Burma and abroad, was (and is) a woman named Aung San Suu Kyi: daughter of the military demi-god Aung San, who led the Burmese in the struggle for independence from the British and for whom there is a national celebration (even now) every year on January 4. From birth, Daw Suu—as she is known—has been an object of fascination to all Burmese, given her lineage, but she took on mythic qualities after the 1988 uprising, when she happened to be in the country (she had been living in England with her family) caring for her ailing mother. Witnessing the events unfold around her, she evolved into a de facto leader of the resistance movement, making speeches and writing what would become the seminal texts in the pro-democracy movement.

She was subsequently placed under house arrest, where she won the Nobel Peace Prize in 1991 (and was unable to accept it, lest she leave the country and never be allowed back in again). In the intervening years, her husband died and her children grew up motherless, but Aung San Suu Kyi remained unbreakable. She would not leave her Burma. She forsook her family, because in this struggle, she understood herself to be more than a woman, a wife, a mother: She represented the hope of freedom for the Burmese people. She was known—to all of us—simply as "the Lady." The great leaders of peace and reconciliation—Mandela and Tutu and Havel—all claimed her as one of their own, and so she was.

Aung San Suu Kyi's democracy, born from the independence politics of her father, was the accepted standard in our household. What she did, we did. What she said, we said. And yet, as it concerned these roots, I knew quite little. I just assumed that because the military dictatorship was so impossibly villainous, the woman who resisted them against all odds was necessarily righteous and infallible.

But what of her political ideology, her ties to a certain Burmese nationalism that remained celebrated into the current day—even by said impossibly villainous military dictators? Aung San, her father, had been assassinated just as Burma was coming into its own, when his leadership might have been put to the test. I knew so little of this history, and how it might inform the movement that my family was now a part of.

As is often the case when it comes to colonialism and its demise, the nationalists were the ones who sounded the battle cry of independence. Aung San was their hero. He led the negotiations with the British to return the country to its rightful owners, but Aung San's political associates were also key players in that ugly chapter of 1938 in which scores of Indians were targeted and killed.

Aung San himself may not have been a xenophobic murderer, but he was a signatory to Thein Pe's pamphlet, the one that made no secret of the thorough disgust felt by the Burmese toward the Indians. It wasn't called *Burma for the Burmese* . . . but it might as well have been. The Indians were a pox, a metastasizing disease that threatened the whole of Burma:

Betel-quid shops were owned by the Indians. . . . Textile shops were owned by the Indians; the big bazaars were owned by the Indians; the wholesale trades were run by the Indians; shoe-repairers were Indians; the hosiery-factories were owned and manned by the Indians; sand-soap was sold also by the Indians; the luxurious perfumed soap was also sold by the Indians; the capitalist money-lenders were Indians; Indians; Indians; Indians—everywhere Indians—nothing but Indians. The darawans were Indians; the High Court Judges were Indians; the compounder (dispensers) were Indians; the Medical Superintendents were Indians; jail warders were Indians; and the Prison Officers were also Indians. Wherever you go you will find Indians, nothing but Indians.[34]

It was like *Invasion of the Body Snatchers*! *Indians were everywhere!*

Thein Pe—and, by association, Aung San—made note of the "approximately one million Indians in Burma. As our population is approximately only twelve millions, there is a ratio of 12 Burmans to 1 Indian. *It is really alarming.*" (Emphasis mine, again.)

It was straight out of a right-wing super PAC ad, this fearmongering, this Us-versus-Them-ing that was happening, sermonized through pamphlets and speeches. And it wasn't just some nefarious political operative with a penchant for sensational YouTube videos who was doing this, it was the leader of Burma's revolution, the hero who everyone in my family revered, the guy I'd known about (if not specifically) since birth, the father of the freedom-fighting woman on whose behalf my grandmother had protested on all those Sundays on the hot pavement outside of the Burmese embassy in Washington, D.C.

In the wake of assassinations (primarily Aung San's) and power grabs immediately following independence, Burmese nationalism continued its fever-induced mutation. Rabid nationalism expelled the Baghdadi Jews and Parsis and all remaining Indians from Rangoon and Mandalay. It reengaged one of the world's longest-running civil wars within the ethnic tribes. Businesses, banks, schools all were forced to adapt: International owners, investments, and curricula were all excised. Nationalism basically shut the country down and stole its sunlight. The British were always implicated in Burma's near century of misfortune, but what about the Burmese who pushed them out?

This dangerous and deadly self-regard did not end when the military junta eventually ceded (at least half of its) power to a democratically elected government, either. Aung San's daughter, the very same icon my grandmother had championed, was now, decades later, turning a blind eye (at best) to the systematic execution and persecution of her fellow countrymen, the Rohingya. Daw Suu, now in control of Burma's government (though constitutionally barred from officially becoming its prime minister), reacted defiantly when faced with news reports that the Rohingya were being targeted en masse and fleeing the country in staggering numbers. "There have been allegations and counter-allegations," the Nobel Peace Prize Laureate insisted in late September 2017. "We have to make sure those allegations are based on solid evidence before we take action."[35]

She pointed to attacks launched by an armed local group calling itself the Arakan Rohingya Salvation Army (ARSA) on Burmese police outposts in the region, limited in number and scope but deemed, by her, to be "acts of terrorism." Was this the justification for a military response that displaced nearly half a million people? Was this the same woman who had been held up as a paragon of justice and human rights just a few years prior?

Most disturbing (and for me, at least, most unbelievable)

was the reaction to this modern-day violence and upheaval by the Burmese themselves. One report described the response in Rangoon following Aung San Suu Kyi's questionable commentary that year. Her words were "met with applause and cheers from large crowds [in the city] who had gathered to watch live on large outdoor screens amid a party atmosphere."[36]

Daw Suu may have been out of touch with the international community where it concerned the Rohingya, but she was apparently very much still in favor with her fellow Burmese—they agreed with her. Buddhist nationalism was hopelessly intertwined with the religious and ethnic hatred that had plagued Burma when her father was alive (and probably well before that). No one knew any better than they had nearly a century ago.

We, as a family, had always maintained that the violence and insanity in Burma was . . . violent and insane, which is why my grandmother could be found in front of the Burmese embassy for so many years, which is why she maintained a steady grip on political news out of Burma, which is why she situated herself at the nexus of the exiled pro-democracy movement, rallying for the release of Aung San Suu Kyi. "Those people!" she would say, in reference to arbiters of her country's decline, too angry or frustrated to summon an adjective to describe their evil, their incompetence. But weren't those people us, in some ways?

I had always assumed we were in no way implicated in Burma's destruction, its internecine killings and brutal subjugations. We had left, therefore we were exempt from examining whether we, too, might have harbored some of the same exclusionary, misguided ideas about Burman superiority—the delusion that allowed a Nobel Laureate to look the other way when ethnic cleansing was happening in her backyard. That sort of behavior, that strain of poison, had always been understood to be someone else's and not ours—despite the fact that those behaviors helped shape our very identity—the identity I was so eager, now, to explore and celebrate, to reignite within my own life.

The profile we had drawn for ourselves was in direct opposition to that of those who'd stayed behind: Burma was repressed, calcifying, broken . . . but we were not. We read the newspapers and studied French and spoke English, but we never stopped to think that these delicious fruits were in some way linked to a very sad harvest, from seeds that we had somehow helped sow. Our family remembered when Burma was the rice bowl of Asia, but not what we had done to precipitate its decline. Instead, we mourned the glorious past and longed for it once again, a luxurious thing to do from the other side of the planet.

But when I'd begun peeking into the spaces between the lacquer boxes and law degrees, what I discovered . . . was turmoil. My grandmother's gentilities belied real problems: deep-seated animus and moral hazards, violence and economic calamity. Not just Burma's, but our own. Aung San Suu Kyi, whose beatific face decorated mugs and T-shirts and keychains, stuff I'd dutifully smuggled back home to show my friends in the West, had turned out to be a fraud. It was like looking in a treasure box only to find the bones of a skeleton. This was the first time it occurred to me that the stories we had told ourselves—and indeed believed—were just that: stories. The truth, as it turns out, was complex (it always is), but more than that, it was fractured, like a stained-glass window that had shattered into tiny pieces and was nearly impossible to put back together.

Up until this point, our story of success had been a necessary and constant rebuke to the narrative of Burmese collapse. But now, as an American (as we all were), I could finally look back and realize that, lo and behold, we had failed, too.

CHAPTER FIVE

—— // ——

The fundamental problem with discovering skeletons in your closet is the impossibility of putting them back in there. Unearth the disturbing lurking among the familiar, and its very likely that you'll keep looking for other, possibly more disturbing things—that you'll find yourself strangely and revoltingly eager to see how many bones pile up. Maybe I was just unusually self-punishing, but the revelations about my family history made clear (to me, at least) that I needed to go back to the source of the conflict and confusion: I needed to go to Burma.

I had a very specific mission in mind: I was coming for my mother's birth certificate, written—as family lore would have it—on a palm leaf, per Buddhist tradition, and left to rot in some unnamed corner of the Burmese archives (maybe) for three-quarters of a century. My mother could be creative with her birthdate (a skill I, too, was perfecting with each passing year), but this recovery was not a bid to prove her right or wrong. It was mostly so that I could reaffirm for her (for us), a birthright that had been dimmed by immigration and naturalization, globalization and Westernization, time and distance. I wanted to give her a piece of home, something that was undiluted by all the history and mileage that had come after.

This trip to Burma wouldn't be my first: I'd done that on New Year's Day 2008, and I'd dragged my mother along with me. The evening newscasts in 2007 had been filled with images of bloodied Burmese monks protesting the brutality of the ruling military regime, and I'd decided that we could no longer sit on our gentrified American haunches, numbly watching CNN. So we'd packed our bags and made a three-day pilgrimage back to her birthplace, careful to stay in family-run guesthouses so as not to funnel dollars to the evil military government, ever-vigilant about keeping a low profile, silently raising our fists in protest as we sped past the home of Aung San Suu Kyi, who at that point was still under house arrest.

It was a heartbreaking trip. My mom hadn't been back to Rangoon since she'd left nearly forty years prior. I remember sitting on the plastic tile floor of our room at the Queen Shin Saw Pu Hotel one night as the tinny local loudspeakers blared an announcement in Burmese. The night sky was dark like pitch, and the fluorescent lights in our room made us both look wan and slightly seasick. We'd visited all of our relatives who'd remained in Burma and made offerings at all the pagodas, but here it was only day two and we had nowhere else to go. My mother didn't recognize what had happened to her city, and all those wistful memories she'd had—the frangipani blossoms and palm leaf umbrellas—seemed to have vanished against the rancid poverty and buckled sidewalks. I couldn't imagine coming home and feeling like a stranger, and so I didn't hold it against her when she said she wanted to go back to Thailand.

This time, I wasn't returning to Burma because I felt guilty or particularly fired up about bearing witness to whatever political and moral savageries were being perpetrated against the citizens of the country. Aung San Suu Kyi's house arrest had ended, and anyway, I'd gotten new perspective on her and her father's nationalist tendencies. A new and quasi-democratically elected government was to be installed in Parliament—the first in over half a century—and the United States had reopened trade relations. Political prisoners were being released. Things, maybe, were beginning to look up.

So I would find her birth certificate, yes, but I was also going to Burma in search of some magnificent and elusive personal connection. So much of my research into our family history had left me feeling adrift, confused, slightly chilled—in the interest of rounding out our family portrait and filling in its details, I had inadvertently changed its composition entirely. I would take one more shot at trying to connect to my blood via the land itself. I would go to the place, set foot on soil, breath the air, and experience a life so different from my American one that it would surely force some sort of epic revelation born of unseen connection, some meaningful intimacy, some sense of belonging, however fraught. Right? I mean that was my intention, at least.

I was not alone in my decision to make a heritage voyage. All over the world, (relatively prosperous) second- and third-generation immigrants were returning to their ancestral homes to hold what can best be termed an Experiential Séance, in which the ghosts of ancestors past would come alive through the touring of homes, monuments, cemeteries, castles, distilleries, and the like. In Ireland, you could take a chauffeured tour of the fifteenth-century Bunratty Castle or have a tipple in Cork—a veritable *Angela's Ashes* expedition that was sure to return you back home with a keener, more tactile understanding of your left-behind blood.

Or you might hop a flight to Accra and revisit the slave traumas of Ghana's past, traveling along the 156-mile southern coastline, where the crumbling castles and forts of the blood trade still echoed with the terrors of the 1700s. There was, after all, something particular and particularly resonant in the land, something that made the past come alive when one put foot to ground. And if it could be this way for those who were removed decades (or centuries) from their personal histories, why not so for us first-generation Americans? Nowhere was it written that family members needed to stay away from their ancestral homes for several hundred years before a long-lost son or daughter might book a ticket back in the hopes of discovering something meaningful or clarifying. Heritage travel, as they called it, might not just be for reminiscences of the long, long ago: Perhaps it would be equally as useful to recall the recent past.

And so: First, I intended to hunt down evidence that we once lived there. I wanted to see the old family homes, imagine my grandfather puffing on a cigarette and making the decision to leave for America under cover of night. I wanted to see the (re-creation of the) teak palace in Mandalay where my great-great-grandmother once served in the shadow of the king. There were so few photographs or heirlooms that survived our exodus from Burma that it was sometimes hard to believe those times had ever really come to pass—the tiffin carriers full of vindaloo and English-style garden parties, the lacquer boxes of hand-rolled cheroots. Everything about the place was masked by the gauze of distance and loss, like a famous shipwreck that everyone talked about but no one could find. Here was my chance to savor whatever was left.

I wanted to touch and see the things that had remained here after we'd left, something that was (unlike us) permanently Burmese, and could, in this way, vouch for our history here. This was, of course, going to be close to impossible, because Burma's information architecture approximated that of a sandcastle: haphazard and frequently demolished by the elements.

I knew that the place I would need to visit was the National Archives of Myanmar, but gaining entry to that building would require navigation through approximately sixty-seven layers of unreasonable bureaucracy born of intense paranoia and general ambivalence to transparency. I knew this mostly because the information available online in the United States— after I risked passage to an archives website that Google Chrome warned was unsafe for my computer—insisted that any requests for entry be accompanied by a letter, sent to the Burmese embassy, detailing what, very specifically, you were researching and why. It might take weeks for a reply, if you got a reply at all.

I was no scholar, and had no academic institution to vouch for me, but I convinced my New York City–based book editor to sign an official-seeming request on letterhead, confirming that I was working on a book and would need access to records pertaining to "Myanmar history and social development," which was as benign-sounding as I could make it without verging into actual misrepresentation. I decided I would need backup in this endeavor (especially because I neither spoke nor read a word of Burmese, apart from questionable kitchen lingo pertaining to dried shrimp and fried summer squash), and so I brought along my Burmese-speaking(ish) and very expert cousin Geoff, who was working on his PhD and therefore had endless oceans of time to spend in libraries, and in fact relished the thought of more of it. I filed a similar petition on Geoff's behalf, hoping his status as a "doctoral candidate" at Columbia University might somehow grease the wheels, or at least endear us to the authorities.[*]

Naturally, we received nothing in the way of response from the Burmese embassy, but I decided not to let this reality deter us in our travel. I had held low expectations regarding any sort of correspondence, anyway, and figured the request must have been lost in a mountain of paperwork piled on a bureaucrat's crowded desk, somewhere. Extensive travel around the world and my personal proclivity for cajoling had taught me that it was oftentimes easier to convince people of what you needed—or wanted—in person. Upon arrival in Rangoon, Geoff and I promptly got to work contacting anyone who might have even passing knowledge about how to gain access to the archives.

To help us navigate the byways of the past and present, Geoff suggested we enlist his former Burmese language tutor, a sassy fixer named Yu Yu, who had assisted a number of de-

[*] The Burmese, including my family, have a preternatural obsession with education degrees. To get a PhD is to be nearer to God, closer to nirvana. When I was growing up, my grandmother always used to specify that so-and-so was a "medical doctor," rather than the (presumed) doctor of letters. "Medical doctors" were equally impressive, and the expectation was that everyone should aspire to be a doctor of some kind.

manding and occasionally pushy Americans during their travels around Burma, including Anthony Bourdain when he filmed
an episode of his big-budget food show in Rangoon. (We made
a point of visiting several of Bourdain's favorite noodle shops
and pestering Yu Yu to order whatever Bourdain had ordered.
I figured it couldn't hurt.) Anyway, Yu Yu understood the general futility of navigating Burmese bureaucracy and agreed it
would behoove us to ask for advice from a visiting scholar who
had already successfully gained entry to the records.

Yu Yu made several cellphone calls that led nowhere, or delivered to us conflicting information about how feasible our
quest was, and we mostly remained hopeless, although not despondent. Until one morning, as we were headed somewhere
else (I don't remember where) and our trio stopped at a money
changer and ran into a very important French guy of many
degrees and affiliations who had basically Gone Burmese (he
was the type of French guy who insisted upon speaking in Burmese to Burmese and English people alike). This French guy
was notoriously dialed in to the System, and practically laughed
us into the street when we asked, with furrowed brows, how we
might ever gain sanctioned entry to the archives—as if it was
asking for the pass code to the Secret of NIMH.

Effectively, he told us (in Burmese) that it was *really very easy*,
and that all we had to do was get this one very famous Burmese
academic to write us general letters of recommendation and
then we could show up at the archives with these letters and
meet with an official on site who would give us the necessary
credentials. It was so easy! (Would it really be so easy?) The
very important French guy grabbed his thick stack of Burmese
kyats and whizzed out of the money changer because (obvi-

ously) he was very busy, probably attaining another achievement of importance.

Yu Yu set about contacting this very famous Burmese academic and requesting a letter of recommendation from a man who had never met us and had no idea what we were doing in Rangoon. As far-fetched as this sounded, it was apparently something the famous academic was accustomed to doing, so much so that his son—who ran a local bookstore—had the template on hand and yes, sure, he could print out two copies with our names and have his father sign them. I'm not sure his father was the one to actually sign the letters, but at this point we were no longer asking questions.* We assumed this was just the Burmese government's delightful protocol—an elaborate scavenger hunt featuring obscure personalities and arbitrary tasks. Impossibly, we got the letters and were on our way.

The archives were located on a drowsy residential street and happened to be far less menacing than I had imagined. Most of the Burmese government buildings I'd seen so far were hulking turn-of-the-century stone behemoths constructed by the English as if to withstand a world war (and indeed they did, for the most part). While this structure was far from flimsy, it sat only two stories high and had the welcoming air of a very large bungalow (a bungalow with a central marble staircase). Geoff and I practically skipped through the main gate, now convinced that we belonged, until we were stopped by a patrolman in the guard house who looked at us askance and demanded our papers.

After presenting our questionable letters of recommenda-

---

* In fact, I am sure: His father did not sign it.

tion, we signed the register (this seemed like progress) and made our way to the bungalow/archive main building, only to be told that we would need to present our papers once again to the deputy director general of the archives. We were ushered into a second-floor waiting room that had the stale and disconcerting air of a 1960s interrogation room. I could have been—but was not!—grilled on my Communist sympathies.

Geoff and I waited quietly, apprehensive about what was to come. Despite whatever connection I had to the country, the unpredictable nature of Burmese bureaucracy made me feel like I might get deported at any minute, never mind the fact that I wasn't looking to uncover anything particularly incendiary. Eventually, the deputy director general, a heavyset man in official uniform, entered the room to review our paperwork and otherwise make Geoff very nervous. He appeared confused about who Geoff was and why he might be assisting me, which Geoff attempted to explain using what I can only imagine was convoluted Burmese. The deputy then demanded to see the recommendation letter from my editor, though I'm not exactly sure if he knew or cared about the actual publishing house or the project or even how legitimate it all might have been. Mostly, I sensed, he just wanted the paper.

Of course by this point, my editor's spiffy signed letterhead, the one that politely vouched for my character, was languishing on the desk of some paper pusher at the Burmese embassy in Washington, D.C., useless to me in Rangoon. All I had on hand—back in the car out front with Yu Yu—was an unsigned Word printout on regular white paper stock. It didn't look very convincing. I excused myself from the room so I could run back to the car and huddle in the back seat and fake my editor's signature on the letter,* hoping that the ink would dry in the time it took me to return to the deputy director's office.

I handed the letter over to the deputy, wincing at my very obvious forgery and noting that my editor's "signature" bore no resemblance to his actual name. But given the myriad indiscretions that had accompanied this comedic process, I foresaw that this would not necessarily be an issue. Once the deputy director general gathered all of our application materials in a cardboard folder, he disappeared once again for an extended period during which Geoff and I exchanged nervous glances and hushed commentary.

"What do you think he's doing?" I asked, in a stage whisper.

"I don't know!" Geoff replied, giving me a look that said *Shut the fuck up!*

To our great satisfaction, the deputy returned with approval, plus notes from the director general himself regarding the specifics of our archive access. My editor's letter appeared to have been read: As proof, there was a red checkmark at the end of it, as if to signal that it had been vetted, though I'm not sure exactly what was being verified, other than ink. The deputy director noted that if we desired any records between the years 1963 and 1965, the request would have to be assessed through an official request, and approved (or not) accordingly. Those were some of the most fraught years in Burma's struggle after independence. The government seized and consolidated power, nationalizing the economy, expelling foreigners, and otherwise laying the foundation for the country's precipitous decline. It was no surprise those years were off-limits.

---

* Sorry, Chris. Desperate times and all that.

Those years were also, of course, the most critical ones in my family history—1965 was the year we finally left Burma for the United States. My grandfather had felt the hand of the government clamping down and realized that if there was to be a future for his children, it would not be in their birth country.

If the Burmese festival of paper had begun with a bang, it was not yet over. After we received our approval, Geoff and I exited the interrogation room and were escorted to the reading room, where another application process began. Here we were handed a sheaf of papers—the first page of which was ominously blank. We were asked to sign a ledger (name, date, address, degree completed—again the focus on academic degrees—subject matter, book title, and records requested). We were then required to complete a two-page application asking much the same thing, and then told to compose a handwritten letter (on that blank sheet of paper) addressed to the director general—once again, saying much the same thing. The woman who was helping us complete this secondary application informed us that we would need to present our passports, as well as two passport-sized photographs, which I did not happen to have on hand. We would have to return the next day.

But before Geoff and I left, we asked about the method by which archival materials were requested. The assistant demonstrated by performing a sample intranet search—helpfully, in English, for the non–Burmese speaker in the room (me). While the Burmese government had reverted most official information back to the native tongue, there still existed a strong English presence, especially in older materials—after all, the country had been English speaking during much of the time that its information architecture was initially developed. The assistant typed in the sample search term "repot." In doing so, I could only assume she meant to type "report" and instead spelled the word the way the Burmese pronounced it—which was indeed closer to *repot* than *report*, with its hard *r*. I was quite sure entering "repot" in lieu of "report" would not turn up any entries, and was preparing myself for an awkward exchange wherein Geoff and I would have to politely spell the word for her, but lo and behold, the search turned up numerous "repots" (police repots, financial repots, and the like). To say that one needed to adopt a Burmese mind-set to begin one's research in this country was an understatement. You had to think Burmese, speak Burmese, and, apparently, spell Burmese. A new hypothesis started to dawn on me: Maybe this whole search was fucked.

A day later, passport-sized photos in hand, we were finally allowed entry to the archives and granted full research privileges (except the years 1963 through 1965), which was both exhilarating and a complete letdown. I was looking for birth records, property records, government records—anything of that sort, really—but what quickly became clear was just how impoverished the record collections were. So little had been kept. It was as if Burma's history since independence in 1948 had been nearly wiped away.

Birth certificates were a pipe dream: If my mother's palm leaf ever truly existed, it had been lost long ago. Property records were virtually unsearchable, and you could forget about any census documents. The British kept organized records of their own citizens who were living in Burma and India but didn't (of course) bother to record the births or deaths or marriages of anyone who wasn't a Brit by blood. England may have been the ruling colonial power, but unless you were from the kingdom itself (or were progeny of the kingdom), your entrance to and exit from this earthly realm were not the concern of official record. And anyway, the bulk of those records, ones pertaining to the governance of the country (where I might find more information about U Myint Kaung and his work, for example) were all stored neatly away in what I could only imagine was a climate-controlled room somewhere in London.

Instead, what I could find on native soil was a motley selection of random records: an omnibus of declassified telegrams from the Burmese embassy in Washington, planning memos for official state visits (including from India's Jawaharlal Nehru and Egypt's Gamal Abdel Nasser), and an excess of paper about the rules governing various state programs. Hidden among these seemingly dull documents I found something that mattered, a glittering diamond document in this bureaucratic rough: a page from my own family's story. A booklet of rules for the state scholars program—a government program that allowed the most promising young Burmese the chance to study abroad and, in turn, broaden their horizons.

One of my mother's cousins, a young man named Maung Aung Lay, had been a state scholar but tragically died in a plane crash on his way out of Burma. He was a physics scholar, bound for the University of Chicago, and my mother could vividly remember learning of the news of his death: "It wasn't night-dark, but light-breaking dark—it was early in the morning. The sun hadn't come up yet," she recalled.

My mother had been staying at her aunt Yee Yee and uncle U Thein Han's house, a frequent occurrence given my grandmother's general lack of interest in spending any considerable amount of time with her own children. (Much of my mother's childhood was spent with these two.) They were Maung Aung Lay's parents.

"I would always sleep with my aunt," she explained. "And when she got out of bed, I'm sure I followed her. I remember that she and my uncle were listening to the radio that morning, one of those funny, old, wood and cloth-covered things. It was rectangular, and it stood on a bookcase in their living room. They were so intently listening to the radio that I'm not sure they knew I was with them. My aunt had her ear close to it because I gather they didn't want to turn it on, really. I knew something was wrong—there was something very troubling and ominous about this radio listening, especially at that hour. It was dark, after all; why would they be listening so carefully to the radio?

"The next thing I remember was that there was a lot of hushed talk and weird crying sounds coming from the bedroom. I don't remember any news coming to me afterward— basically I sort of put it together. But I don't remember a scene where I found out."

Maung Aung Lay had left for America a few days before. He flew from Rangoon to India, and his plane went down upon takeoff from India en route west.

My mother had told me this story countless times, and it always struck me as both eerie and tragic: the bright future Maung Aung Lay had ahead of him, and the terrible end he met just as he was starting this new life, but also that scene back at home, with the radio in the early morning darkness. My mother couldn't remember the aftermath, but it clearly haunted her for the rest of her life.

"I remember being in a red sweater that morning," she told me. "And for years after, I had a hard time wearing that color."

For me, reading the rules of the program that ultimately took him away from us (forever) was a way to get a little closer to him, however indirectly. I wanted to envision his application, the anticipation as he left home for the first time. Among other things, I found out that there were certain conjugal taboos imposed upon Burma's youngest and finest minds: "No state scholar shall marry during the tenure of his course and if he does so, the scholarship shall be terminated." You could imagine the lovelorn scholar, away from home for the first time, an easy mark for a tragic or complicating romance.

As a state scholar, my cousin faced a rigorous physical exam prior to departure, one that checked for all the diseases of the era (scarlet fever, smallpox, syphilis, and so forth) and required a rather intrusive assessment of everything from his respiratory system ("Comment more fully on the condition of the applicant's lungs") to his endocrine system ("Urine: Specific gravity? Reaction? Albumen? Sugar?"). I couldn't remember the last time I had been asked about the specific gravity of my urine as part of an academic scholarship application.

I giggled through most of these rules, but they managed to convey an impression that the world, at that moment, was a huge place. It was not the planet that I'd grown up on, one that had been casually shrunken by the Internet and Cathay Pacific airlines. Sixty-five years ago, the crossing of borders and commingling of cultures was a deeply serious thing.

I'd come to imagine our family as a cosmopolitan clan: a great-grandfather who wore Saxon shoes, a grandmother who preferred American motorcars, a mother who went to see

French films with her English school classmates. But these rules made me remember that we were also ordinary Burmese; we were stripped down to our skivvies and made to say aah, blood tested and language screened like everyone else who wanted to try their hand at America. I could imagine my cousin poring over this little rule book, itself the only constant in his soon-to-be-new life (a life, alas, he'd never begin). For a moment, sitting in the archives reading room, I felt a tingle of the dread and excitement that he must have felt, knowing that the world would never be the same for him again.

There was also a page of my grandfather's story in this little booklet. He oversaw the state scholars program during a short embassy stint in Washington in 1956. At that point in his long career as a Burmese bureaucrat, he was the undersecretary for education, but he also had personal experience with studying abroad: In 1951, my grandmother and grandfather had both been awarded Fulbright scholarships to study in the States.

According to my grandmother, she was not sure how this came to pass; the government "just selected about ten of us," she said. She remembered that she took Trans World Airlines to Bombay and stopped for a week in Paris.* The only French my grandmother knew was *"Je voudrais une omelette avec champignons et un verre du vin blanc"* ("I would like a mushroom omelette and a glass of white wine"), a phrase she managed to butcher spectacularly whenever she uttered it out loud in the years hence, which she did more frequently than made sense.

---

* The children—my six-year-old mother and her four-year-old brother—were not advised of their parents' yearlong sojourn, and were left with their aunt and uncle and given no explanation. "They were happy to have them," was my grandmother's assessment. My mother is still outraged to this day.

She recalled that for their one-week stopover in Paris, she and my grandfather stayed at the Hotel du Lys on the rue Serpent, and that she immediately fell in love with French press coffee and croissants. "I couldn't have cared less about what my husband did," she said, and by way of explanation offered, "We were very close to the Champs-Élysées."

My grandmother had been fearless, of course. "I wore Burmese dress," she explained, "but saw Parisian ladies in their spring coats and went and bought a short coat in green at the Galeries Lafayette. They had perfumes and colognes there and I bought a bottle—Arpège, I think?" How easily, how seamlessly, she had managed the City of Lights. But no, she protested: "I was a hick! You know," she added, "the Burmese really can't pronounce 'Champs-Élysées.'"

They flew into New York and took the train to Washington, and then my grandmother was off to study for a few months at Kansas State Teachers College in Pittsburg, Kansas. That was followed by a brutal winter at the International House at the University of Chicago ("I liked it because I could get good Chinese food!" she said), and then it was on to Maine, where she stayed with a Mr. and Mrs. Nielsen in Augusta and tried skiing and chicken noodle soup for the first time. "Sebago Lake was nearby," she recalled, "and the salmon caught there was sent to the White House!" (The American harvest made a deep impression.)

My grandfather, meanwhile, was completing his graduate studies at Indiana University. News clippings from the United States detail "Burmese visitors" who stopped in at several American universities in the winter of 1951. In an article detailing the apparently close relationship between Burma and

Bucknell University in Pennsylvania, the Bucknell student paper made note of a recent group of scholars from the region, including one U Thant Gyi, my grandfather, whose pastimes included "scouting and photography."

How curious it must have been to live in Augusta or Indianapolis, coming—as my grandparents were—from the leafy delta of Rangoon. And yet how easily they had done it. Perhaps it was destiny? The village elders told my grandmother that, growing up in the tiny, dusty town of Pakokku, she used to always say, "When I grow old, I'm going to America." My grandmother couldn't remember where this desire came from, exactly, but she insisted it was true. The elders of her village were sure, even then. She recounted their conversations: "Mya, you know, she was always talking about going as a child."

I asked my grandmother if it was hard when she finally arrived in America. In those long, cold months in the middle of nowhere, did she miss home? "Oh," she said, "there was no time to miss Burma." For those six months, she never wrote home or called her children—not once. I'd always thought assimilation was an act of valor that required self-sacrifice and a strong heart. But my grandmother suggested you had to be a certain type of cutthroat, too.

After they returned from that year abroad and before they left Burma for the last time in 1965, my grandmother worked as the head librarian at the U.S. Information Service library at the American embassy in Rangoon. I scanned the archives' intranet for anything that might shed some light on the happenings at the embassy compound, in the hopes that she or the library might be mentioned. There were a few reports, but nothing revelatory.

From the period in which my grandparents were stationed at the Burmese embassy in Washington, D.C., declassified cables revealed not much more than intra-staff skirmishes. One particularly spicy report detailed the "administrative gangsterism [!] that already exists among subordinate staff," presumably relating to a certain third-tier secretary who had been pressing for a salary increase.

The seemingly hunky-dory account was odd. In the late 1950s and '60s, the Americans were locked in a pitched geopolitical battle to stop the spread of Communism around the world, and wanted to ensure that Burma wouldn't turn into another Vietnam. My grandmother knew this, and her life was, in some ways, shaped by it. She revealed that she'd first gotten the job at the USIS library because the soon-to-be-former librarian was suspected of having Communist ties. Her husband had been targeted as a possible sympathizer and the home office in Washington made clear the position was to be filled by someone else. In stepped my grandmother. It was not a point of family pride that she gladly stepped in amid a witch hunt against her colleagues—one wonders what she would have done if she'd been called before the House Un-American Activities Committee—but it was her posting at the USIS library that eventually led the U.S. State Department to get our family out of Burma after the government fell.

My grandmother and grandfather, former Fulbright scholars who'd tasted the West, their home a center of Rangoon society where Burmese and non-Burmese mingled easily, were easy targets for a military government that had announced its course as the "Burmese Way to Socialism."

After General Ne Win regained power in a bloodless coup in

1962, westernized Burmese, especially officials who had served in the previous government (my grandfather had been an official in the education department shortly before the coup), were eyed with suspicion. My grandfather was soon demoted to the post of a high school principal. Shortly thereafter, my mother was observed taking French lessons, and a government representative made clear that this sort of thing was not permitted: Burma was returning to her roots; foreign elements were not tolerated. Amid the nationalization of the banks and the closing of the universities, it was clear then that the life they'd had in Burma was no longer—and so they looked to America as their next (and final) destination.

The Library of Congress needed an expert on Pali, and here was my grandmother—available and ready to move. They held the job for her for nearly two years while she got her papers in order (she never did get a passport, but the U.S. government didn't mind). And so, taking up that post at the USIS library several years prior was, in the end, a move worth making for my grandmother—all things considered. But you wouldn't have known from the archive's cache of cables (at least the ones that I had access to), that McCarthyism had made its way up the delta to Rangoon.

I had been hunting for some paper trail that would lead me back to my people, something I could touch with my own hands—whether a birth certificate or land deed—that would prompt a profound spiritual revelation about my heritage, but I was not going to find it in these archives. The elements, however man-made, had washed our particular sandcastle away.

I was annoyed (we'd really had to hunt down the very important French guy and that famous Burmese academic . . . for this?) but ultimately, I suppose it wasn't all that surprising: Did I really think that a military junta that had driven the country's economy into the ground, shuttered universities, and otherwise prevented the free exchange of ideas and conversation . . . did I really think *those* guys would take the care and expense to preserve historical record of their mayhem and the events preceding it? Probably not.

I was disappointed. Angry, even. Yet I'd also seen glimpses of the family story—my story—in at least a handful of documents cloistered away in the Burmese archives. And in those moments, I felt some small frisson, a mild but nonetheless decidedly unearthly vibration of familial recognition—the thing I'd come halfway around the world hoping and searching for. Of course I wanted more. Fortunately, the archives weren't the only source of information for this sort of emotional ancestral quest.

Yu Yu told us about someone named U Aung Soe Min, Rangoon's own Renaissance man. U Aung was an art dealer, musician, bon vivant, and connector of people and places in the former capital city; a collector who—through patience and networking and luck and curiosity—had amassed an impressive collection of primary historical documents, one of the best around. One afternoon Geoff and Yu Yu took me to his gallery, a rabbit warren of rooms, each crowded with eight-foot-high stacks of vintage newspapers, magazines, posters, documents, pamphlets, property titles, propaganda, and paintings. There was absolutely no organization to the collection, with trade ledgers from the late 1800s stacked alongside Burmese agitprop from the 1960s. You had to be guided through each document—or stack of documents—by the man himself. There was no intranet, only the musty air of a hoarder's lair. But, then again, the man did know how to spell the word "report."

I wanted to know how U Aung had managed to obtain all this . . . stuff. He explained that after the military took power in the late sixties and nationalized the country, most of Burma's libraries had been shuttered and destroyed. Some remained as tools for socialist propaganda, and were open for individual research projects. These were essentially socialist libraries. There were private libraries and private collections, as well. "But in 1993 and 1994 and 1995," he explained, "everything was destroyed."

Those years in Burma were ones of (particular) tumult. The international community was calling for the release of Aung San Suu Kyi. The junta declined. It continued to arrest and jail political opposition figures and other pro-democracy reformists. And the crackdown was not—apparently—limited to people.

"The libraries, the old books and documents, they were just on the streets. People sold them on the street," he said. "I witnessed this. Archives of the Japanese occupation? On the street. Those valuable documents, research, interviews, collections of local history—both social and economic—were totally gone. The socialists wanted to erase that history."

U Aung (wisely) thought there might be private collectors interested in the material, and started buying the documents from the street-side book merchants.

"I wanted to start the most serious collection," he explained. "Most are not my interest, but they may be needed in the future."

Rangoon's de facto archivist collected as much as he could

from these haphazard fire sales and document dumps. When old or famous writers and academics passed away (the type of men and women who would have had sizable private libraries), he'd hear about it on the streets from the booksellers. "They sold everything," he said. "It's very sad in Burma; the generations don't maintain their previous generation's work. It's very bad."

The work of purchasing and archiving Burmese history wasn't just arduous and heartbreaking: It was also kind of illegal. U Aung told me that many of the books from the 1970s (presumably political manifestos) were hidden until the pro-democracy movement really gained steam in 1988 and '89. "Someone brought those books to me, donated them to my library—because the government didn't like those books," he said. For this, U Aung was arrested. "They didn't give a reason. They just said, 'He has some affiliation with the underground movement.' The government," U Aung concluded, "doesn't encourage libraries."

And so, piled up in his various rooms (there was more stocked away in U Aung's apartment and at other locations around town), I found . . . all sorts of things. There were political cartoons with a distinctly national subtext: "Nyo, darling, this is the time when our country really needs her sons . . . and there is no greater duty than to fight for her freedom." Indeed, "Nyo, darling!"

It was sassy and camp, and it was unlike anything I'd seen before. There were motion picture yearbooks from the fifties: evidence of a flourishing and occasionally insurgent Burmese cinema. There were happy-looking illustrated guidebooks to Burma's ethnic minority groups. There were pop-art pamphlets and cheeky photo illustrations of bosomy Burmese pin-ups, enticements for I'm not sure quite what. There wasn't a shred of evidence of my grandmother's Fulbright program, nor was there even a dim hope of finding my mother's birth certificate, but what I found in U Aung's collection was maybe, in a way, even more valuable.

Here was evidence of Burma's flourishing cultural and intellectual life. Here was comedy and irony in full color. Here were ways of writing and thinking about government and society that I could understand. No doubt this was due in part to the fact that Western references were paramount—"Nyo, darling" was more Lichtenstein than Lichtenstein—but also because the documents were sophisticated and funny and suggestive.

I'd never thought about Burma like this before, primarily because my relationship to the country had always been dusted in regret or confusion or reverence. There was so much distance between that world and my own—a childhood filled with Garbage Pail Kids and episodes of *Real World*, an American mishmash of the goofy and ironic—and indeed I had come back to Rangoon looking to exploit this chasm for spiritual revelation.

But looking at the film stills from the heyday of independent Burmese cinema, I could easily imagine what it might have been like to *be Burmese*. I hadn't ever thought about this in a practical way: not just identifying with Burma as an ethnic and historic designation, but actually living life *as a Burmese person*. With U Aung's cached material, I could envision a Burmese life, as I had thus far lived an American life. I could see myself at revival and art house theaters, opining about obscure Burmese directors, collecting vintage posters for my teenage bedroom or writing thinly disguised political manifestos for campus publications—just like I had growing up in the States, experimenting with vegetarianism and trying desperately to develop an appreciation for Truffaut films and Constructivist art.

What I learned in this moment was that Burma wasn't all palm leaf birth certificates and mohinga* hawkers at the night market. It was also breasty pinups and campus poetry. I should have known that, of course—how stupid it had been to assume otherwise—but I'd had no proof. So here was my revelation: I could now imagine a vivid interior life as someone who'd grown up in Rangoon rather than in Washington.

As exciting as this was, it also made me angry—because these piles of artifacts were just that: remainders from a golden era, a bygone worldview, a discussion that had ended (abruptly). There were plenty of expats and experts who might lecture me on the vivid Burmese intellectual life that existed even now, in spite of (and in reaction to) the political realities of the day. But from my admittedly brief time traversing the information highways and byways of Rangoon, this particular brand of interesting and occasionally joyful cultural output seemed to have met the same end as Burma's libraries: It had been tossed out on the street. At least as far as I could tell from my entirely abbreviated research sojourn in the homeland. I'd visited the university library, which had archived some interesting campus publications from the 1940s, '50s, and early '60s, but those, too, had come to a grinding halt once Ne Win shuttered the

---

* Mohinga is the national noodle dish of Burma, sort of the Burmese answer to pad thai.

campuses, suspicious that they were hotbeds of revolution and unrest (and indeed they were).

The only remnants I could find of this funny, freaky, hidden past was U Aung's haphazard collection, scraped together by one man who understood the loss. Did societies really unwind themselves like this? Who spoke fluently and with vivid language, only to revert back to Morse code? It didn't seem possible, but here was proof that it was.

And, I wondered, who was at fault? What idea took hold that would burn a thriving culture and scatter its ashes? Was it the same culprit that was behind the slaughter of Muslims and the expulsion of Indians? The same menace that prevented my mother from improving her French and smeared my grandfather for his cosmopolitanism? The same power that insisted on nationalism as the ultimate virtue; that valued blood over every other form of identity? Could it be the same thing that I was now embracing, if in a seemingly more benign form—the force that sent me hurtling back to Burma in the first place?

Maybe—but I wasn't ready to land on that damning conclusion just yet. Instead, U Aung's words echoed in my head: "It's very sad in Burma; the generations don't maintain their previous generation's work."

With this loss as motivation, I was increasingly antsy to see as many artifacts as I could before they were tossed out on the street or demolished or otherwise forgotten by nearly everyone. At the top of my bucket list were the old family homes: I would crisscross as much of Upper and Lower Burma as I could, in the hopes of verifying that they existed, proof that we'd really been here. So much had already turned to vapor; here was my chance to savor a remnant of the past before it, too, evaporated. Before I left for Burma, my grandmother had given me vague directions that weren't much more than a trail of anecdotal bread crumbs: "We lived across the street from Saint Xavier's church," she said, "and near my school, the Wesleyan Methodist mission school." If I asked for any more specifics, my grandmother tended to get a faraway look in her eyes and change the subject because she really didn't remember much more than that, and anyway I'd be lucky if I remembered half as much as she did by the time I was even forty-five.

Armed with little more than her coordinates, I flew from Rangoon to the ancient capital city of Bagan, and took a boat up the Irrawaddy River to Mandalay with my husband, Sam, my newly wedded partner in crime, recently off a six-year stint in the White House and therefore conveniently blessed with some time to engage in things like taking a boat up the Irrawaddy River, for no reason other than his wife thought it a good thing to do. In addition, Sam was an inveterate traveler who had, among other things, gotten lost in the Malaysian jungle and bartered for fish in Croatia, and so the prospect of a (possibly) daring river adventure must have piqued his interest.

I, meanwhile, thought the boat ride would be romantic, a voyage back in time to the era when the Irrawaddy Flotilla Company had escorted my grandmother and her family out of Rangoon during war. At the outset of the trip, just as we boarded the hulking ship in the warm, dark hours of an early Burmese morning, Sam looked wistfully out a porthole and announced that this reminded him of a trip down the Amazon he'd taken several years prior, a multiday journey wherein he was forced to hunt and kill some sort of Jurassic river animal for dinner. I didn't want to kill any reptiles, just to commune with the past—to feel the churn of the waters of Burma's longest river, in the hopes of summoning the ancient vibrations of my family story.

As it turned out, the twelve-hour boat ride was painfully slow and remarkably lacking in scenery—the Irrawaddy in this stretch is no rushing river. She lazes and curves, shallow and silty, through much of the featureless terrain between Bagan and Mandalay, at depths of sometimes merely a few inches. Sam drank approximately seventeen beers over the course of the voyage and fell asleep for many, many hours while I "took notes" and refreshed myself on all of George Orwell's observations about my mother country. The trip really had only a plate of shipboard noodles cooked by the first mate to recommend itself. I spent much of my time praying for snacks to issue forth from the tiny mess.

While those were good noodles, all of the Burmese associates I ran into later asked why we didn't just drive. "It's much faster!" they would say, not accepting this silly desire for nostalgia. And in truth, when we finally stepped away from the sluggish waters of the northern Irrawaddy, I was happy to be in the former capital of Mandalay, smaller than Rangoon but still bustling with industry, thanks to the heavy investment of Chinese business.*

Mandalay was where my grandmother had lived after her birth in Pakokku (near Bagan) until she was sixteen, when she

---

* The takeover of the Burmese economy by the Chinese was cause for consternation, but had the advantage of ensuring wide availability of excellent Chinese food, which was not a bad thing at all.

and her parents decamped for Rangoon and all the glittery things the capital had to offer. One of the only photos from her childhood shows a seven-year-old Mya Mya standing with her siblings and parents in the front yard of a large teak house, saluting her father in awkward fashion, possibly custom when it came to formal Burmese family portraiture.

I wanted to find that house, assuming it was still a house.

The Internet revealed to me that there was one Saint Francis Xavier Church in Mandalay, which I hunted for (and found) because I knew my grandmother's elementary school, Wesleyan Methodist Mission School, was supposed to be nearby. Sam and I walked around for a few blocks before stumbling upon it and were then shooed away from taking any photos by a very friendly security guard who explicitly shut me down, and did so with a beaming smile. "No!" he enthusiastically called out to me as I held my camera aloft. "No!" (He looked so happy about the denial I had to check twice.)

In the yard of the mission residence next door, I made enough noise poking around the grounds and speaking loudly to Sam about the likelihood or unlikelihood that this was the place my grandmother had gone to school that the headmaster's daughter, a cheerful and sleepy young woman named Gracie, came out to see what was going on and offered to introduce us to her father, the Reverend Dr. Zaw Win Aung. The reverend later informed me, to my great chagrin, that the original church, mission school, and mission residence had all been destroyed during World War II. This did not bode well for our family house, which had been located within blocks of all these buildings.

My great-great-grandmother, an attendant in the court of

King Mindon Min, had purchased the home from one of the queens (there were several of them), an imperious woman who would sell the property only to my great-great-grandmother, presumably because she was already vetted through her years of service. The house, not surprisingly, was located on the outskirts of the palace compound, which was a magnificent teak paean to opulence and the shameless harvest of natural resources. After the British gained full control of the country in 1885 and the last Burmese king was exiled to India, the British took hold of the palace and renamed it Fort Dufferin, effectively converting it into a military frat house, where soldiers lived among the remnants of the palace and generally broke shit. During World War II, both the Allies and the Japanese bombed Mandalay to smithereens. Almost nothing survived.

And yet, I walked and walked and walked that damn neighborhood, looking desperately for this house, even though the chances of it still standing were slim to none. I'd look down at the old photo taken from the front yard, then look up along the streets for anything even vaguely resembling that house—convinced that it had to be standing, somewhere; that history couldn't keep disappointing me; that all of our time in this country hadn't simply turned to vapor and ash and dust.

And I think I found it.

Masked by laundry lines and fencing and disrepair, here was an old teak house on a corner, in roughly the right area, with a yard the right size to have once grown hollyhocks and jasmine. There could be no unimpeachable proof, of course. I had to make an independent decision to believe that this was our house, and to further conclude that I was satisfied with this decision. Which was unnerving. All along, I'd thought this journey would offer definition and certainty. But what I was learning was that when it came to heritage, where it concerned identity, there was no hard stop. In fact I would have to decide—on my own—what was enough, what was proof, what was an answer worth accepting. As with the house, I'd have to determine that I'd found what I was looking for: There was not going to be a finish line.

I didn't stop looking in Mandalay. I went on the hunt to find any place I could, knowing that "finding" was an inherently subjective concept. Back in Rangoon, I had general coordinates for my grandmother's first apartment in the city, the one that had running water and an English toilet. It was on East Fifty-first Street, and it had been located "around the corner" from the post office. I found the post office, which was (amazingly and impossibly) the same one that had stood in 1933, but all the apartments around it had been refaced or rebuilt.

I knew that I wouldn't be able to determine exactly which building had been hers, but I hoped that I'd see some façade or otherwise timeworn structure, one that looked like it *could* have been hers, and might therefore allow me to imagine it indeed had been. But nothing exuded any sort of lingering scent of our Burmese history; nothing looked as if it had withstood the decades in between the last great war and the present day. The trail was cold. I nearly got run over trying to take pictures of some random street corners and eventually went back to the hotel, where Sam was busy scouring the neighborhood streets for a plate of delicious Shan noodles that would rival the ones we'd had on our float down the Irrawaddy.

After my grandparents returned from their two-year embassy posting in Washington, D.C., my grandfather was made the undersecretary of education in the administration of Prime Minister U Nu—a well-intentioned but unfortunately ineffective leader. A contemporary of Aung San's, he became a proponent of democracy and democratic ideals in the years following Burma's independence, but none of this would come to pass in Burma's tumultuous mid-century climate of civil war and social unrest. When the military coup d'état ousted U Nu's government in 1962, my grandfather was "demoted" (my mother's term) to a position as headmaster of the former Saint Paul's English High School in Rangoon, which was subsequently glamorously renamed Basic Education High School No. 6.

Basic High No. 6 was a sprawling, proto-Hogwarts-style academy, where the children of the British, Burmese, Anglo-Burmese, and Anglo-Indian elite were schooled in preparation for their eventual leadership roles as captains of industry and government. My grandfather took his diminished posting in 1965, and I returned with Geoff nearly fifty years later, to see what was left of this tenure.

The first thing you could say about Basic High No. 6 was that it was pretty far from basic: The structure took up an entire city block and was a magnificent sprawl of marble hallways and turn-of-the-century brickwork, surrounded by giant athletic fields for cricket and football and whatever other sports the men and women of superior lineage liked to play.

But it was clear that time had laid a heavy hand on the school, and that the upkeep had been impossible, given what else was going on in the country. The part of the campus still in use was shabby and in need of repair: Cobwebs and thick soot coated nearly every surface, paint was peeling on the walls, classroom furniture was rickety and mismatched. The part no longer in use looked like a sunken ship. Former classrooms were filled with stacks of broken chairs, discarded sinks, vintage electronics, and piles of nondescript yellowing paper. Geoff and I managed to nonchalantly usher ourselves into the wings of the building not open to the public (security was not particularly tight, which is to say it was nonexistent). The walls were covered in black mold, the cornices and eaves home to pigeons and other noisy birds, the glass windows long ago broken out. Athletic fields had been completely taken over by vines and weeds. It looked fucking haunted.

The school was open that day—apparently students were sitting for some sort of exam that morning—and we found our way to the principal's office (the only time I had willingly and enthusiastically sought out the principal's office) to see if U Thant Gyi, my grandfather, had somehow left his mark.

Yu Yu came to meet us and, with her ineffable charm and fluent Burmese, managed to get us into the offices and into the correct room. On the wall of Principal Kyaw Kyaw Tun's office were older watercolors and newer photos of all the esteemed Burmese headmasters of Basic Education High School No. 6: There were Tun Aung and Captain Ba Hein and Myat Htun.

Kyaw Kyaw Tun was enthused and we were interested. But there was nothing for U Thant Gyi, the first headmaster of the school when the government seized its reins in 1965. Surely there had been a mistake; we asked and asked. We even had Yu Yu come in and ask (again) in more official and therefore intelligible Burmese. But no, there was no trace of U Thant Gyi. Only Wikipedia seemed to remember, on its list of the school's headmasters since nationalization. There, at the top, my grand-father's name. But it was nowhere else.

Maybe it made sense: He'd stayed for only one year, after all. The government wouldn't let U Thant Gyi leave for America with his wife and children, and so he'd stayed behind in his de-moted position for only as long as it took him to find a route back to the States. The Library of Congress had already guar-anteed safe passage and a new American life for my mother and grandmother and my uncle; he alone needed to find a way out. (He emigrated in 1968 and never looked back.)

But if I was being cynical, it was no coincidence that he'd been wiped from the record. He'd forsaken Burma, and in re-turn, he was ghosted (as far as public record was concerned). Disrepair and overgrowth and black mold notwithstanding, the Burmese government still considered its Basic High No. 6 to be a breeding ground for the country's leaders, and why would they champion a man who had so cavalierly left this all behind? Here was their retribution.

I thought about it and figured that my grandfather, one of the gentlest and most good-humored men on earth, would probably have laughed, or shrugged it off. They could have their broken-down Burmese public school; he got America, after all. I—the American granddaughter and presumed bene-ficiary of this decades-old trade-off—would have to satisfy my-self with that. (Looking at that wall, I still felt a sense of loss.)

Another day, Geoff and I went to Rangoon University to find my grandmother's old campus dorm at Inya Hall. We rolled up in a sputtering taxi (there was no other kind) to find that the whole dorm complex had been repainted a flat burnt sienna with a fresh gleaming white trim that made the building look brand-new. The marble floors had been polished, and sunlight was streaming in. Young women—co-eds, I guessed —were chattering on the upper floors. Clean laundry was fluttering on the small balconies, and giggling conversations wafted across the grassy, palm-filled courtyard below. I could almost see and hear what it must have been like to be a student at Rangoon University.

After all the soot and mold and birds-roosting-in-the-cornices that I'd experienced thus far, I hadn't expected to see any kind of modern-day hustle or bustle. It was disorienting—and somewhat depressing. I talked to Geoff about this sinking and semi-despondent feeling, about how I felt cheated by the spanking rehabilitation, the glimpse into a diorama of living history. As much as all the broken chairs and moldy documents elsewhere were depressing, they'd also felt real: This was what happened with the passage of time. (Time was fairly elastic; one man's minute was another man's hour.) In most of what I'd seen so far, there was unadulterated evidence that time had ravaged the landscape. For those who left, this was reaffirming, even if it was tragic (to think of what might have happened to us if we'd stayed!). But the rehabilitation, the erasure of evidence that something chaotic and destructive had gone down, and instead that everything was *just as it always was*—this seemed to be the worst kind of lie.

We'd grown so accustomed to seeing things exactly how our parents had left them—the weird luxury of decay—that to see a place where time had ticked on, where repairs had been made and indentations fixed, was disappointing. Maybe even distressing. Because people had continued moving forward with their lives. The past had been reclaimed, and there was no part of it left for us. As it turned out, even though we left . . . maybe we were the ones who'd been left behind.

If there was one place in the whole of Burma where history and tragedy lay largely untouched for half a century, it was the Secretariat building. Here was the place where the father of modern Burma, Aung San, was assassinated (along with six cabinet ministers) on the nineteenth of July in 1947, less than a year before the British Union Jack was lowered for the final time and the Burmese were granted control of their own country.

Aung San's death was a cataclysmic event, the gunshot that changed the course of a nation. (Imagine if Lincoln had been killed before the end of the Civil War.) When the military staged its coup in 1962, it closed off the Secretariat to public view with wire and locks. Security guards and packs of wild dogs acted as pretty convincing deterrents to any would-be amateur historians or otherwise snoopy citizens. Word on the street was that the bullet holes were still in the wall of the council chamber, and that the room itself had been made into a shrine. But the rest of it—all sixteen hectares of the complex, the cupolas and domes and wrought iron staircases and parliamentary halls—had been locked away for fifty years, left to the elements and destroyed in sections by cyclones and earthquakes. The Secretariat had become—through neglect and endless gossip—the place of legend, of ghost stories, of conspiracy theories.

Naturally, I wanted in. To see the room where Aung San had died; to examine this perfectly preserved vestige of Burmese history. But not just because, duh, of course *any* sentient and self-directed detective would want in, but because we had family history in that building, too. (And unlike evidence from all the other disappointing and inconclusive attempts we'd made thus far to revisit that history, this relic was likely intact, if for nothing else than people didn't generally fuck with roving packs of wild dogs.)

My mother emailed me while I was in Rangoon:

> I vaguely remember visits to the Secretariat with Poh Poh [my mother's father] when I was very young. Distinctly remember walking that long passage, along the balustraded balcony. I don't know if Poh had his offices there, but the building was among the places that anchored our world.

It was a place that had anchored our world. Maybe it still could.

I set about trying to sort out who could get me in. I knew that the Yangon Heritage Trust, run by a scholar/author/shot caller named Than Myint-U,* was working with the Burmese government to determine what, exactly, to do with the building. It was a prime specimen of colonial architecture, one that hadn't been messed with in a very long time, and was ready (according to the government) to be repurposed.

Rumors abounded about the hotel group that was going to turn it into a luxury respite for French, British, and American

---

* Than Myint-U was the grandson of Burmese diplomatic legend and former UN secretary-general U Thant. He had also written a few books about Burma, including *The River of Lost Footsteps*, that most every Burmese person had read or held an opinion about. Generally, he made me terrified about my own half-Burmese inadequacies regarding language, culture, and history.

tourists, but in fact it was leased to the Anawmar Art Group, with plans to turn it into a museum showcasing what could only be a staggering private collection—one that, as yet, no one had seen. It would take a lot of art to fill a space that massive, to say nothing of its quality or provenance. It surprised me how much everyone else was convinced of the goodness of this endeavor.

Than Myint-U was gracious enough to meet with Geoff and me and give us an abbreviated schooling in the history of Rangoon's most extraordinary colonial buildings; he sent us on a walking tour with YHT guides who revealed some of the city's most impressive gems. But as far as opening up the Secretariat, he was noncommittal. The last person to tour it had been a high-ranking U.S. official named Barack Obama, and while Geoff and I were clearly very important cultural ambassadors, it was not exactly the same thing.

At the time of our visit, the American ambassador in Rangoon was a lionhearted man named Derek Mitchell—who, together with his impossibly organized and convivial wife, Min—managed to make serious headway in improving Burmese-American relations (and supporting Burmese democracy in general), *and* somehow found the time to offer certain wayward travelers (me) excellent bowls of homemade mohinga.

I decided to push my luck and plead with him to get us into the Secretariat. I employed obtuse suggestion ("I hear the Secretariat is nice this time of year!") at first, before descending into outright begging ("I cannot leave this country without seeing the Secretariat!") until the ambassador relented/indulged and made a few calls to see what might be done. Barack Obama had been a distracting guest, I could only presume, so here was a chance for the ambassador and his wife to tour the grounds uninterrupted. They could thank me later! Several days before the end of my sojourn in Rangoon, we gathered at the gates of the Secretariat a few minutes before twilight and, miraculously, we were let in.

In the magic hour, the building was startling in its scale and deterioration. A story-high clock was stuck at eight o'clock, the numerals mostly missing, a family of pigeons nesting below. Whole wings of the building had seen their roofs cave in, the windowpanes long since gone, as bats cruised through the hallways before the sun dropped. But around another corner, things would be largely intact, in need only of a good mopping to be once again functional. A Victorian-era staircase, with its massive curving metal frame and the ghost of a dome that once topped it, was like something from an ocean liner. Vast, empty rooms were everywhere—rooms so big they suggested a Soviet-era gymnasium, with barrel-vaulted ceilings and iron pillars. You could almost smell the cloud puffs of hand talc.

Walking through the Secretariat was like a waking dream, and not necessarily a good one—one of those night-sweat-inducing anxiety dreams where you stroll through the halls of school, but everyone has already left for the summer and you've missed the final and now where are you? Lost. It was a vast, melancholy building, full of memories that weren't mine but still too palpable to ignore. I thought about my mother's stories about her father, and could hear the shuffle of feet, the thrum of typewriters, the hustle of a government office readying itself for its next act. The sound of life, of busyness, felt as if it had just momentarily drifted away—but how? I was sad and lucky to be inside.

When we finally got to Aung San's assassination room, I was nearly hyperventilating with excitement. For so long I had known this man, or at least his legend. My research had complicated and distorted that legend, but I still couldn't escape the sheer Holy-Shit Factor of walking into a room where one of the most important people in the country's history had been shot.

If I couldn't retrieve my mother's birth certificate, if our family homes had been destroyed, here was something concrete that might bring me back to the thing I'd been looking for since I landed at the Yangon International Airport: a reflection of who I was, indelible proof of my belonging. My outsized expectations for some sort of heritage supernova had diminished considerably; I no longer expected a whiz-bang revelation that would knock me sideways. But I still hoped there could be some sort of quiet reconciliation, where I could at last place myself in the context of these people, this place, their blood, this land. Here was my last shot at finding myself in a national myth.

We took off our shoes, per Burmese custom, and stepped into the room. It was not what I had expected. The walls were covered in wood-grain contact paper and linoleum, apparently papering over the bullet holes—some of the only physical testimony to Burma's bloody and violent transition out of colonialism. Linoleum! It was so corny and unbelievably hokey that it was almost funny. At the front of the room were garishly blinking colored lights surrounding a shrine to Buddha. I nearly winced at the sight of all this, trying to imagine the same room in America. What we might do to "fix" something broken but still central to our history. No amount of imagination stretching could really convince me that anyone would ever put just *a little* putty over the crack on the Liberty Bell or dry-clean Jackie's pink suit and sell it as a vintage piece.

But then Geoff the PhD student reminded me that my reaction was predictably and obnoxiously Occidental: Who was I to say what an appropriately "historical" treatment should be? To begin with, keeping the shot marks on display would have been tacky and gruesome, no? It wasn't as if we kept JFK's bullet-riddled car in the Smithsonian, after all.

Secondly and perhaps more important, the Burmese had a different understanding about time (and especially artifacts), in no small part dictated by Theravada Buddhism. I had experienced it during my visit to Bagan, where eleventh-century stupas and shrines had been casually "repaired" with slapdash twentieth-century brickwork. Historians and preservationists, the folks at UNESCO, they were all horrified. Bagan might have been a World Heritage Site if not for its crappy and widespread masonry fixes.

But Burma's Buddhism stipulated that one accrued merits from building one's *own* pagodas and stupas, and so it was in nobody's best interest to spend a disproportionate amount of time, money, and concern on pagodas and stupas built by someone else. If you weren't going to get credit toward nirvana, what was the point? It was crass by Western standards and I couldn't shake the feeling that I was witnessing a tragedy, but, then again, it came from a genuine belief about priorities, about the things that held weight in this short, terrestrial existence of ours. It made me think about what mattered to me.

Buddhism taught freedom from material objects, which, of course, is why it's so widely adored by the shopping-obsessed

West, but here was an instance of its converse: Why spend too much time worrying about what happened to these old piles of brick? The government knew that tourists wanted to see the ancient structures, and therefore they had some monetary value, but wouldn't the tourists prefer to see artifacts that weren't crumbling? Enter the repair crews. (And when it came to anything outside of filling its own coffers, the military junta was cheap. It was no surprise they hadn't sprung for UNESCO-certified restoration.)

Maybe some or all of the same forces had been in play during the whole trip—the poorly kept archives, the indifference to historical records, the absence of my grandfather's photo on the principal's wall—and were at work again when it came to the room I was presently standing in. I tried hard to reconcile these spiritual, political, and economic realities, but I realized I was just too deep into this epic voyage to find a meaningful bridge to my heritage to let it all go now. It was, in the end, somewhat devastating that all the things I'd hoped to find—echoes and shards of some life we'd once had that I might use to conjure a connection—had been lost or repainted or thrown out on the street or papered over.

The Anawmar Art Group told us it was planning to complete its rehabilitation of the Secretariat in what its well-coiffed representative estimated was "two to three years." This seemed effectively impossible unless the Anawmar group was somehow able to bend time, or limited themselves to a pretty surface renovation of the massive building.

Somehow, many people—smart people, I might add—were convinced that Anawmar would actually restore Aung San's assassination room and allow the people of Burma to live with their own history for a few minutes. And that the restoration wouldn't be crude or ham-handed or somehow further degrade the integrity of the building. And that the spending of tens of millions of dollars on the project would be driven by an unstinting belief in progress, not profit, and history, not vanity. Maybe it was my own jaded and increasingly bitter outlook about Burmese restoration, but the plan seemed implausible. Everyone else seemed okay with that.

I thought about my mother's email once more as we walked out of the building: This had been our anchor, she'd written to me. It had been left to bats and dogs and potentially shady art world denizens, but the Secretariat was still standing. I could take issue with the state of affairs across the board, but at least I had seen these places, slid my hand down the same balustrade that my mother had as a little girl, hand in hand with her father.

The Wesleyan Methodist mission school of the 1920s no longer existed, but I'd put foot to ground in Mandalay, the city where my grandmother lost her first teeth and learned how to read. I never found my mother's birth certificate, and my grandmother's dorm hall had been repainted and replastered, and Aung San's bullet holes were no longer visible, but I had learned something about my heritage and my people and my relationship to both, which came as a surprise.

These were not eureka moments, nor any of that immediately tangible heritage recovery stuff I'd arrived in Burma hoping to experience. Connecting back to my people was more complicated than a series of meaningful encounters over exotic noodles and nostalgic tours of former stomping grounds, as it turned out. But after all the searching and seeking and cajoling and sneaking around, I managed to get a glimpse of the past (our past!) in its most unlikely and unusual iterations. I had—however impossibly—felt the vibratory echoes of my family's history.

Still, I was going to be angry about Burma and dislike a lot of it, just as I had gotten angry about our family history, and disliked a lot of that, too. I questioned decisions made by the Burmese people and thought—in many cases—that they were stupid and unwise ones. I felt compromised and confused. And now I just wanted to go home, where my connection to place and people was unquestioned, where things were less heavy and less fraught with the emotional weight of loss. And home, for me, was America.

I'd stepped foot where my people had lived and breathed and taught and fought—but what of that astronaut without a base station? Here I'd visited a new planet, but I hadn't found an old home. There was no recognition like the one you hear from those who've traveled the galaxy—that moment when they spy Earth from thousands of miles away, peering through that tiny glass portal of the space shuttle and know, with ten thousand percent certainty: That's home, and that's where I belong.

Maybe, then, it was time to try the other side of my knotted family tree, the all-American one whose more distant branches had lately grown even more gnarled, the Catholic intertwined (maybe) with the Jewish.

I'd gone east—so now it was time to go west.

PART III

THE AMERICANS

CHAPTER SIX

Thomas Wolfe had it right: You can't go home again (especially if that home was never yours to begin with). Burma, with its slapdash reconstructed stupas and molding colonial relics, its informal archives of comic books and agitprop, had upended my ideas about what I was looking for. I'd assumed that I could unwind my mother's immigrant story and return to her roots, comingle myself with the Burmese by exploring our left-behind blood and land, and claim both for my own. I'd hoped I could scavenge the remains of Our Family Before America and find something resonant and true there that would leave me less lonely, more sure of my place in the world.

What I found, instead, was that I was a damn Yankee. By the end of the trip, I was ready for pizza, or, at the very least, soft cheese. I was tired of trying to communicate in Burmese. I was fatigued and angry about the punishing heat on the Tropic of Cancer that made me listless and exhausted. I sounded like a spoiled American brat—maybe because I was one.

Begrudgingly, I conceded that I was not "American" in the way my mother was "American." She, unlike me, was Burmese first, and then she was American. She lived in the United States, and she was happy to live in the United States, but she was, and would always be, Burmese first—whether she chose to acknowledge this or not. I was not Burmese first, as much as I had hoped to be, as much as I hoped that my Burmese half might compensate for my confused whole. But even if I cared deeply about my mother's roots, I still couldn't muster a deep sense of identification with them.

Perhaps I had more in common with immigrants who'd disposed of their earlier selves and histories, and thought, effectively, "So what?" when it came to what their ancestors had left behind.

In other words, immigrants like my father's family.

Europeans who came to America were drawn to these shining shores in part for liberation, after all. They were looking for the opportunity to become something different than they'd been in the Old World; to shed the constraints that defined the places they fled. Or that was the story, at least.

When they got here, America struggled to integrate each European wave: the German and Irish, the Southern Europeans. The Jews. Each one was accused of diluting the country, of lowering the average IQ, of breeding quickly and without adequate resources, of being cultural usurpers. But nativists eventually found a way, in time, to make sense of these masses yearning to breathe free. One by one, they were tossed into the great melting pot and made American. Or, some might argue, generically white—a critical designation, as it would turn out. The point is, to reap all that America had on offer, European immigrants assimilated into new constructs of identity: one part joining, one part forgetting. We, the children of this cultural amnesia, were now keen to (of all things!) remember, desperate for clues that might lead us back to the very place that our ancestors had left behind.

My father's family had taken a few elements of their Irish Catholic heritage—the church, the European names, the penchant for dishes involving boiled cabbage—and held on to them in the New World, small keepsakes around which to organize their American identities. They told wistful and probably inaccurate stories about the old days—because to be an American was to be an immigrant, and it was common understanding that every second- or third-generation immigrant had to be in possession of at least one or two discreet, heartwarming chestnuts from the Old Country. Those keepsakes, in turn, became totems of shared American identity—but that was about it, as far as family history was concerned. They assimilated. And in the process, those elements of their identity—religion, language, and culture—had become "American," and not alien.

I wondered what got lost in this. In sanding down the differences, something *must* have been forgotten or thrown away—potentially something of value. With the research I'd done and conversations I'd had, my sensitivity toward the negative space in our family stories had grown. I felt drawn to the thing that might be missing—the thing that might have pointed my family, and me, toward a deeper sense of self and community than anodyne multiculturalism or assimilated identity could ever offer. And for my family, that might have been . . . membership in the Tribe of Israelites: the Jews.

Were we, really, Jewish? I had rumor and anecdote on my side, but I didn't have irrefutable proof. Where my mother's side of the tree had necessitated the unwinding of something irreconcilably exotic—where I worked to find myself in Bagan and Mandalay and Rangoon—my father's side of the tree required the very opposite approach. Take an inherently basic history and confuse it. Mightily. (Possibly.) Burma had left me feeling that perhaps I was nothing more than simply American—the experience had placed me back at square one solitaire. But my father's story still offered some redemption from that loneliness: a gang of bearded ancestors, a tribe of one's own, if you will. It was time to start sleuthing around and bothering strangers for obscure information. Again.

Iowa, my father's birthplace, was impossibly Rockwellian. His portrait of home was a simple triptych: family, church, and community. Here was a place where children carried hot baked potatoes in their hands to keep warm and belly-full during wintertime, where the mailman (my grandfather) knew each and every home, where neighborhood children played stickball in the twilight hours of summer and sat down to home-cooked meals of steak and corn each night. It was hard to imagine unwrapping this golden folklore to find some molten core of hidden identity.

Our family weren't farmers, exactly, but, as my father told it, much of his home life revolved around food: the growing, harvesting, cooking, and eating of it. With six children, a stay-at-home mother, and only a mail carrier's salary to support them all, much of what the family ate was from the land.

In the sizable kitchen garden and orchard, herbs and vegetables and fruits were grown: endive and cabbage and potatoes, dill and thyme, peaches and apples. There was a summer kitchen where the food they grew was pickled and canned or made into jams. My grandmother rendered her own lard and fried doughnuts in it on Sunday. She baked her own pies and breads—bread purchased at the grocery store was designated specifically as "store-bought" and consumed with a certain amount of disdain. Meat came from the local butcher, but even in that transaction there was an old-timey element of the personal: A phone call from the butcher shop would alert my grandmother to the fact that a pig had just been slaughtered and would she like some pork chops? In these retellings, stories that I grew up with and could recite like they were my own, you could smell the scents wafting from the family dinner table . . . and they were delicious.

As for my great-grandfather Henry Wagner, the man who had brought the Wagner family name to the shores of the United States from the Old World, the very reason our clan was able to spread its seed in the land of opportunity in the last quarter of the nineteenth century, there was remarkably little to share. When I asked my father about Henry, he replied, uncharacteristically stingy in his recollection, "I have no memory of my grandfather at all. I'm not even sure I was alive when he was." (Turns out he wasn't.) The only memory he could conjure about my great-grandmother—Henry's wife, Anna—was her death. "My father came home," my dad explained. "It was a cold day and his glasses were all steamed up. And he was crying."

From the evidence I'd heard thus far, I imagined Henry Wagner to have been a sort of stern character. From photos, he had a thatch of white hair and a formidable, do-not-fuck-with-me mustache—the kind of facial hair that meant business, not irony. (I enjoyed the fact that I was vaguely scared of him; it gave our family history a sense of weight.)

When the Jewish Theory presented itself, I hatched a hypothesis that Henry had been an educated Luxembourger who'd had reason to flee the Old Country with only the savings he could carry on his person, driven by scandal or necessity or curiosity to the shores of America, where he started over— never once looking back. He was a mirthless and highly focused man (probably) who had no time for remorse or nostalgia, and when he arrived in a state filled with Christians, well then, he decided to become one, too. Not because he was scared of being singled out or otherwise intimidated for his Judaism, but because to be Christian was to make a pragmatic break with the old and assume full membership in the new. This theorizing was held on tenterhooks—but this is the outline I drew for myself, eager to fill in corroborating details.

What my father did recall with clarity were details about his grandparents' home. Henry was known as a businessman and "a merchant." He owned a local establishment on Main Street, Wagner's Bar and Grocery (of course), a small market with an adjacent saloon. In the bar, someone had painted a big mural of people wasted in a tavern, toasting one another with steins of ale. It was framed in mahogany, my dad explained, traces of wonderment still evident in his recollection, "and there was a big, long beautiful bar."

Henry and his wife lived in a "really big house." My father, not usually one known to notice home décor, offered that there were lace curtains and real silver for dining, "very nice" plates and crystal glasses. A formal dining table, chairs, and—hanging on one wall—a portrait of Henry in bow tie and suit. "He was very dignified," said my father. "Henry and Anna were very European." By way of an aside—or a clarification—or maybe both, he added, "It never occurred to me that I was from the working class, or different from the banker."

If my father had been insulated from the discomforts of class consciousness, something similar was apparently the case with race. "There were no people of color in Lansing—none," he told me. "A handful of Native Americans were the most ethnic people in town. The only person of color I saw before college was the dry cleaner. [He] was an African American man, and I remember being sort of struck by it. He was an incredibly nice guy," my father noted, "and my mother liked him a lot. But we never talked about race." I raised an eyebrow when my father said this—I've found in my adult life that it's always a little iffy when someone white finds the only person of color (a person in some sort of servile position, no less!) "incredibly nice."

In fact, he went out of his way to tell me that if Lansing had a persecuted population, it wasn't based on skin color or religion. In the wake of the First and Second World Wars, "the pressure put on people not to emphasize their German origins was tremendous," he explained. His father, Carl Wagner, Sr., was a rural mail carrier, and "there were numerous people who corresponded in German. Dad could read it because he spoke it as a kid." But with the advent of war, speaking German became "one hell of a liability. And there was also a very subtle anti-Catholicism. I used to think of myself as being a minority."

In this town, at this moment, my father would have me believe that the outcasts were more likely to be the German-speaking Catholics than the only Jewish family or the single black guy cleaning laundry. How was that for an ethnic alley-oop?! Here I was, assuming that the all-white denizens of Any Town, Iowa, would secretly harbor ill will for the traditionally persecuted: the Jews or the black people. But it turned out that that wasn't really an issue: It was the *Germans* who got the sneers and sideways glances. Could it have really been this way? It would be a relief to believe that we weren't implicated in the country's foundational racist crimes: slavery, Jim Crow, anti-Semitism. It also seemed pretty unlikely.

After all, how could we have managed to reap all this—the bounty of America, with its peaches and dill and freedom—without extracting some price, taking something away from someone? Did the universe simply act with benevolence in the case of my father's wholesome family, imparting gifts with no blood or plunder? My father explained Henry's choice of Iowa as his destination because, "They were giving land away: forty acres if you could farm it. The land was free."

Here it was, the snag. The unseen "they." How had "they" acquired the land they so freely gave away? I knew that Henry Wagner arrived in Iowa somewhere in the 1870s or '80s, but I had no idea what he found upon arrival—and I had already learned that the most interesting (read: complicating) truths were to be found in those snags. I set out to determine where, exactly, this land came from.

Lansing, Iowa, is in the farthest northeast quadrant of the state, situated in Allamakee County. On the east the county is bounded by the Mississippi River, and to the north it's hemmed in by the state of Minnesota. The first Iowa history book I consulted had a fairly matter-of-fact explanation about how the area came to be settled by the Germans and Irish and Norwegians of the mid-nineteenth century: "Allamakee was long held as a peaceful hunting land over which hostile Indians pursued the chase without collisions. It was given to the Winnebago Indians in 1833, when they were forced to surrender their Wisconsin homes."[1]

"Forced to surrender" didn't sound very good—in fact, it sounded possibly terrible, and so I began looking into histories about the Native Americans in Iowa to find out how the Winnebago ended up in Allamakee County—and what happened to them once they got there.

Flush with manifest destiny, the country was emboldened in the early part of the nineteenth century by a populist, racist Democrat named Andrew Jackson. Jackson, known popularly as "Old Hickory," was a hero in the War of 1812, a successful lawyer, an unapologetic slave owner, a founder of the Democratic Party, a destroyer of the Second Bank of the United States, and a guiding hand behind the forced removal and displacement of tens of thousands of Native Americans from their home soil. In his most famous decision, Jackson—who had been greatly aided by the Cherokee against the Creek at the Battle of Horseshoe Bend in 1814—nonetheless ordered the forced removal of fifteen thousand Cherokee from their ancestral lands east of the Mississippi so that American settlers could have sole dominion over the land. In so doing, President

Jackson defied a ruling from the U.S. Supreme Court that had affirmed Cherokee sovereignty, and set a deadly precedent for the treatment of Native Americans elsewhere in the country. The expulsion of these Cherokee—as well as several other tribes of native peoples—and their long, forced march westward, was known as the Trail of Tears: Nearly four thousand Cherokee lost their lives along the way, felled by disease, exhaustion, and starvation.

Up in the Midwest, under Jackson's guidance, the U.S. government in 1829 negotiated with representatives of several tribes[2] the sale of eight million acres of land extending from the upper end of Rock Island, Illinois, to the mouth of the Mississippi—lands that are now most of Missouri, Iowa, and Minnesota.[3] In some cases, the federal government made these kinds of agreements with tribal leaders who were more receptive to the idea of land cessation, and (according to certain historians) more receptive to bribes, as well.[4] The sale of this land resulted in a massive expulsion of native people from their ancestral homelands—and it was, not surprisingly, a deal that few were happy with.

Here's a letter from Potawatomi chief Senacheewane to Jackson:

Father, we wish to be shaded by one tree. The black cloud has long since disappeared—and we were in hopes it should never return. It is, Father, in your hand to keep it off, to let the Influence of that great tree keep us in unity & friendship. To go away from our home is hard. But to be driven off without any hopes of finding home again is hard to think of, and the thought is equal to death. You do not know, Father, our situation and if you did you would pity us, for these very same woods that once made our delight, have now become the woods of danger. The river where we once paddled our canoes uncontrolled, has now become the river of alarm and of blood. Several of my young men have been killed by your white children & nothing has been done to cover the dead.

Father—we cannot go away. This is our land, this is our home, we sooner die. Come Father, speak to us, and we shall try to please you.

I am done.

May the great Spirit above give you health and a long life—is the wish of all your red children.

I speak for my people—who are many.[5]

The Winnebago Indians back then were known as the Ho-Chunk Nation, for *Hochungra*, meaning "People of the Big Voice." As part of that massive sale of tribal land,[6] the Ho-Chunk were forced to give up nearly a third of their land for $540,000 dollars[7] (payable in thirty annual installments) to make way for miners who had their eyes on the territory, especially the mines in southeastern Wisconsin—though that didn't put an end to encroachment and hostilities.

Certain factions of the Winnebago remained resistant even after that sale, splitting with the rest of their tribe and taking up arms to reclaim their land in the Black Hawk War of 1832. When they lost, the Winnebago were forced to cede remaining homeland in Wisconsin in exchange for "neutral ground" in Iowa (plus $270,000 in twenty-seven annual payments). This "neutral ground" was a forty-mile-wide "buffer zone" in the northeast part of the state, where the feds insisted that the tribe would have protection from predatory settlers, frontier hustlers, and other warring tribes. The government assured skeptical tribespeople that they would be relocated to "better lands" when those became available. (They never did become available.)[8] In the meantime, America set about "civilizing" the Winnebago children in Indian schools.

That so-called neutral ground included what is now Allamakee County—and it was hardly neutral. The Winnebago were forced onto territory that was being battled over by the Sauk and Fox tribes (also known by their tribal name, the Meskwaki), and their common enemy, the Sioux. While the Winnebago had ancestral bloodlines that linked them to the Sioux, they were effectively people without a home, caught between warring factions, and unsafe in their new territory. I read this and was reminded of Senacheewane's plea: *"To be driven off without any hopes of finding home again is hard to think of, and the thought is equal to death."*

Some resisted this forced exile and traveled to Washington, D.C., to make their case in 1837. Tribal elders purposefully sent representatives who weren't designated to sign treaties, as a sort of insurance policy against crappy deals. It didn't work. The representatives were told they couldn't leave Washington without signing a treaty—one that would give away the rest of the Winnebago lands. It didn't matter that these particular tribal signatures were meaningless, nor did it matter that the feds said they'd give the tribe eight years to pack up and move out. In the end, the Winnebago were allowed only eight months to relocate. I thought of Senacheewane again: *"Father—we cannot go away. This is our land, this is our home, we sooner die."*

This chapter took a deadly toll—standard operating practice, as far as the history of Native Americans was concerned. What happened to the Winnebago is what happened to the Cherokee and Seminole, the Choctaw and the Chickasaw. In 1829, the Winnebago were estimated to number 5,800. By 1837, that population was reported to be 4,500—smallpox had killed off nearly a quarter of them.[9] Less than two decades later, in 1855, the tribe numbered only 2,754. A quarter century of warring, negotiation, settlement, and expulsion had failed to yield any redemption for the People of the Big Voice.

Offering a grim assessment of the times, a resident and writer by the name of Alexander Fulton concluded:

> Contact with our civilization seems to have wrought only misfortune and disaster to this once proud and independent tribe. The large amount of money annually paid them by the government attracted about them many mercenary white traders and liquor-dealers, and they were subjected to the temptations usual under such circumstances. Many of them became dissipated, and in consequence of the mortality induced by drunkenness, sickness and disease, we find them, in 1855 diminished. When the Winnebagoes first became known to the whites, they were described as of good stature, noble and dignified bearing, and as having straight black hair, piercing black eyes, and superior mental capacity. Contact with civilization seems not to have improved them, either mentally or physically.[10]

Decimated in number, diseased in body, broken in heart and soul, the Winnebago, who whites saw as a threat to their westward expansion, had been violently contained. By 1846, the tribe was uprooted yet again, moved out of neutral ground and over to Minnesota. Not surprisingly, the first white settlements in Allamakee County were established somewhere around this time. The town of Lansing was claimed and settled in June 1848.

The Homestead Act of 1862 opened up the great expanse of the American West to white settlement—and Allamakee County was no exception. If the fight to claim this land had been bloody and protracted, the process by which it was given away was, ironically, remarkably easy for most Americans (excepting, of course, native people, who weren't considered citizens until 1926). Even immigrants could claim their acreage, provided they swore their allegiance to the United States, swore they were no longer faithful to whichever king or queen had once ruled their dominion, and further swore they would obtain proper American citizenship within five years.

All that swearing aside, the relative facility of this process was remarkable—the inherent generosity of giving away land, even to, ahem, illegals! (From the vantage point of the early twenty-first century, in the gust and swirl of the roaring debate over immigration, it is nearly impossible to imagine any president ordering American land to be given away to "illegals," refugees, or the undocumented.)

The Homestead Act was passed during the Civil War—and one of the driving forces behind it was slavery. Earlier attempts to parcel out western lands were met with resistance from Southerners, who feared the rise of small farmers on free land was a threat to their way of life: plantation slavery. What if the opening up of the West attracted anti-slavery Europeans or poor Southern whites? Many Northerners, meanwhile, wanted to ensure that the practice of slavery ended in the South and aimed to prevent it from corrupting the westward expanse of the United States, precisely by populating it with small farms owned by free persons, rather than wealthy landowners with slaves. (Not all Northerners were fans of this plan, however; some were concerned that the parceling out of free land would drain their factories of cheap labor.)

Anyway, there were several failed attempts to pass a homestead act, most of which were scuttled in Congress by the Southern states—until they seceded from the Union and departed the legislature. Once that happened, Lincoln was free to pass the law sans Southern resistance—and did.

So what did all this American bounty mean for the slaves themselves? My father had mentioned the lone black dry cleaner in town—shouldn't there have been black-owned businesses sprouting up all over the Midwest once it was opened to homesteading and closed to slavery? Indeed, under the Homestead Act, and once the Civil War ended, former slaves were technically able to claim parcels of land for themselves. And with a southern landscape where racism and violence remained the order of the day, no doubt the West seemed enticing. But to migrate hundreds or thousands of miles required resources and networks that many newly freedmen and -women didn't have—and so some were forced to stay put and work (for wages, this time) in service of those who had once enslaved them.

But there were other, nefarious reasons that the great American heartland remained monochromatically white: Southerners made it very hard for newly freed black folk to leave the region. The exodus of former slaves to the Midwest was greatly complicated by racial animus.

The National Park Service oversees many of the records relating to the Homestead Act, and details the various pernicious challenges that kept Southern blacks from leaving the South during Reconstruction:

> Southern whites continued to oppose the exodus. . . . Many went to extreme measures to try to keep blacks from emigrating, including arrest and imprisonment on false charges and the old standby of raw, brute force. African-Americans suffered beatings and other forms of violence at the hands of whites desperate to keep them in the South. Though these typical forms of intimidation did not really prevent many freed blacks from leaving, the eventual refusal of steamship captains to pick them up did.[11]

It was hard to settle a new place if you weren't allowed to leave the old one.

When my father said the land was free, he hadn't thought about—or cared to know, particularly—the price that had been paid by someone else. All that free land wasn't really free, as it turned out.

I called the National Park Service to find out who had taken parcels of Allamakee soil for themselves, following passage of the Homestead Act. There were six settlers: Two men named John Carroll and James May took land in 1874; Melvin Lang in 1886; William Clark in 1890; John Thomas in 1894; and Charles Widman in 1927. A very helpful man named Blake Bell from the NPS reiterated that none of these men were named Henry Wagner. While this undermined my father's proposed reason for Henry Wagner's choice of Iowa as his new home ("They were giving land away"), it also absolved me of some guilt, although not entirely.

Ultimately, I couldn't get away from the fact that we had accepted, at face value, the notion that all this had been somehow easy, or miraculous; that golden opportunity had shone itself precisely at the right moment, and that there were no strings attached. It wasn't as if I now expected Carl Wagner, Jr., to pay reparations to the Winnebago of Wisconsin, or to offer a family plot to the families of former slaves, but, in retrospect, the ho-hum narrative about our Iowa origin story seemed lazy, if not foolish—and it made me wonder what other self-serving, just-so stories were woven into our family history, ready to be unwound.

"A handful of Native Americans were the most ethnic people in town," my dad had said. What a wonder this was, his lily-white Lansing, his monochromatic Main Street. "The only person of color I saw before college was the dry cleaner."

Well, there was a reason for that.

CHAPTER SEVEN

So what had been lost in the happy story of Henry Wagner's assimilation? What did I really know about Henry? What did he do in the Old World, why did he leave, and why did he (possibly) conceal his religion when he arrived in America? Why did he come to Iowa, of all places?

His life was largely the province of myth: According to my father, he was erudite, some sort of multilingual translator, a man of the merchant class who appreciated crystal and lace. But where exactly did he come from and how did he end up in northeastern Iowa, which was, at the time of his arrival, very nearly the American frontier? Why leave what was presumed to be a very comfortable existence in Luxembourg to decamp for the wilds of Allamakee County? And who the hell had led him there?

I wanted to know the answers to these questions not just for curiosity's sake, but because it had become clear that things were more complex than our Rockwellian family tableau and its homemade doughnuts and hopscotch Saturdays would suggest. I didn't want the Hallmark version of our family story. Survival and success almost always necessitated something breaking along the way—and the harmony of our origin story smacked of delusion.

Admitting this motivation probably makes me sound like a person with many issues (and I certainly am), but the complexities and subterfuges that characterize Twenty-first-Century American life (WMDs, catfishing, electoral college votes versus popular votes) had taken their toll on me, and it was impossible to reconcile such a simplistic narrative with what I had learned about survival and success. I was discovering through this research that my American origin story—and, for that matter, probably everyone's—was messy. My father's story—generically, the White Immigrant Origin Story (WIOS)—was a familiar one: Most of my white friends had one. "We came from Ireland, and my great-grandfather made a good, honest life in America, and now we have Super Mario Bros. and a sport utility vehicle."

This is what I'd grown up understanding; this was the family history in circulation when I went over to Meredith Mullen's house after school to feast on hard salami sandwiches with French's mustard and take a dip at her mother's country club's swimming pool. It was a benign story during my childhood years, but the WIOS is nonetheless a source of much horror and grief in American life: It is a story about virtue, freedom, fairness, opportunity, cheerful assimilation, and hard work, and it is a lie. Even after my most rudimentary investigation—a few calls to the National Park Service and some extensive Googling—my own family's WIOS had collapsed. That experience drove home this truth: Almost no one achieves their success or secures their place in this country in singular, godly fashion.

The typical WIOS is filled with easy lines like my father's explanation for his grandfather's destination: "They were giving away land." Of course they weren't—someone a few years earlier had stolen it and killed the people who once lived on it and then given it away to someone else—and we had conveniently decided to gloss over that reality. But because enough people agreed to the WIOS, enough people didn't ask questions or look under the rock, it didn't matter that the land was stolen and its shepherds slaughtered. It didn't really matter how many brown folks and black folks raised an eyebrow or a hand or a fist in complaint or caution. Nor did it matter how many of those people asked for the same things that defined the WIOS and were denied—or worse.

Ironically, the WIOS didn't even work for white folks, in the end; all the erasing and revision, the rounded corners and sanded edges, left its inheritors with something flat and blanched, full of empty calories. It wasn't nourishing, it was generic and forgettable, and, most crucially, it eventually wore thin. And when the truth inevitably started to emerge, however many years later and at whomever's hand, it became cause for shame and denial. Who wanted to be born of the people who'd ousted the Winnebago? Who wanted to be the kin of a former slave owner? Nobody, really. You couldn't find a new family, couldn't choose your own roots (if only!)—and so, instead, you had to dig deeper into the mythmaking of the WIOS, double down on its fantastical origins: Once upon a time, things in America had been great, and simple, and pure—how else would we have made it?—and, dammit, we need to get back to that time.

Here was a dangerous proposition: If you went too far down this rabbit hole, you'd realize there was nothing much on the other side. But this simplicity—the belief in the goodness of a certain people and their inherently superior nature, their infallibility, the notion that nothing fetid or rotten preceded them—it was intoxicating. When people speak of these simplified lies as manifestations of white privilege, we sometimes forget that *privilege feels good*—and a lot of people are willing to pay a price for it.

When I was in college, my mother moved to Europe and married a tall Dutchman named Joost who enjoyed two things above all else: smoking and driving at high speeds. Every summer I would visit them in Amsterdam and inevitably we would take a vacation in some nearby European country. Joost's preferred method of transportation was the car (of course), and so one summer we piled into his ride: Joost, my mother, my grandmother (in town to buy Amsterdam diamonds and complain about my mother's disorganization around the house), and me.

These drives were not short and necessitated many stops at European rest stations, where you could purchase a full roast chicken and Swiss chocolates for the road. One day, Joost decided it would be beautiful to take a detour to Alsace-Lorraine: We would forgo the rest station and stop instead for dinner at a Michelin-starred restaurant. Joost could then smoke too many cigarettes at his leisure.

We exited the car—Mya Mya Gyi, Tin Swe Thant, Alex Wagner—three generations of Burmese women (one half-Burmese), and walked into the restaurant. It was the sort of place that offered small tufted seats for the pint-sized manicured dogs that some women preferred to keep as companions once their husbands grew tired of talking to them and their children had left the house. The clientele was more German than French, and it was decidedly chilly when we three Burmese Queens entered the room. The maître d' wouldn't look at us and said something snooty (and very likely racist) to Joost—which he declined to translate. (He was the only one of us who spoke German.)

The women eyed us icily, as if we had somehow polluted the air of the restaurant. The dogs looked on, passive. But what I remember most about that moment was how mortified I was to be with my Asian mother and grandmother. How much browner they made me feel, how different they made me seem to other people, and therefore how much more out of place I felt. If I had just been sitting with Joost, perhaps the atmosphere would have been warmer, the service better, the experience easier, the dogs friendlier. I would appear less obviously brown, less obviously from some other place. I can see, looking back, how enticing it was to simplify, to blanch, to wish the darker or seemingly more *complicated* parts away. And it shamed me. (We suffered through dinner on principle, then vowed never to stop in Alsace-Lorraine again. To be clear, this was not any kind of hardship.)

For the sake of all of us—not just brown people or black people or white people—it is imperative to shatter the lie that anyone's origin story is a streamlined thing born of virtuous behavior or fortuitous decision-making, and that anything different is somehow lesser. For me, this meant finding out as much as I could about whatever the Wagner clan might have forgotten, and top of the list was the possible forsaking of Our Jewish Roots. A discovery here would confirm that there was indeed a lie at the heart of my family myth, that there was a complicated story about race within my seemingly white family, and within its (false) construct, there was (major bonus) a place I belonged beneath the bleaching.

Interviewing family members for their admittedly subjective recollections of our possible Jewish heritage had been useful to a certain point. But now I needed specific confirmation from some sort of independent authority. That meant documentary evidence: things such as birth certificates and marriage licenses. Census data! I had been through the proverbial paper mill in my travels to Burma. I fought hard to reclaim documentation about our people—looked high and low for evidence about what we'd lost—and the search had turned quixotic, in the end. That which I did find had been wholly unexpected, had sent me off in a different direction altogether.

But I had faith that the paper trail in the West might be better preserved: For one thing, Western Europe hadn't fallen prey to a repressive military government that had systematically destroyed records in a bid to rewrite history. No, Western Europe had fallen prey to a fascist dictator who had systematically destroyed whole countries! And yet, Europe's libraries, I knew, had not been ransacked, pillaged, or left out on the streets: There were legendary research archives across the continent. America's records of who had arrived here and when

were still intact—as far as I knew. I had hope, however unin-
formed, that the records I was looking for had been preserved.

As much as I knew about Henry Wagner's place of arrival in
northeastern Iowa, I had little information about the man himself. When did he meet and marry his wife? (Was it really a
shipboard romance?) Was his last name really Wagner? Apparently, he spoke several languages, among them, French, German, and Yiddish: Would census forms from the Old World list
his profession and therefore suggest how he came to speak all
three? Why did he leave the Old World to come to America?
Was there any evidence—here or in Europe—of his flight from
home and why he'd made it? Surely such a thing wouldn't be
listed on, say, a utility bill, but perhaps there was some kind of
legal record that I could find in the Luxembourg archives. And
then, of course, the central mystery: Was he Jewish?

The easiest place to start was Henry's arrival in the United
States. There would be an immigration record that would list
his name, birth date, and birthplace, and from there I might
trace his steps backward or forward. I knew I was looking for
a Henry Wagner born in Luxembourg around 1849—my father had mentioned something about Henry having been involved in the Franco-Prussian War but didn't know any of the
details. Luckily, and for reasons far more important than my
little heritage research project, this was a short war. I had the
years 1869 to 1871 to play with (I figured it would be all the
more comprehensive to include the years immediately preceding and following the war itself).

How many people emigrated from Luxembourg to the
United States in this time period? As it turns out, not all that

many. According to the archives of the main entry point for immigrants arriving in America pre–Ellis Island—the Castle Garden database—only 561 Luxembourgers arrived in 1869.[1] A mere 277 left for America in 1870. And 829 departed for the New World at the conclusion of the war in 1871. From Henry's alleged hometown of Esch-sur-Alzette, only 187 males departed his district that year. I started my research online— digitized immigration records had already revealed this much. I hadn't even stepped out of my house yet: This was going to be *so easy*!

Unlike my Burmese travails, genealogical research in the twenty-first century for descendants of Europeans means mostly a lot of Internet surfing and chat room kibbitzing. The bulk of government records, including passenger manifests, naturalization forms, birth and death certificates, marriage licenses, and census surveys, have been digitized by private, for-profit companies (and, in some cases, the National Archives), and after dutifully entering my American Express number in a series of required fields, I gained entry to a portal into the past.

As it turns out, it wasn't so easy.

At first glance, I came across several "Henry Wagner" characters who fit the proverbial bill. One—twenty-three years old at the time of arrival—landed at the port of New York in May 1869 on the SS *Paraguay*, entering not via Ellis Island (which had yet to open) but at nearby Castle Garden, now known as Castle Clinton. The last time I'd been to Castle Clinton National Monument, it had been converted to a public performance space where I'd seen Cat Power sing to an audience of sweaty millennials. I wonder what this potential great-grandfather would've made of his Burmese American descendant going to see plaintive indie rock in the building where he'd entered the New World over a century prior.

Because this Henry Wagner was described as a painter, I imagined he would've been a creative thinker, which is exactly what made me dubious that this particular Henry Wagner was actually my great-grandfather. Nothing about the stories I'd heard thus far suggested he was a man of the arts, though, of course, you never knew. Nothing suggested he'd be a fluent speaker of Yiddish, either. The man was a mystery.

Another Henry Wagner arrived July 25, 1870, but apparently came from Prussia and had been born in Germany, so this seemed to make him, at first, an unlikely candidate. But I couldn't dismiss him out of hand, because I soon learned that men from Luxembourg were often listed by the U.S. government as German, because they spoke German, or had German accents and otherwise possessed a passing familiarity with German culture. The German Empire, properly speaking, didn't even exist until 1871—which meant that the roughly sixteeen hundred Luxembourg-born men who immigrated to America in my targeted time frame could have been lumped in the immigration rolls with the approximately seven hundred thousand to one million men of German stock who did so from 1860 to 1870. (By the 1880s there were nearly 1.5 million of them.)[2] And there were a lot of Wagners in the German world! It was a massive Wagnerian headache.

I looked and looked at the immigration records online and found many Henry Wagners who'd arrived in New York from Germany over the years in question—ones who came here professing to immigration officials that they were farmers or merchants (duly noted on the intake rolls but not, apparently, a mandatory question) or, more often, nothing at all, because in the end they were coming to America to become whatever they would be. They left from the ports of Boulogne-sur-Mer and Hamburg and Liverpool and Cherbourg and entered America mostly through the port of New York (there were also lesser numbers entering through Philadelphia, Baltimore, Galveston, New Orleans, San Francisco, and Boston), and they came in on ships named *Etruria* or *Phoenicia* or *Normannia*, hulking steamers operated by White Star and Cunard and Inman, with two or three coal stacks to power them through the one- or two-week voyages across thousands of miles of Atlantic Ocean.

There were so many Henry Wagners that (sort of) fit the bill that it was nearly overwhelming. But as confusing as this became for my research purposes, it was also beautiful, in a weird way. The multitudes of these men with the same name, all coming to the same place to start anew—or fleeing their various disasters. "Henry Wagner" became, for me "John Q. Public." The name meant nothing; it was just a placeholder for the experience.

So if there was a surfeit of Henry Wagners in the passenger manifests of the late 1800s, I figured it would make sense to start looking for other records from later on in my great-grandfather's life. If I had more biographical details, that might narrow the search for his arrival year in the United States. From there, I could establish his date of departure from the Old World, and then possibly trace more of his life back in Luxembourg using whatever census forms ye ole Grand Duchy made available to nosy, patriarchy-shattering amateur genealogical detectives like myself.

And anyway, since most of Henry's adult life was spent in

America, it figured that America was likely to have the longest paper trail. I widened the search—and came across two documents that gave me pause.

Among the digitized records available online at Ancestry.com (the King Kong of digital records archives, and, not coincidentally, accessed through a pay portal) was a naturalization certificate for a man named Henry Wagner dated March 1, 1886. I knew this had to be him because it was signed in French Creek, Allamakee County, Iowa. (The county had been settled only three decades earlier, and the Norwegians who did most of that work numbered only five hundred or so in the whole county; it was not exactly a bustling metropolis.)³ There could be no other recent immigrant named Henry Wagner in a place that small (right?).

I was surprised at the date: 1886, by all accounts, was a good fifteen years or so after Henry had first set foot in America.* After his first children had been born. And, presumably, after he had opened Wagner's Bar and Grocery on Main Street. To imagine him still a citizen of the Grand Duchy of Luxembourg —and even possibly an undocumented immigrant in America! —for such a prolonged period of time, during such formative years of our family history, complicated my conception of our American beginnings. As it turns out, up until 1906, there was no formalized recordkeeping around immigration, or the naturalization process; it wasn't until 1906 that the Bureau of Immigration and Naturalization was even created. The process of becoming an American changed to some degree from the postcolonial era up until 1906, but, effectively, would-be Americans

---

* The Franco-Prussian War ended in 1871.

had to have resided in the United States for at least five years, and in their home state for one. (These requirements increased and decreased through the decades, depending on the political climate of the day.)

When they applied for citizenship, immigrants had to prove they met the residence requirements; they were asked to renounce allegiance to any foreign governments, pledge their loyalty to the United States, and take an oath. It did not seem like a particularly arduous process—but, perhaps more interestingly, there was no apparent mandate that it even take place. No deportation task forces were on the hunt for Luxembourg illegals who were theoretically pilfering off the largesse of the American government. There was no mandatory period in which immigrants had to file for citizenship; some did so as soon as they could, while others, like Henry Wagner, waited almost twenty years.[*]

In fact, the process of becoming American seemed relatively open, unless of course you were a Chinese laborer—in which case you were specifically barred from even entering the country, thanks to the Chinese Exclusion Act of 1882—so there were some aspects of the process that would be familiar to a twenty-first-century American. Of course, these were the most disturbing parts.

In the absurdist here and now of America today, when the suggested deportation of eleven million men and women without proper paperwork has an inherently brown subtext, Henry Wagner's belated naturalization is an urgent reminder that the "illegals"—those tax-avoiding, coattail-riding outsiders—from two or three generations ago were mostly white men and women. And American law enforcement, it seemed, was pretty relaxed about it. Henry Wagner, whatever his immigration status, was a token of that reality. Most every white American family—even those urging the construction of a wall to keep "Them" out—has a Henry Wagner in its past. If only they knew.

But mostly, this piece of paper (this scan of paper) stirred my heart. Laying eyes on my great-grandfather's 130-year-old naturalization certificate reminded me of the thing we constantly say but never seem to realize: We are a nation of outsiders. I always knew this as it concerned my mother's side, because her arrival story was never not with us, never not with her. I was reminded of it by virtue of her very being: She was Burmese and then she became American, and you could see that history in her face, hear it in her voice, feel it in her conception of the world. But I had never really understood the same to be true on my father's side. His whiteness, his American ordinariness, masked the fact that he, too, came from someplace else.

In this moment, it became quite clear to me (as obvious as this was, it was still revelatory) that any claim anyone—who wasn't a Native American!—made to being a *true* American was a lie. To say that you were the "real" American and that someone else—an outsider—was not wasn't some sort of bright-lined immigration policy. It was merely a power grab: Everyone in this country was an outsider.

Henry Wagner and his white descendants were allowed to lay claim to the title of "American" because somewhere along the way, the country had decided that white American outsiders, if residents for a sufficient amount of time, were not outsiders; they became, simply, Americans. But brown American outsiders were—and would always be—brown American outsiders. They could (eventually) be ennobled with the "American" title, but only in hyphenation: African-American, Burmese-American, Mexican-American, as if the hyphenation clarified that these people were not exactly *full* Americans.

When, for example, had I ever heard the Wagner family referred to as Luxembourger-Americans? Precisely never. And yet my black friends who had families here for centuries—some for long, hard centuries—before Henry Wagner alighted on this land would forever be known as African-American, occupying a slightly lower place on the American power grid. And so it went. I didn't forgive this injustice, but it did make me wonder about the inverse: What did it mean to suddenly conceive of my white, Western, Wagner European roots as something out of the "ordinary"? To place them in the same bucket as my Burmese roots? What exotic, Luxembourgian strangeness did I come from?

When I discovered that my great-grandfather was naturalized in 1886, I had my first important notch on the family time line. Now I began to look for other, earlier milestones so I could start to plot out a story that explained this man. After going bleary-eyed over archives and records to scrape together the little I'd discovered thus far, I wanted to find the answer to a salacious unknown, one that might shed some light on Henry Wagner's ethno-religious background: When (and how) exactly did he marry Anna Wagner? Could she have been Jewish, too? Was their marriage one of convenience? Was it religious? Where did it happen? In the Old World or the New?

Cousin Karl had mentioned that he thought Henry Wagner

had taken his wife's name, in part to disguise his identity after the Franco-Prussian War (where Karl believed Henry may have engaged in treasonous activity), but I secretly thought that maybe Henry had taken his wife's name to disguise his true, Jewish background. I wanted to see what the records showed about their life together and went on the hunt for census data, which would give me information about their marriage and the children born from it.

I first found census records from 1880. In curlicued English script, they accounted for Henry Wagner, a self-described thirty-two-year-old farmer from Allamakee County, born of parents from Luxembourg stock and married to a twenty-two-year-old woman named Eva Wagner. I had always been told that my great-grandmother's name was Anna, but Eva seemed close enough—and if Henry had been alternately referred to as Heinrich, maybe Eva was some Teutonic derivative of Anna (a stretch). Or perhaps it was her middle name (less of a stretch), or maybe whoever was taking the census was one of those name takers who inadvertently altered future generations of American families by virtue of crappy handwriting or bad hearing or just plain Yankee laziness (likely).

Anyway, I went with it, and did so because the math mostly fit: I knew Henry had been born roughly in 1848 or 1849. According to this census record, he and his wife had three children, a two-year-old son named Heinrich and two daughters: one year-old Catharina and six-month-old Mary. And I knew from our family records that the eldest of my great-aunts and -uncles were Henry, Catherine, and Mary. This was the Wagner clan.

Once I was able to pinpoint the names of a few key family members (Eva Wagner was known as Anna Wagner, Catharina as Catherine, and so forth) and establish a timeline to work with (Henry and Eva/Anna were having children by 1878, so they must have married before that because children out of wedlock in the nineteenth century seemed like something that simply *was not done*), I was able to narrow my search for other biographical documents, including, most important, a marriage license. It wasn't hard to find.

Dated April 4, 1877, Allamakee County records showed the wedding of Henry Wagner to Eva Wagner. It did nothing to point me in the direction of the Tribe. Henry and Eva/Anna had married officially in the state of Iowa, and with the blessing of the Catholic church—no synagogue in sight.

But weirdly, unlike so many other marriage records, the bride was not listed by her maiden name. Unless her maiden name had happened—also—to be Wagner. This might explain why my millennial cousin Karl believed that Henry had changed his name to hers, perhaps to disguise his identity after the Franco-Prussian War (where, again, Karl insisted something had gone very badly wrong), or perhaps because he was trying to hide his Jewish identity in the New World (which was my preferred operating thesis). Or perhaps they had just been born with the same last name.

I knew I needed professional help—of all kinds, which was abundantly clear. Specifically, I knew I needed professional help for *this project*. Through exhaustive and specific Googling, I stumbled across Anne Kenne at the University of St. Thomas in St. Paul, Minnesota—there was a limited number of Luxembourg experts in the United States, apparently—who was a university archivist and the head of the school's Special Collections department.

From my Internet research, I could see that Anne was America's de facto Luxembourg whisperer, and so I sent a rather feeble email to her, begging for help. She suggested a few books and Web resources, but most important, she turned me on to a site called Luxroots.org. Who knew there was enough of a community of Luxembourger genealogists to warrant its own site? Before long, I would realize *of course there's a community of Luxembourger genealogists.* But at the moment, I was aware only of the peaks of the world of genealogical research, not the massive mountains below the surface.

Luxroots.org has the organizational chaos of an early '90s riot grrrl zine, which had the net effect of both confusion and heightened expectation. It was effectively the Web equivalent of the bargain bin: You were sure there was a treasure buried in there, somewhere—something that might fit the bill for whatever you'd been searching for. In this case, that thing was a name: Jean Ensch, a man who I will dub the Sherlock Holmes of Luxembourger detective work. Ensch monitored the site and acted (as far as I could tell) as the wizard behind the grand duchy's genealogical forum.

Again, I sent a rather feeble and desperate email into the unknown. Could Mr. Ensch help me in my search? I was looking for information about my great-grandfather Henry Wagner of Esch-sur-Alzette: specifically, if he tried to change his name or otherwise alter his identity in the wake of the Franco-Prussian War, reasons unspecified (to Ensch) but quite clear (to me): I wanted to know if my great-grandfather had been Jewish. I crossed my fingers.

Ensch did not reply.

I waited.

I waited longer.

Eventually, I gave up hope.

More precisely, I went where any good Inter-nerd on the verge of losing hope goes: to chat rooms, specifically genealogy chat rooms where various self-styled ancestry experts are waiting to comment or reply to all manner of inquiries. On Ancestry.com—where most of my key digitized records were available to me, as long as I was able to afford $29 a month in subscription fees—there happened to be a particularly chatty community of amateur genealogists, and so I posted my query: I was looking for any records pertaining to a certain Henry Wagner, born circa 1849 in Esch-sur-Alzette, Luxembourg, and/or his marriage to Eva/Anna Wagner.

Someone from Aurora, Illinois, with the handle *chi1k* responded within four hours. *chi1k* found birth records on FamilySearch.org for someone named Henri Wagener, born July 31, 1849, in Esch-sur-Alzette. Amid several lines of terrifyingly medieval Germanic script, I found the handwritten name "Heinrich."

I couldn't read any of the rest of it, but *chi1k*, already the most useful and generous virtual stranger I'd ever come across, explained that He(nry)(nri)(inrich)'s mother was a twenty-two-year-old named Anne Wagener. As with "Anna" and "Eva," or "German" and "Luxembourgian," online genealogy research tips told me that "Wagener" could have eventually become "Wagner"; specificity was sanded down through the generations, especially when it came to immigrants who were both leaving so much behind and trying to assimilate into a new culture (and/or had a new culture foisted upon them). Anne's father, Peter (also known as Pierre) Wagener, sixty-six, was the only other male name listed on the document. There was no record of a father for the newborn.

Meaning: He(nry)(nri)(inrich) Wag(e)ner was an illegitimate child.

Supporting that point was this piece of evidence, scrawled in the margin of the birth certificate, according to *chilk*:

Michel Mueller of Grevenmacher and Marie Anna Wagener married in Esch-sur-Alzette on 28 Aug 1856 (making Henri a legitimate child of the couple).

Not that I necessarily needed further proof of this, but *chilk* then posted a census document from 1867, which showed Michel and Anna Mueller, née Wagener, and their son Henri Mueller.

By the year 1871, another Luxembourg census revealed that Henri was no longer living with Anna and Michel Mueller. But of course he wasn't: He had already left for America—and was on his way to becoming Henry Wagner (again).

As fantastically helpful as *chilk* had been, I was slightly worried that I was too reliant on his/her reading of the paper. No amount of magnification rendered the nearly two-hundred-year-old script legible to my farsighted eyes, and besides, I didn't know any German beyond the kind of cutesy greetings you made to shop owners in Berlin boutiques so they wouldn't think you were an uncultured American tourist. Was I too dependent on this random chat buddy's explosive reckoning of our family history? Probably. I could imagine presenting the illegitimate origins of our forefather to my dad and his sisters, and then citing the source as someone named *chilk*. They would likely frown or otherwise make clear that an anonymous online personage was not the person to trust with a significant rewrite of one's own family history. I, too, had some doubts.

But then, six months after my initial email, the elusive Jean Ensch surfaced, like a submarine rising out of the dark sea at the least expected moment.

Apparently, the email address I'd used to contact him had been (essentially) shut down five years ago and was presently in use mostly as a "spam trap" (his description). I was lucky Ensch had even bothered to check it.

The wizard had checked the birth records of Esch-sur-Alzette and found the same one that *chilk* had sent to me. He, too, concluded that my great-grandfather had been born a bastard:

Peter Wagener declared that his daughter Anna Maria Wagener, aged 22 years, had given birth to an illegitimate child, whose given name was Henry. A marginal note specifies that a recognition of fatherhood and a legitimation by marriage was performed at the marriage of Michael Muller and the mother Anne Marie Wagner (spelling now Wagner in marriage record), which occurred 28 Aug 1856 in Esch sur Alzette.

Henri Wagner was henceforth known—for some unspecific number of years—as Henri Mu(e)ller. As Ensch put it:

> The groom recognizes the fatherhood of the child and allows that the child shall bear henceforth the name of Muller and have all the rights attached to the status of a legitimate child.

Knowing nothing about European social mores of the mid-nineteenth century, I hazarded a guess that it was not an easy thing to be a bastard son at that time. I further supposed that Ole Peter/Pierre Wagener was probably not puffing on a celebratory stogie in the newborn ward when he confirmed to the state that his daughter was an unwed mother. This presumed trauma, this illicit history, stood in stark contrast to what I knew about my great-grandfather, a patriarch who had fathered a Catholic clan of thirteen children who bore his (mother or wife's) name. These children, in turn, fathered a next generation of Catholic sons and daughters who hadn't even the faintest inkling that their grandfather himself had been born out of wedlock. And then adopted! With obfuscations like these, it wasn't hard to imagine that Henry had perhaps been covering up other biographical details of kaboom-like quality: namely, Judaism. The introduction of Michael Muller would provide another branch of the family tree to explore as it pertained to Our Jewish Roots.

Furthermore, for a time—at least from the age of seven until he left for America—he was known as "Heinrich Muller." It was unclear whether Henri Muller officially became Henry

Wagner before he immigrated to America or after, when he wed Eva/Anne Wagner. If he did so prior to landing in the United States, it suggested something dubious. Perhaps he was, as Karl had suggested, shedding "Muller" for personal reasons; possibly, to escape his past. But if he'd taken his wife's name upon marriage, then that was just sort of unusual—though by all accounts, it was also his original last name, so not entirely unprecedented. I paused in my research to grapple with a slightly less pressing issue: Did this mean, in some alternate universe, that I was really . . . Alex Muller?!

But back to the point: The women of Henry's life—his mother and his wife—played a determinative role in his public identity, one that was completely ahead of its time. Women, after all, were the ones whose names were forgotten by history: They lost their maiden names after marriage, and their children bore their fathers' names. In the Victorian era, the so-called spheres occupied by men and women were completely different (if complementary): Men were deemed the breadwinners, the leaders, and women were their helpmeets, keepers of the home fires. The Victorian subtext was, basically: You can't change the world without a good wife (and indeed, it was the husbands who changed the world, not the wives).

Anne Marie Muller and Anna Wagner may very well have given their wifely services to their respective husbands, but they had also—unwittingly—established a lineage in their common name. (Given how complex our retention of the Wagner name was, I was particularly satisfied in my decision not to take my husband's name after marriage—not that it was ever really a debate.)

So Ensch, a person with a real name, had confirmed *chi1k*'s research. A few days after her/his initial response, *chi1k* offered an addendum to her/his post. I had read it with interest at the time, but now that so much of her/his research had been confirmed by another source, I was even more inclined to follow it:

> Henry Wagner and his father in law Henry Wagner came to the USA together. There is one passenger list which agrees with this and matches up pretty well with another Wagner family from Esch-sur-Alzette.

So Eva/Anna's father was also named . . . Henri Wagner. And my great-grandfather He(nry)(nri)(inrich) Wag(e)ner, né Mu(e)ller, had traveled with this other clan of Wagners to the United States, posing as one of them—otherwise, you had to figure, he would have been listed as He(nry)(nri)(inrich) Mu(e)ller. Apparently, this was the moment when Henri Muller became Henry Wagner—not at a wedding, not in Europe. En route to America. This, in turn, suggested something possibly shady: Henry Wagner was immigrating to the United States undercover. Why else identify himself with a clan of Wagners—and enter the New World using their last name (which, to be fair, happened also to be his birth name)?

Maybe Karl's rumor about something questionable happening during the Franco-Prussian War hadn't been so off the mark. Perhaps Henry Wagner, né Mu(e)ller, had something he wanted to get away from back in Luxembourg—and wanted to make sure it couldn't follow him across the Atlantic to America. So he found a new family.

Chilk next provided a link to a manifest from the ship *Algeria* of the Cunard Line, which arrived in Queenstown, New York, on June 5, 1871.

Traveling on board was a large family by the name of Wagner:

Henri Wagner, age 50 [born about 1821]
Catherine Wagner, age 42 [born about 1829]
Eva Wagner, age 16 [born about 1855]
Eliza Wagner, age 11 [born about 1860]
Nicolas Wagner, age 8 [born about 1863]
James Wagner, age 5 [born about 1866]
Herman Wagner, age 3 [born about 1868]
and
Henri Wagner, age 22 [born about 1849]

As far as we could divine, my great-grandfather, born Henri Wagener, had, at some point in his early twenties, decided to leave his birthplace and travel to America as "Henri Wagner" . . . in the company of someone also named Henri Wagner. Henri Wagner the Younger apparently got along well enough with the family of Henri Wagner the Elder that he followed the Wagner clan to a tiny town in northeast Iowa and married one of his daughters, Eva Wagner (also known occasionally as Anna Wagner) several years later.

There were therefore *two* Henri Wagners that settled in the same region of the state: One was my paternal great-grandfather and the other was my paternal great-great-grandfather, but the two were not related by blood (as far as I knew!). I was infinitely confused about how this had all come to pass. Had

Henri Wagner the Younger found this family of Wagners by happenstance? Or did Henri Wagner the Younger target this family specifically because he would have cover—both in name and circumstance—as he tried to escape whatever the hell he was leaving behind in the Old World?

What exactly was the relationship between Henri Wagner and Henri Wagner?

I hoped that American records might clear some of this up. *Chilk* pointed me in the direction of an obituary from a local paper circa 1926, detailing the death of Henry Wagner, "the uptown grocer":

> Deceased was born July 4, 1849 at Ech, Luxemberg [*sic*], where as a young man he followed the occupation of teamster, being so engaged during the Franco-Prussian war of 1870 and captured by the Germans on the borders of his native land, which afterwards became part of Germany and so remained until the World Wars restored their independence. In 1871, Mr. Wagner came to America and Allamakee County with his employer, also a Mr. Henry Wagner, but no relative. Business called him back to Luxemberg shortly afterwards, but he did not remain there long, joining his employer in French Creek township, Allamakee county where the latter had purchased land and on April 4th 1877, marrying his daughter Anna. . . .
>
> Shortly after their marriage Mr. and Mrs. Wagner came to Lansing and have continuously resided here ever since. Both were honest God-fearing people, and by industry and

frugality they succeeding in rearing a large family and establishing a model Christian home. . . . [P]rior to the death of his son Frank, [Mr. Wagner] said that his six sons should be his pall-bearers. Now the five boys, Henry, Joseph, Gus, Carl and Leo, and son-in-law James O'Malley of French Creek township will act as such. His eight daughters are the Misses Anna, Katherine, Josephine, Lizzie, Rose, Martha (Mrs. Bowles), Melinda, (Mrs. O'Malley), and Clara.

Funeral held at I.C. Church in the shadow in which he lived for over 30 years and in whose faith and teachings he was a practical and life long adherent.

Short of confirming everything I knew about Henry Wagner's travel to the United States, the obit conveniently explained how Henry Wagner the Younger had gotten his start once he'd arrived here: It was all thanks to the largesse of his father-in-law and employer, Henry Wagner the Elder. Years before he was legally a member of their family, the Wagner clan had effectively adopted this young stranger Henry as their own, and given him the tools (a partner, a job, and land) to begin anew—to flourish, even—in the United States.

Together, Henry the Younger and Anna had fourteen children and established what was by all accounts a "model" Christian home (and with fourteen children, you could specifically say it was a model Catholic home; birth control was clearly not in play). The Wagners of Lansing had lived—according to the local paper, at least—in the shadow of the Church of the Immaculate Conception in Lansing (IC = local shorthand). Christian religiosity was arguably the most noteworthy achievement of Henry's life: More text was dedicated to his faith than the business for which he was the proprietor.

Reading an obit like this made it increasingly hard to imagine any validity to Karl's theory about some dark and tortured Luxembourg past being my great-grandfather's driving motivation out of Europe. It was hard to imagine him as some sort of Franco-Prussian War criminal; Henry Wagner the American seemed like a pretty stand-up guy. Not to mention a fairly religious one, too. How was it that I could have ever imagined the patriarch of this clan to have some sort of dark wartime secret and a Jewish background to boot? The obituary summed up a Catholic life, lived devotedly, with room for nothing else.

So, yes: At first glance, my wild theories flew in the face of all the evidence I'd amassed. But if you looked at this with my now well-trained and paranoid gimlet eye, it could also strangely support them. If one was indeed Jewish by heritage, if not practice—insofar as one spoke Yiddish and drank Passover wine—and one did not want to be seen by society as Jewish by heritage . . . then perhaps devout Catholicism was our Wagnerian version of a religious smokescreen. The strategy, basically, could have been: "out-Christian the Christians." By establishing a model Catholic home and populating it with a horde of children, Henry had fooled everyone. Lansing society would never have thought to question the Wagners' Christian bona fides.

Was there any historical precedent for this kind of hoodwink? I rang up Barbara Kessel, who had written a book called *Suddenly Jewish: Jews Raised as Gentiles Discover Their Jewish*

Roots.* (Although my hopes to become suddenly Jewish had gotten more complicated than initially estimated.)

Speaking to me by phone from Jerusalem, Kessel explained that it was common for Jews to hide their religion during and after World War II. In the wake of the Nazi pogroms and death camps, Kessel said that there were certain Jewish immigrants who gave up on their religion: It had cost them too dearly. "From here on in," she explained to me, "they decided, 'We are not Jewish or staying in touch with our Jewish family.'"

But she added that hiding one's Jewish faith just wasn't as common in the years in question—the "1880 to 1919 experience" when He(nry)(nri)(inrich) Wag(e)ner, né Mu(e)ller, would have immigrated to the United States and presumably hidden his heritage.

There were reasons other than Nazis, of course, to hide one's Jewish roots. Kessel posited it might have advanced one's career and social standing to be affiliated with the church community. And, she added, there was certainly anti-Semitism: "It was not so healthy or beneficial to announce your Jewish affiliation."

Then there was the pressure to conform. "There was something romantic about being American," said Kessel. "It was aspirational." Of course, being Jewish should not have precluded being American—the American identity (and American citizenship!) was not predicated on being a gentile, after all. At least not officially. But, even today, it doesn't take much work to see that if you're something other than a white Christian in

---

* My husband opened the mail the day the book arrived and immediately assumed it was for him, courtesy of his polite but still despondent extended Jewish family who seemed to me to want little more than for him to return to the faith.

these United States, you're a good candidate for American hyphenation (Muslim-American, Mexican-American), a designation that sets you outside the mainstream, however innocuously or conspicuously so. Was it any surprise that, over a century ago, it might have been easier to conform—to drop the thing entirely that signified your difference—if you wanted to be known as generically, simply American?

The obituary raised questions as much as it answered them. Henry had indeed been entangled in the Franco-Prussian War—but what exactly had happened? If you didn't remember what happened in the Franco-Prussian War (I sure didn't until I started reading up on it), here's what went down: In the second half of the nineteenth century, the world was in flux, thanks in part to an epic land grab by various European empires. Prussia was looking to consolidate by annexing the German states of Bavaria, Württemberg, and Baden. The French weren't keen on this Prussian power move right in their own backyard. In the middle of these two powers was Luxembourg—caught in an epic dick-swinging contest.

It gets more complicated: In 1870, Prince Leopold of Hohenzollern-Sigmaringen, who had Prussian ties, made overtures to take the Spanish crown and thereby create a Spanish-Prussian alliance. The French, already wary, did not like this *at all*. Thus began the Franco-Prussian War of 1870. Tiny Luxembourg was smack-dab in the middle of any invasion routes, and the war played out in the country's backyard. In the end, the Prussians triumphed—led by a superior military and better technology—which resulted in German unification, a political development that would have major repercussions in the European years to follow, to, ahem, say the least.

So how could Henry Wagner have gotten caught up in it from his perch in Esch-sur-Alzette? This line in his obit stood out to me: *As a young man he followed the occupation of teamster, being so engaged during the Franco-Prussian war of 1870 and captured by the Germans on the borders of his native land.*

The Teamsters: It was in their Washington, D.C., union offices where my mother once worked in the 1970s, the locus of her happy reminiscences about mob bosses returning stolen cars, and the French chef who worked on-site to prepare lunches for all the employees. (This was back in the day when big labor had big power, and—in addition to negotiating fair wages for its members—provided certain "creature comforts" for those in HQ.) The Teamsters horsehead logo was as familiar to me as Garfield's cartoon cat face, and just the mere mention of it conjured the twin ghosts of youth and loneliness. I'd spent countless hours looking at that logo while playing solitaire, trying to understand why you wouldn't necessarily want a horsehead on your playing cards if you were somehow connected to the mob. But in this context, the horsehead wasn't some inadvertently ironic graphic flourish, but a reminder of the union's origin story, when teamsters didn't drive eighteen-wheelers to deliver their goods, but instead drove teams of horses. Thus, "teamster." Which is apparently what He(nry) (nri)(inrich) Wag(e)ner, né Mu(e)ller, was doing when he was "captured" by the Germans.

If he had indeed been held by the ultimately triumphant enemy army, why, as his obituary stated, did Henry Wagner return to Luxembourg "shortly after" he'd arrived in America? The obit explained away this bit of unlikely travel by saying that "business called him back," but who'd ever heard of going *back* to the war-torn Old World once you'd stepped foot in the New? It was expensive to go back and forth across the Atlantic; I scoured the Internet for immigration logs of return from America to Europe, and there were virtually no records. This was not done in large numbers; so few passengers could afford the trip that it was really a voyage of luxury tourism more than anything else. So why go back? What kind of international "business"—run from a tiny town in northeastern Iowa!—would necessitate a trip to Luxembourg in the late 1800s? What had Henry left behind that called him back?

I'd become increasingly aware, through all this travel and research and Inter-nerding, that I'd unwittingly developed a theory: *In becoming American, something is lost.* I knew what we'd lost in Burma (and indeed what Burma herself had lost since we'd left), but I didn't know what Henry had lost, what our family had lost, when he came to America.

I'd need to go back to the source, to Esch-sur-Alzette—to pay a visit to the grand duchy herself to find the answer to that question. I'd see what kind of records were still left. Possibly there would even be a local census that surveyed the Jewish residents and the Catholic ones, and from there I could glean the answers to the initial mystery that was now being crowded by so many others: Were we Muller/Wagners actually Jewish? I'd put foot to ground and stomp around, hoping to land on those elusive and resonant vibrations of my family story. I'd find out what we'd lost.

CHAPTER EIGHT

I knew precisely one significant thing about Luxembourg when I boarded the train bound for Luxembourg City from Paris: Businesses liked the place because the corporate taxes were low. Low taxes begat company headquarters, which in turn begat men and women of indistinct European provenance in sharp suits wearing the disinterested gaze of the twenty-first-century wealthy. And indeed, if you needed piqué cotton toddler clothes or fur throws for the living room couch, there were plenty of haute-bourgeois accoutrements to be purchased on the cobblestone streets of the capital.

The National Archives of Luxembourg were situated on a hairpin turn overlooking a walled fortification over the Alzette River. Given the land assigned to American government offices, it was pretty commanding real estate for a mostly humdrum research building, but maybe this was just the way things were in the bountiful land of low taxes and many luxury goods. Either way, I didn't have time to enjoy the views: I was on the hunt for evidence about Henry Wagner's departure from this duchy and then his return sometime in the mid-1870s—as well as possible clues as to why he'd made this mysterious departure in the first place.

Had Henry left, like so many others, lusting after the gleaming promise of America and her waving wheat fields? Or was there a boot in his ass, chasing him out of the country under dark of night? Maybe he'd just been lovestruck, ready to follow his eventual wife wherever she might go? Beyond that, I wanted verifiable evidence that Henry Wagner had left the country under questionable circumstances—and, um, Judaism: Did they have any record of Henry Wagner's faith buried somewhere in the microfilm?

What had he left behind that he tried to gather again? Was he after the same thing I was after, to reclaim some sense of who he was, an identity that Henry Wagner had prematurely abandoned and possibly lost?

I was one of only a handful of researchers in the place and realized quickly that everyone who worked in the building (and was presumably there to help me figure out whatever I was trying to figure out) spoke a strange dialect of Luxembourgish French German.* This was a tricky and seemingly unwinnable combination, especially for someone (me) who had only a few years of college French under her belt.

As I pretended to do research on the first day, various strange personages revealed themselves to me, including a po-

---

* There was one young woman who spoke English, but her teeth were jagged and sharp, as if they had been chipped away in a terrible fight. These teeth proved such a distraction that I was unable to concentrate on anything she was saying, therefore rendering her English language skills moot.

nytailed, ear-cuffed archivist who was responsible for retrieving the really old books that were too delicate to sit in the stacks. He had the intellectual workman look of a Phish roadie, and things were proceeding fairly smoothly between us, until he involved me in a conversation about the global divide on matters of personal history. Or at least, I am fairly certain that's what our conversation was about, because it was entirely in attempted French—the language we were both aspiring to speak.

ME: These archives are very well—uh—very good!

ARCHIVIST: Well, that depends.

ME: My mother is from Burma, and nothing exists there.

ARCHIVIST: Burma!

ME: Yes, in Asia. And nothing exists.

ARCHIVIST: Well, that's because in those cultures, the past is the past. When it's over, it's over.

ME: Yes! Even the birth certificates, they don't exist.

ARCHIVIST: Each culture is very different. In America . . . in America, I'll tell you a story—I was in America and— [*proceeds to launch into unintelligible conversation that maybe involved the following*] and everybody called each other "dude"—as if everyone was a dude and that was it! [*Or possibly, it was something relating to McDonald's? The word for "dude" in French is* mec, *and French slang for McDonald's is* Mac—*so it could have been either.*]

ME: Yes, it's complicated. Thank you very much!

Eventually, through a mix of the aforementioned rudimentary language skills, pantomime, and occasional onomatopoeic sounds meant to elicit pity and/or patience, I was able to gather that I needed to consult with an archival expert named Mr. Nilles on the matter of passport information that may have been collected when Great-Grandfather He(nry)(nri)(inrich) Wag(e)ner, né Mu(e)ller, departed Luxembourg, for both the first and second times.

As it turned out, Mr. Nilles had no particular idea about how to find Henry Wagner, except for a series of government records entitled "Mouvement de la Population Luxembourgeois," a (limited) collection of papers detailing population movements in and out of the country. But Nilles's old books (unsurprisingly) revealed to me that a lot of Wagners left Esch and returned to Esch and otherwise traveled around Luxembourg in the 1880s. In 1871, only a handful of people departed for other countries—nine, to be exact—though there were no records of their names. I held out hope that one of them was Henry Wagner, but had no way of knowing for sure. And I could find nothing documenting his return home.

I'd hit a wall and therefore did what any self-soothing amateur genealogist with a limited command of the local language often does: I started drinking. That evening, after I was plied with mediocre Bordeaux by a strangely friendly maître d' at the cozy hotel restaurant,* the stout night clerk came in and walrussed his way around the restaurant, eventually settling in my vicinity. By way of the generous maître d', this portly fellow discovered that I was in town to research my family from Lux-

---

* It was a place that reminded me of the sort travelers might stop at in Sleepy Hollow. Actually, a lot of Luxembourg reminded me of what I imagine Sleepy Hollow to be like: the genteel patterns and stuffy Old World airs and surplus of white folk.

embourg. I wasn't sure whether it was the fact that I was "Chinese" (as far as most Luxembourgers were concerned) or the fact that I was roughly three decades younger than the average tourist/genealogist, but this admission seemed to delight everyone who heard it. "Famille en Luxembourg!" they'd say, as if this reality was so outlandish as not to be believed. A Chinese girl! With family from Esch!

The night clerk gave me a brief socioeconomic history of Esch-sur-Alzette, and noted the extraordinary wealth created by a so-called Iron Boom in the second half of the nineteenth century. I knew little about this apparently significant historical moment, but I'd had "reasons to return to Luxembourg in the second half of the nineteenth century" on my mind, and this information made me think perhaps Great-Grandfather Henry had returned home in the hopes of making a fortune. After all, he returned sometime between 1872 and 1877—the very same years of the Iron Boom. The night clerk suggested I might look to see if family land was sold during this time to a mining conglomerate, in an effort to put some much-needed cash in the Wagner/Muller pockets.

I spent the following day looking for any evidence that might suggest the Esch family had eventually struck it rich—or had at least been in the market to strike it rich—during Luxembourg's Iron Boom. In the 1871 census, I could decipher that Michael Muller's listed profession was "mine worker" (*ouvrier mineur*). Mining was crushing, backbreaking labor that left you with time for little else: If Michael Muller was mining well into his forties, there was little likelihood that he had enough capital to be a landowner. And if he didn't own land, he wasn't selling anything to the mining concerns, nor was he cashing in on any sales—regardless of whether the Iron Boom was happening in his backyard or not.

By 1880, it appeared that there were three other people living with Michael and Anne Marie Muller, possibly boarders to help cover rent. Not something people of means would do, and certainly not people who were newly rich. It was evident that Henry's people had never gotten the big payday.

As I discovered this, the microfiche man who had been helping me decipher the very nearly illegible census script proclaimed loudly (and haughtily, I might add): "Ah, but your family was very poor!" as if to put me, the linguistically challenged Chinese American impostor, in my place.

Defiantly, I responded: "Yes, but in America, my great-grandfather was very *rich*!"

This was mostly untrue, of course. Wagner's Bar and Grocery was not exactly Trump Tower, though it certainly informed my father's invocation of Henry as a "cultured" man and a "translator." My dad—long an advocate for the poor and working class—always trumpeted his own humble (if storybook) Iowa beginnings.

But in my dad's retelling the story of his forefather Henry, what always struck me as hypocritical, or at least odd, was his appreciation for his grandfather's wealth, his formality and expensive furniture. There was always something Warbuck-ian about this, the way my father—the nobody son of a rural mail carrier—spoke about Henry Wagner's possessions with such undisguised materialism. Though my father always maintained that it never occurred to him that he was from the working class, it certainly occurred to him that the things in Henry Wagner's house were not the same as the things in his house.

Henry's crystal and silver and mahogany were a source of pride. Being a corn-eating, stickball-playing, Catholic church–attending American was very important to my dad and his conception of self, but so was the fact that his people were "dignified" Europeans from the "merchant class." People who spoke multiple languages and dined with silver and drank from crystal. Maybe this was the most natural reaction for someone who grew up with little, an acquisitiveness born of meager circumstance, like Ricky from *Silver Spoons*. But I had always wondered if it wasn't somehow also fraudulent: proposing to be one thing and then simultaneously aligning yourself with its opposite.

This was in many ways the crux of the American immigrant story: the penniless arrival who made his way up the economic ladder, the Horatio Alger bootstrapper who became not only the backbone of our society, but was living testament to the fact that divine providence shone down on the American Project. To be close to that—presumably the rags, but most certainly the riches—was very important to us Americans. To be somehow connected to affluence, as my father insisted he had been, was a repudiation of those who thought little of your family and its prospects. Even if that wealth had ultimately evaporated, it was something later generations held on to (as my father had), a reminder that they were once great.

And what if that capital came from someplace sordid? What if the foundations of that success were built on someone else's land, what if it required the blood and sacrifice of entire nations who remained unrecognized (and poor!) even after all that fortune had been created? My father was a well-intentioned liberal who promoted equality and espoused egalitarianism, but he still clung to his connection to prosperity and "high culture"—treasure he knew nothing about, a fortune amassed in the dark, as far as he was concerned. It compromised the very things he proposed himself to be.

And now that fraudulence deepened: Those classy beginnings and that imagined European education were both probably fakes, stories we'd told ourselves that had little in common with reality. In fact, Henry Wagner was the bastard son of a miner, a man who worked as an ox-cart driver in a crappy little mining town and smuggled himself the hell out of Dodge with the first folks who would give him a ride.

I went in search of photos from the era in the Luxembourg National Library collection, black-and-whites from the heyday of the country's mining era. Industry may have been booming, but you wouldn't know that from the look of the land and its people. Downtown Esch, with its dirt roads and empty streets, was hardly bustling; the businesses appeared few and far between. Mining factories on the outskirts of the city were hulking industrial wastelands. The men—miners of indeterminate age—posed outside the mouths of the mines with a look of bleary resolution.

I could only imagine the terror that accompanied a descent into the earth each day: Here was a day's work. And these were the *boom times*. Seeing these pictures, as much as unraveling any other part of our family history, made me comprehend the absolute and piercing poverty of the Wagner homestead. The darkness of soot and coke, the meagerness of this existence, it was as far away from lace and silver and mahogany and a goodly Christian life as you could imagine. Those trappings of wealth were all set design for our American play, and if you pushed just a little bit, the scenic background gave way to reveal dust and wires and filth behind it.

I'd uncovered Henry Wagner's economic background but had yet to unravel the central mystery of this European sojourn: Was he—or anyone in his immediate family—Jewish? Having discovered the truth about our formerly high-class roots, my natural inclination was toward skepticism as it concerned our deeply Christian faith. If in retelling his story, we had papered over Henry Wagner's mean beginnings, it didn't seem like much of a stretch to guess he could have rewritten the script on his religious education, as well.

In an 1867 census, Henry's mother and father were listed as Catholic. The same went for the family Henry eventually married into: the *other* Wagner clan. All registered Catholics.

I wondered whether Henry's mother, Anne Marie, perhaps might have been raised Jewish, and later converted to Christianity after her marriage to Michael Muller? After all, Judaism was transferred on the maternal line. I began looking for census records for Anne Marie's father, Pierre Wagener, the presumably grumpy grandpa who'd attested to his daughter's single motherhood on Henry's birth certificate. Anne Marie; her father, Pierre; and her mother, named Anne Hentgen,* all lived under the same roof until their daughter entered lawful wedlock, and so presumably a census record would provide some insight.

---

* Were "Anne" and "Henry" the only names in Luxembourg, or was this a cruel intergenerational joke meant to throw me off the scent?

The Luxembourg government was not in the practice of asking about religion until nearly the mid-nineteenth century: If I wanted information about Pierre's faith, I'd have to search for records after 1867. Which wasn't going to be easy: Pierre Wagener was born in the year 1782. That was a long-ass time ago, and a census in 1867 would theoretically find Pierre at the ripe old age of eighty-five (!). For someone whose listed profession was "mine worker," it was hard to imagine that Ole Pierre would have survived into his eighties, given the backbreaking labor of the era, and the poverty in which Pierre presumably lived. I gave it a shot anyway, but the only Pierre Wagener of Esch-sur-Alzette listed in the 1867 census was twenty-seven years old. Unless Pierre was Benjamin Button, this was not him. And thus the search for Jewish origins seemed done and over. I'd followed the increasingly poorly marked trail right into the mists of time, where everything vanished.

But before I departed my position in those featureless mists of time, I stood for a moment and wondered: What was I thinking, traveling to this strange little tax-free duchy, with scant knowledge of French or German, no archival research skills to speak of, and complete ignorance about how to conduct genealogical detective work? I decided to retrace my steps out of this fog and go home to the familiar, a place I could navigate. Where the names of the people were not an endless variation of Henry, Heinrich, Henri, Anne Marie, Anna, and Anne. Where it did not seem so impossible and curious that an Asian-looking woman might have European roots. Where the streets were not paved with cobblestones, and stores were open on Sunday, and the brown people in town lived in places other than the outskirts, and ran more than the doner kebab shop by the train station.

Home: a place full of chaos and ambition! And relatively high taxes! A place with many different kinds of brown people with many different grandparents. To a place I felt like I understood, a place where I could see myself. I could not see myself in Luxembourg City. Ever. It was, technically, my family home—but for other people, a long time ago. There was no vibration left in these streets. Nothing resonated. The national motto of Luxembourg was "We Will Remain What We Are." Well, as it concerned my family of Luxembourgers, we sure hadn't remained what we were: I could look in the mirror and know that we had become something else.

But I wasn't done yet. Once I got home to the States, I decided to take what I knew and enlist someone who spoke the language, who might approach this process with a degree of professionalism, or at least literacy: someone who could uncover, with certain finality, what our religious roots were, and whether there had been any reason to forsake them along the way.

Using online databases at the National Archives and the Association of Professional Genealogists, I called as many experts in Midwest American/Western European genealogy as I could find, hoping to hire someone for the job. Most of them looked at the scope of my research and the dead ends I'd reached, the sheer number of Henry Wagners that had been uncovered, and issued a polite but firm rejection. But just as I began to get demoralized, an angel of mercy descended from the genealogical heavens. Julie Cahill Tarr was a genealogist who spoke the language *and* had family from Luxembourg *and* was based in the Midwest. Together, she and I distilled my abject feelings of confusion and despair into a few distinct and presumably answerable questions:

Was Henry Wagner Jewish—or was there any evidence of Judaism in his family?

Why did he leave Luxembourg, and was it, in fact, under questionable circumstances?

How did Henry, a teamster from a mining town, come to be a man of the merchant class once he arrived in America? (Where did all that fine china come from? How'd he get the cash to open Wagner's Bar and Grocery, aka our version of Trump Tower?)

Cahill Tarr went to the Luxembourg American Cultural Society Research Center, located in Belgium. Belgium, Wisconsin. The nomenclature here was no coincidence: In the 1850s, thousands of Belgians and their Luxembourger neighbors left Europe for greener pastures and greater economic prospects in America. Attracted to cheap and newly vacated land in the Midwest (courtesy of the removal of its original Native American tribes), these settlers made home in places with considerable tracts of arable soil, like Wisconsin. A large number of Belgian residents in one particular part of the state resulted in a town called . . . Belgium, Wisconsin. Luxembourgers, aligned with the Belgians in history, cultural traditions, and religion, settled in many of the same places. Belgium, Wisconsin, was ground zero for all things Luxembourg in the United States.

Cahill Tarr combed through old copies of the *Luxemburger Gazette* and consulted colleagues who knew about German military history. She examined auction notices and passenger manifests and even more census data than I had. She even read

nineteenth-century city liquor and bond permits from Allamakee County. But still, there were questions left unanswered.

To begin with, she could find no evidence that anyone
in Henry Wagner's family—neither his in-laws, nor his
stepfather—was Jewish or practiced Judaism. The families of
Anne Marie Wagner and her husband, Michael Muller, were
listed as Catholic on all available government records. This,
combined with the exceedingly Christian obituary written for
my great-grandfather Henry Wagner—including his funeral
at the Immaculate Conception Church and burial at Geth-
semane Cemetery—led Cahill Tarr to the conclusion that the
Jewish mystery of the Wagner clan was solved.

The Wagner clan wasn't Jewish.

She posited that my great-uncle Leo, the one who had referred to himself as "just an old Jew" all those years ago, might
have converted. But this seemed unlikely. Leo had remained in
close proximity to his family throughout his adult life. It was
he who was tasked with taking care of the family business until
it was put up for sale. Nothing about his known biography
would suggest a desire to break away from family tradition
(and identity) for reasons unknown.

So maybe he was just drunk on Mogen David wine and felt
particular kinship with its Jewish vintners when he claimed
membership in their faith? I didn't know. Maybe Henry Wagner learned Yiddish as one of the tools of his trade? I realized
I knew close to nothing (which is to say: nothing) about the
Jewish diaspora in Luxembourg—an admittedly very specific
field of study—and so I emailed Neil Jacobs, a former professor
of Yiddish linguistics at Ohio State University. The good professor immediately disabused me of certain ideas.

Firstly, he explained, Yiddish was not an obscure form of communication. It was a hugely popular language: In the years preceding World War II, it was arguably the third or fourth most-spoken Germanic language, with eleven to thirteen million speakers. Secondly—and more important—was I sure that Henry Wagner actually *spoke* Yiddish? "When you say 'spoken,' " Professor Jacobs said, "that could mean 'really good at it for three minutes, but not three hours.' "

If Henry's command of the language was more the former (three minutes) than the latter (three hours), Jacobs added, then it was indeed possible that he might have picked up certain Yiddish phrases as part of his trade. "Non-Jewish cattle dealers in Germany," Jacobs explained, "over the years, incorporated Hebrew and/or Aramaic vocabulary through their contact with Jewish cattle dealers. From there, it took on its own life."

Perhaps Henry had crossed paths with these folk in his commerce? Or perhaps he picked up his Yiddish in *other* circles. By way of an aside, Professor Jacobs added that "many words of Hebrew and Aramaic vocabulary worked their way into marginalized groups." In the underworld, in other words, there was Yiddish slang.

So there was that: If Henry Wagner had been involved in unsavory activities with unsavory characters, then perhaps this explained his command—however notional—of Yiddish. Which is to say yes, he might have had some Yiddish vocabulary, but in the same way that some of us know Yiddishisms from watching *Seinfeld*. It doesn't make you Jewish.

My thus-far-imagined kinship with the Tribe of Israelites— the dream of disruption I'd harbored this whole time—was indeed a dream deferred. The Jewish Theory had animated a deep spelunking into my ancestry, which introduced me to other, equally compelling mysteries. I didn't necessarily need to be Jewish to be something other than what I thought I was. There were plenty of family realities that set me apart from who I imagined the Wagners had been, among them: mining, poverty, and possibly criminal behavior.

There was (different) identity in these tribes, but they were tribes nonetheless: the laboring, the poor, the unlawful. The latter was the most disjunctive of these possible realities, going against the grain of every story I'd heard about my family so far, its godliness and goodliness (in fact, we might have been a band of thieves!), and therefore I wanted/needed more. Were the Wagners chased out of Europe for high treason? Was Henry Wagner a wanted man? Why'd we leave?

In my mind, this is how it went:

Henry Wagner, born into poverty in the coal-mining town of Esch-sur-Alzette, Luxembourg, was a bastard child who'd never known comfort. His adopted father worked several miles deep underground, swinging a pickax in the mines for much of Henry's adolescence. The son knew nothing more of life than grime and boiled potatoes. But he had ambition (he was a Wagner!). In his early teens, he began carting goods in and around town, a trade for the unskilled but energetic. This offered Henry's first glimpse into the finer things in life—the lace curtains and china and crystal goblets that decorated the homes of the wealthy, items that he would covet and mark down as the things he would one day—*someday*—buy for his own family. But how? He had nothing in this meager existence, and he was a nobody.

Then, like a gift from the emperor himself, war broke out.

The Franco-Prussian War was fought on tight battle lines, and Luxembourg stood firmly in its course. Far from a province of blood-soaked armaments, Henry's hometown was instead bustling, chaotic, exciting, as people and things crossed its borders, headed one way or another. He loved war! And war, in the end, loved him—insofar as it gave him the blessing of opportunity. Supplies were needed—dry goods, ammunition, weapons—and Henry Wagner had a horse and wagon. In the trade itself he was unskilled maybe, but he was energetic and undeniably so.

He became a young man in demand, shuttling supplies to the French on Monday, to the Prussians on Wednesday. It was miraculous how easy it was—but he knew it wouldn't last forever. By the end of 1870, there was already talk that the war would soon be ending. The Prussian army—to whom Henry had ingratiated himself, on days when he wasn't ingratiating himself to the French—was filled with commanders who were less enthusiastic about the black market teamster who continued to hustle his way back and forth across enemy encampments, helping them one day, their enemies the next. It was insulting to the Prussians, and they did not like being played the fool. They saw his split allegiance, the rifle butts poking out of his wagonload headed in the opposite direction, where they would eventually be turned against the Prussians. It was an abomination! They started asking questions.

Henry, who had by now amassed a sizable savings, squirreled away underneath his hay-filled mattress (or inside his rough-hewn chest, this part was still fuzzy), began thinking about the next chapter, his escape from Esch, its grime and boiled potatoes. He considered other parts of Europe, but the

Prussian empire was growing inexorably, and punishment (if it was indeed treason) could follow him across the borders. And anyway, Europe was dead. He was young, and he wasn't ready to forsake the bustle and the chaos and the excitement—he had gotten a taste for this life. He wanted something new, something where his future could be shaped as easily as his allegiances had been during the war. He'd heard stories about America. But how to get there? He knew no one in the United States, didn't even speak the language. He would need people, resources.

Another man on the teamster circuit, older and slower but still strong, mentioned that he intended to leave soon. He'd had enough of this place, he said: He'd heard of the American bounty, too, and he wanted a piece of it. It was too fortunate, as if God himself had decreed the plan: This other man happened to have the same name as Henry's mother's family! It would be easy to change the papers and make it look as if they were one family. In exchange, Henry would pay the older man a lump sum of his savings; the rest he'd hide somewhere safe. Could they leave soon? Yes, said the elder Wagner, they would leave soon. Better to get out now, while everyone is still distracted by war. (Better to get out now, thought Henry, before they find out what I did.)

You could already imagine Tom Hardy playing the lead role in the movie adaptation of this life, the swelling strings of the score, the title credits rolling slowly at the end.

It was not quite what happened.

Cahill Tarr explained to me that the records about Franco-Prussian prisoners of war were not exactly in tip-top shape. If Henry had been captured by the Germans and/or accused of treasonous behavior during the war, there were few records to prove it.

But she did stumble upon information that at least pointed in the *direction* of salacious and possibly illegal activities that might have driven Henry, his future father-in-law Henry Wagner the Elder, and his family out of Europe and over to America.

The Wagner team traveled to America from either Liverpool (in England) or Queenstown (in Ireland). Cahill Tarr explained that this was not the norm: Most of their fellow countrymen left from Antwerp (in Belgium) or Le Havre (in France). She thought, perhaps, that leaving via England or Ireland might have been a bid to evade whatever or whoever was after them in Luxembourg.

Supporting the idea that their departure had been made in haste—and therefore perhaps not under ideal circumstances—was the fact that several weeks before their departure for America, Henry Wagner the Elder put his home up for auction. The old man was getting his affairs in order before heading west, but also, he wanted to sell his home quickly—and thus a public auction. This fact, wrote Cahill Tarr, "suggests an urgency to leave."

And where did Henry Wagner the Younger get that money to start Wagner's Bar and Grocery, aka the Mar-a-Lago of Lansing, Iowa? How, exactly, did he secure the financial backing to enter into the so-called merchant class? Henry Wagner the Elder's home sale offered one clue.

This future father-in-law's home was no hovel: It was listed as a three-story home with a slated roof, a cellar, and a stable for twelve (!) horses. The house was located near the local church, which suggested it was in a good neighborhood. And it came with a separate garden plot, also for sale.

I couldn't compare this property to the overpriced converted yuppie loft complex that I lived in and yet simultaneously despised, but I sensed, even from my limited understanding of equine financials, that having a stable big enough for twelve horses meant that you were doing Just Fine.

Julie Cahill Tarr came to the same conclusion: "The proceeds from the [home] sale were probably more than enough for the family's passage to America and may have been enough for them to get a head start settling in Iowa," she wrote to me. (It also suggested a reason for Henry Wagner the Younger's return to Luxembourg not long after his arrival in the United States: He might have been buttoning up his father-in-law's affairs at home, following the auction.)

But all of this raised the question: How did Henry Wagner the Elder, who was listed in census records as a *voiturier*—French for a carter/carrier—make the cash to buy a home like this in the first place? During the period in question, mining in Esch-sur-Alzette was just beginning to be big business. There wouldn't have been enough time for the elder Henry to cash out of a carting business affiliated with the soon-to-be-booming coal mines. Perhaps, then, Henry the Elder had been engaged in what I loosely categorized as a side hustle, aka *a little of this* and *a little of that*. And maybe some of this (or that) involved selling on the black market, or, later, hauling goods for both the French and the Germans during wartime. Equally involved in this side hustle might have been his employees—and who was working for him at the time, but my great-grandfather: Henry Wagner.

What I hadn't understood until this point was precisely how close Henry Wagner the Younger had been to Henry Wagner the Elder (no relation). Cahill Tarr revealed that the younger man had been in the employ of the older as far back as the Old World. Therefore, if one of them was engaged in a duplicitous and/or criminal side hustle, so might the other have been— giving both a reason to hightail it out of Esch as soon as the going got tough. But would they really have intertwined their fortunes so closely in the long-term? After all, it was one thing to work for a guy; it was another thing to start a whole new life with him (and his family) in America.

As it turns out, the bonds between the two men were even deeper than I'd thought.

Cahill Tarr, reader and speaker of non-English tongues, had determined that, according to the 1867 Luxembourg census, Henry Wagner, formerly Henry Muller, *lived in the same house* as Henry Wagner the Elder—his eventual father-in-law. On both of their (separate) census entries, the same address was listed—a fact that slipped by my eagle-eyed-yet-unfortunately-illiterate reading of the same document. This meant that for a time, Henry Wagner had lived well—or at least not in a hovel with only grime and potatoes to animate his meager existence. Perhaps this is where he got his taste for the finer things in life.

My heretofore semi-sympathetic scenario of a coal-dusted dreamer with his nose pressed to the window of the high-class homes . . . was probably an illusion. In fact, Henry had been inside one of those well-furnished homes himself, drinking from actual glasses, sleeping on a mattress and not a cot. Perhaps, then, it was less ambition than entitlement that drove him to do whatever he had to do to get out of Esch—he knew from a twelve-horse stable, and dammit, he wanted one of his own.

The knowledge that the two Wagner men, Elder and Younger, had once shared the same roof was, in effect, the key to the biggest mystery of them all: Why the hell had my great-grandfather ended up hitching his wagon to that of a random family, forever linking his fate and fortune with theirs? It also explained how he met my eventual great-grandmother, Eva/Anna Wagner. He'd come of age under their roof!

Anna and Michael Muller, Henry's parents, had also lived in the Wagners' house, and presumably sent their eldest to work with its patriarch in his carting and carrying business. While the two families didn't live together for an extended period of time—a census three years earlier shows them living separately—they clearly forged some kind of a bond, enough of one that Henry Muller became, in effect, an adopted son.

This clarified a lot. Nearly all of the big, looming questions, in fact. But there were all kinds of subtler questions I'd never know the answer to, including: Why? Why did they live together? Did something happen to the Muller family, or the Wagner family? It amused me that we were members of a proto-kibbutz (there I was with the Judaism again), a sort of high-class Luxembourger mini-commune, but I wanted badly to know the dynamics at play inside the house. Was Michael Muller a friend of Henry Wagner the Elder's? Had my great-grandfather always had his eye on Eva/Anna, the woman who would become his eventual wife in America? Was theirs a romance for the ages, or did Henry just marry her because it would secure his share of that Wagner money?

Or was there something more explosive happening here: Could Henry Wagner the Elder actually have been the real father of Henry Wagner the Younger? This would explain why the two men lived in such close proximity, provide a reason as to why Wagner junior had moved into Wagner senior's home. But it would also mean that my great-grandfather . . . had eventually married *his half sister and had thirteen children with her.* I shuddered to think about this possibility. It kept me awake enough that I tried to push it to the deepest recesses of my mind. And also, most important and certainly most frustrating: I'd never know. Julie Cahill Tarr and the Luxembourger American Cultural Society Research Center couldn't tell me what my great-grandfather had known—or connived—when he forged his bond with the Wagner clan. There were no census records that documented love affairs or friendships or intentions, either good or bad.

I'd mistakenly believed that all this sleuthing would give me an answer key, with which I could paint by numbers to get a full-color image of our family and its characters. What I got instead were fragments of pigments long since faded, from which you could hazard a guess about the original hue, but would never truly know. Too many of the papers had degraded or were lost or never even existed in the first place. The things that would have been most illuminating in the search, the conversations between people, were long since forgotten. I would have to fill in the blanks and decide for myself what I believed, which one of us was probably a bad guy and which one of us was probably a good one. Just as in Mandalay, I would have to determine my end point; there was no finish line to cross.

Still, I had enough information about what we'd done and

how we'd lived, the choices we'd made along the way and (most probably) why we'd made them, to conclude that we were not who I'd been told we were, paragons of virtue, defenders of the faith, as American as peppermint ice cream. We lied and cheated and did our best to survive. We told one another stories that made us seem somehow of better character than most other arrivals in our United States. And so, this is what it meant to be an American, as far as my family was concerned: a neat homily about tenacity and piety, iconoclasm and grit. We could exfoliate the rest. But the "rest" was a seriously determinative part of who we were, and what our true community was.

I may not have been Jewish, but I could already see a new kind of identity forming. From these harebrained trips to Esch and Rangoon, these cities of lost blood, I understood that my people were flawed—in some cases, deeply. They elided their own histories. My mother's family held the past closer—the Old World was very much still with her in custom and in language and on stove top—while my father's side had become more generically American. But both sides had crafted an identity that buried the uncomfortable truths of the past: My great-grandfather U Myint Kaung played a role in Burma's economic calamities; my grandmother Mya Mya Gyi harbored racist sentiments that underpinned the dark side of Burmese nationalism. Henry Wagner buried the truth in Esch-sur-Alzette: his struggle, his possible crimes, the debts he owed to others.

Even the land on which we'd grown food, that had instilled in us a certain pride with its American bounty, had once belonged to someone else. The soil wasn't really ours; its fruits were the rightful property of another tribe. The success we'd had in later years had been lopsided: We'd won because others had been forced to lose. We'd flourished in a country that excluded black and brown people from the very same possibilities. What sort of honor was there in that?

I was not Jewish, I didn't feel particularly Burmese, and Luxembourg might as well have been Pluto. But in all these places, all these cities, I saw glimpses of who my real people might have been. Carved out from the negative space of my family history, I saw who we actually were. We were storytellers, revisionists, liars. We built our future selves on deceit and half-truths, we plastered our cracks with omissions—as well as genuine courage and smarts and will. In this act of re-creation, we became Americans. And, I guess, there was some kind of belonging in that.

PART IV

THE CROSSHAIRS

CHAPTER NINE

—//—

I belonged in the crosshairs. This realization struck me—forcefully—when I found myself in London, doing some ancillary research on my Burmese family history. (The Rangoon archives had proved so fruitless that I'd gone west, just to see what the colonial powers had preserved of Britannia's time in Burma.)

I was focused in on the United Kingdom's National Archives in London: This was the storehouse for records of the conquered Burmese. The British loved books, after all! Maybe there would be journals or photos that could shed light on my great-grandmother Daw Thet Kywe's era, the heyday of British rule. (The irony of this was not lost on me—that the British might have more records about the Burmese than the actual Burmese.)

But I was also drawn to the fact that Europe was the place where both of my (unlikely) bloodlines intersected: It was the proverbial nexus of the crosshairs. I'd long since assumed that nothing, other than *me*, connected Rangoon and Esch-sur-

Alzette. After all, if you stretched a wire from one of the cities to the other, it would span more than half the globe. Seventy years separated Henry Wagner's decision to leave the Old World and Mya Mya Gyi's to become a Westerner.

Inside the archives, I found yellowing manuscripts: numerous accounts of imperial Burma from the mid-1800s, written with various levels of curiosity, disgust, unvarnished racism, and distinctly British humor. Many were compiled by British officers stationed in the country, some tasked with official diplomatic duties. Of the information I could gather from this brazenly Occidental point of view, during his reign, from 1853 until his death in 1878, Mindon Min, the last great, non-fratricidal* king of Burma, the second-to-last ruler of the Konbaung dynasty, was understood by the British to be both effective and apparently enlightened. Among other things, Mindon Min created the world's largest book, a canon of Theravada Buddhist teachings known as the *Tipitaka*, and published a newspaper, the *Mandalay Gazette*, which first rolled off the presses in March 1874. He also—perhaps more important— believed in freedom of speech.

Mindon Min, according to these texts, was a shrewd leader who never accepted the word of his courtiers as truth and therefore had spies everywhere. According to historians, they included "monks, queens, princes, princesses, ladies-in-waiting,

---

* Slaughtering scores of relatives is unfortunately not uncommon in the Burmese *Game of Thrones*. King Thibaw, Mindon Min's heir, was credited with a coordinated, timed family bloodbath following his ascension to the throne, though in all likelihood it was his future wife and her mother who were behind it. Also, Mindon Min, together with his brother Kanaung, overthrew his half brother to gain control of the throne. So I suppose he wasn't entirely innocent.

senior and junior officials, members of the ahmudan class [crown service groups], holy men, nuns, medicine men, masseurs and barbers." It was *Homeland*, if Homeland had been set in a palace compound in northern Burma.

Among the cohort of men and women who made it their duty to attend to the whims of Mindon Min and his four wives was my grandmother's grandmother, an attendant to the court. In our family, recounting this fact was always accompanied by the communal basking in hushed glory, but as I discovered in a listing of the various personages . . . there were a lot of attendants at Mindon Min's court.[1]

PERSONAL ATTENDANTS IN THE COURT:

35 pages who carried the royal insignia on state occasions
40 royal tea servers
60 bearers of the royal betel box and other personal
    utensils
100 royal slipper bearers
40 bearers of the royal white umbrellas
10 lectors who read aloud from religious books
15 grooms of the chamber who acted as messengers
450 gentlemen-at-arms
220 bearers of the royal swords in state processions
155 chamberlains or lictors, a company of men chosen for
    their height and whose duties also included the policing
    of the palace

That was a lot of royal slippers. As the British detailed it, Burmese court life was regimented to a very nearly absurd degree—betel box carriers were lower on the ladder than stewards of the royal white umbrellas. Shoes were never to be worn in the presence of the king, and the buttoned-up, be-wigged British unsurprisingly found this practice appalling (so much so that this became the topic of intense diplomatic dissent).[2] But an accounting of these courtly flourishes tended to distract from the larger point of Mindon Min's rule: He managed to shepherd Burma through the last, truly golden days of a semi-autonomous state. It sounded like my great-grandmother had worked for a fairly decent boss, insofar as the king was her boss.

After the southern half of Burma fell to the Brits in 1852, Queen Victoria (or at least her advisers) was increasingly interested in expanding her dominion north. Mindon Min, seeing the long fingers of one imperial power closing over his kingdom, reached out for the hand of another, in the hope that partnership with a different—but equally ambitious—crown might serve as insurance against total annexation by the other.

Mindon Min thus attempted to deepen his alliance with the French, the mortal enemy of the British. By 1873, Mindon Min's corps of diplomats had signed a commercial treaty with France.[3] This partnership did not make the British particularly happy, given all the success (if you could call it that) that the French were having in Indochina, subjugating native cultures and introducing baguettes and so forth.

As I was reading this, a fairly small citation in a dusty British history book, I realized there was indeed a connection between Burma and Luxembourg that had nothing to do with me: Both countries had been bystanders in the same feud of nations, tested for loyalty and exchanged as a show of power, like children in a divorce. Daw Thet Kywe and Heinrich Muller had more in common than I'd realized.

As the English saw things, it was time to contain the French, who were making tracks elsewhere on the planet, too, particularly in Europe's backyard—specifically, *Luxembourg.* At nearly the same time as Mindon Min's emissaries were inking that trade deal in Paris, the French were coming off a war over several German states. The French were ambitious and tenacious during this particular period (what imperial power wasn't?): Remember that French concern over German unification under the Prussians eventually led to the Franco-Prussian War. And just three years earlier, the same two powers had been fighting over control of Luxembourg.

On the other side of the planet, back in Burma, the English saw this French aggression in Europe, coupled with the French advances in Indochina, and they didn't like it. Nor did they appreciate Mindon Min's new trade partnership with France.

It didn't help matters that Mindon Min was getting ever older and more infirm. Sensing his imminent death, his son Thibaw—more accurately, his son Thibaw's future wife and her mother—orchestrated the coordinated slaughter of any and all royal children who might pose a threat to Thibaw's ascension to the throne. Fratricide and patricide were not uncommon measures to secure the crown (in Burma and elsewhere[*]) but the scale of the slaughter made it one for the

---

[*] Too many countries in Europe to count, plus lots of Asia and the Mideast (and Africa, Latin America, and Oceania undoubtedly?).

Burmese history books. Upon learning of it, the British were both horrified and skeptical, although crown carnage was not exactly an alien concept to them.

British-Burmese bilateral relations under Mindon Min, while largely peaceable, had frayed, especially where the French were in the picture. Where did the new king Thibaw's sympathies lay? (And also: Was he a sociopath?) Thibaw, increasingly in debt, took a page from what was now a fairly well-worn playbook: He made overtures to the French.

The British had tired of Burmese efforts to play one imperial superpower off another. They issued an ultimatum effectively demanding the king cede sovereignty and hand over Upper Burma . . . or else.[*] Perhaps unsurprisingly, Thibaw—a king who had overseen the slaughter of the entire royal family in order to take the throne—understood the implications of this ultimatum, and refused.

With one side woefully overpowered and outgunned, the Third Anglo-Burmese War did not last long. In fact, its brevity was an expression of its asymmetry, and there's no substantive accounting of it that doesn't contain certain pathos, even if you believe that monarchs are tyrants. The end of the Konbaung dynasty—a dynasty that spanned 133 years—was brought about in precisely thirteen days. On November 27, 1886, the British annexed the whole of Burma.[*]

It was, apparently, a day like no other.

According to the account of one Brigadier General G. S. White, a British officer in attendance as his country's flag was raised over Mandalay, where it would hang for nearly half a

---

[*] Exactly ninety-one years—to the day—before I was born.

century: "The sun was pouring a flood of golden light on the last hours of Burman independence."[5] (Of course, the British *would* see the light as golden.)

Thibaw and his queen Supayalat were sent to spend the rest of their earthly days in India, the other country ruled under the British Raj. The Burmese royal court was no longer, and the men and women who once bore slippers and white umbrellas, carried royal betel nut boxes and acted as messengers, astrologists, and advisers, were killed or cast off to live as common folk in the capital city of Mandalay, outside the palace gates.

Among those who survived this wildly tumultuous period of Burmese court life was my great-great-grandmother, Daw Thet Kywe's mother. We don't know exactly when she left the court—whether she stayed on until the end of Thibaw's reign or left after Mindon Min died; we just know that somehow—as part of the spoils—she was sold that teak house across the street from Saint Francis Xavier Church and around the corner from the Wesleyan Methodist mission school. The very same house I'd seen in photos, and maybe the same house I'd found a few months prior, as I was stumbling around Mandalay on a wild-goose chase for memories.

What dawned on me at this moment, sitting in the climate-controlled stacks of the British Library, was both the absurdity and the synergy of my dueling family histories. If there had never been a bloody European land skirmish in the nineteenth century, there might not have been a Franco-Prussian War. If Henry Wagner and his future father-in-law had never gotten tangled up in the Franco-Prussian War, they might not have left for America.

If there never had been a bloody European land skirmish in

the nineteenth century, the British may well have left Upper Burma alone. The Burmese court would have stayed intact, the British would never have gained full control of the country, and the military junta that seized power in a coup and subsequently drove my grandmother and mother off to the United States . . . might never have come to power.

In other words, the Europeans—and their territorial aggressions—had upended two people on opposite sides of the globe, for very different reasons at the very same time. Multiple helixes of my great-grandfather's and great-great-grandmother's deoxyribonucleic acid ultimately came to be physically intertwined in the fourth quarter of the twentieth century (that is, through me), but the comingling of fate and fortune had begun much earlier, thanks to the sabers and cannons of Western Europe.

America was the beginning, a new chapter as far as genetic science was concerned—but in a weird way, it was also the conclusion of a story that had begun a long time ago.

CHAPTER TEN

—— // ——

From this globe-encircling history I'd gathered in the overly air-conditioned stacks of the British Library, I concluded that there might be no better testament to an existence in the cross-hairs than my DNA itself. The information I'd uncovered had given me a firmer grasp on my family history, but parts of it remained abstract. I'd set foot in the cities where vestiges of our lost lives still lingered, like contrails and poltergeists—yet rather than finding spiritual peace or a sense of belonging, some lifeline that inextricably linked me to my heritage, I had amassed a complicated, confusing (but inarguably more truthful) understanding about who I was, about my people. Still, I had settled on stories that I could only reconstruct by sparse paper trails before they vanished into the mists, and I was forced to imagine important connections and motivations.

But there was another way, less reliant on imagination and decaying paper. It spoke a universal language that could pinpoint me—and only me. It was my genetic makeup: the indelible evidence that bore testament to exactly where I'd come from.

DNA could reveal precisely who my people were—and whether (ahem) there were any more chapters that my family members had glossed over or otherwise deleted from our history. Beyond that, science would tell me exactly how wide—rather than narrow—my identity truly was. The movements of empires, the costs of war, the ambitions of peoples would be mirrored in my blood. I'd know irrefutably where I came from and to whom I (at least technically) belonged—and in a scientifically precise way. No more reliance on chat boards or archivists or reams of godforsaken microfilm: The information was within me! In my saliva and in my veins, I would be revealed as futureface or Cosmopolitan Everywoman or a Jewish Burman.

What would science have to say?

Thanks to technology and its overserved handmaiden "innovation," there were multiple DNA test services that offered exclamatory, brain-freezingly incredible promises in their online advertisements for this particular aspect of self-questioning: Validate Uncertain Relationships! Confirm Family Lore! Gain a Genealogical Leg Up! and, perhaps most urgently, Determine Your Neanderthal Percentage! I was quite sure that my Neanderthal Percentage was very, very, very low.

At this point in the marketplace search, there were several options for such endeavors—three of the most popular were Family Tree DNA, 23andMe, and AncestryDNA. I didn't know which one of the myriad, brick-breaking DNA-based ancestry tests might return the most comprehensive information and therefore decided to do several of them. I figured I'd combine the results and determine at least the general coordinates of my heritage, if not the pinpointed locations.*

On my mother's side, I wondered how closely the results would correspond with what I'd determined over the course of the past several months about my Asian heritage. It was possible that the DNA wouldn't show me anything new, but that seemed delightfully unlikely, given the general proceedings of this entire project: I could only imagine an unforeseen or otherwise inexplicable result—Parsi bloodlines or Chilean DNA—and the dismissal and loud scoffing that might result. My mother and grandmother were not just Burmese—they were unquestioningly Burmese, in the same way that someone was allergic to cashews or left-handed. As far as they knew, we had never lived anywhere else, never been anyone else. My father had a story about his heritage, but it was never airtight: He had grown up knowing that we came from Someplace Else, and this offered an opening, however slight and untested, for an origin story that might be different than what he'd imagined. No such possibility existed on my maternal line. The people who had come to America were still alive, and they could attest to the fact that there was no mystery surrounding our roots, about who we'd been before arrival on these shores. And their answer was this: They were Burmese. They had never bothered to consider anything else, mostly because there was no need to.

As it concerned my paternal line, I had essentially given up

* All of the information that follows about the genetic-ancestry industry is true as of the time of writing; the specific science and practices are, of course, in a state of constant flux.

on the Jewish Theory at this point, though some tiny part of me still hoped that DNA would offer a rebuttal to all the evidence I'd gathered thus far and reveal that I (somehow) had Ashkenazi blood. This was the same part of me that hoped we would one day get rid of the electoral college and the penny: It wasn't a particularly sane or significant part of my rational brain, but it existed nonetheless. But mostly I wanted to see if—in between the Irish and Luxembourg blood, the Western/Continental histories we'd been passing down through the generations—there might be something unique or exceptional hidden away.

This is what DNA testing offered most people: the suggestion of mystery, of strangeness, of singularity. That maybe you were, in fact, descended from the Pharaohs, that your particular blackness wasn't born of slavery but of untouched African blood—as if your people had miraculously escaped the horrors and the rapes, the exiles and escapes, the flights and trauma, and existed as exceptions to the American rule. Perhaps your Mexican roots were royal Mayan, or your red hair was from the Vikings, not the Scots.

Part of me wondered about all this. Was this a scholarly search for the truth—come what may—or was it just an adjunct to the rest of our mythmaking about the past: a search for evidence that might confirm that we're made of special stock? If I was being truthful, that's exactly what I still wanted to have confirmed. The more I knew about my family, the more information I had about their compromises and crimes, their weaknesses and failures . . . the more intense my yearning became to find, buried among these newly unearthed facts, something extraordinary, mythic, unreal. As if to balance out the mundane, messy reality of this family history: I wanted an epic. Don't we all?

The Family Tree DNA test, cited in various ancestry forums on the Internet, boasted the "most comprehensive Y chromosome, autosomal, and mitochondrial ancestry DNA database for genetic genealogists." Was I a "genetic genealogist"? I supposed I was. Family Tree DNA's website assured me—in decisive, graphic headlines—that it would trace ancestral lines with scientific rigor, suggesting itself to be the most clinically comprehensive of the most widely used tests, though at this point I had no idea what made an autosomal test different from a mitochondrial one or, for that matter, how the Y chromosome fit into all this. (I just knew I didn't have a Y chromosome, right?)

If Family Tree DNA positioned itself as the most clinically comprehensive of the top tests, the service offered by a company called 23andMe* was the most user-friendly—and the most seemingly high-tech. The company began operations in 2006 with the goal of providing its customers specific, personalized DNA-based information about genetic predisposition for various and wicked cancers and other possibly debilitating diseases—with the stated aim of sharing this data for increased collective citizen health power and awareness.

Critics of this relatively newfangled practice made the point that society should also consider how factors unrelated to genetics—variables such as environment and economic stability and access to health care—might inform someone's health outcomes as much as, say, his or her genealogy. And that, not

---

* 23andMe, if you were wondering, is a reference to the twenty-three pairs of chromosomes that most humans are born with—and that carry the DNA within which the genetic code is written.

insignificantly, you had to be careful when giving people potentially devastating information: Were they prepared for it? Was
society prepared for it? Which is to say: What happened if you
started marginalizing entire communities based on their DNA-
based proclivity toward something terrible? Health data could
be heavy stuff, handled improperly.

But wasn't it better to have people aware of various hideous
and wicked illnesses than . . . to have them unaware of various
hideous and wicked illnesses, false positives notwithstanding?
Genetic scientists made the argument that their conclusions
wouldn't necessarily damn entire subsets of American society,
and indeed that their goal was to do the very opposite. Give
people the information, get them the help they needed. Society
wouldn't stigmatize carriers; it would allocate research and
medicine to help them. Information was power! I certainly
thought so—but then again, I was the person that opted in for
extensive bloodwork every time I went to the doctor *just in case*
I had contracted killer bee flu or some other unlikely ailment
that was hiding just under the surface, ready to send me to the
grave in a matter of hours.

The FDA disagreed. According to the government, consumers could misread the health data (or indeed the health data
could be flawed: "FDA is concerned about the public health
consequences of inaccurate results"), with disastrous consequences. In its letter to 23andMe, the FDA conjured certain
apocalyptic scenarios:

> For instance, if the . . . risk assessment for breast or ovarian
> cancer reports a false positive, it could lead a patient to un-
> dergo prophylactic surgery, chemoprevention, intensive

screening, or other morbidity-inducing actions, while a false negative could result in a failure to recognize an actual risk that may exist. Assessments for drug responses carry the risks that patients relying on such tests may begin to self-manage their treatments through dose changes or even abandon certain therapies depending on the outcome of the assessment.[1]

Unnecessary mastectomies, forsaken drug therapy—the FDA was concerned that this could turn very dark, very quickly. In late 2013, the feds put the kibosh on 23andMe's carrier gene testing services, which had—until that point—been the company's focus.[2] Less than a week later, the company was hit with a class action lawsuit, alleging that the science was faulty and hadn't received the necessary approvals, and that the test results were being compiled into databases that were then sold to third parties.

According to the lawsuit:

Defendant uses the information it collects from the DNA tests consumers pay to take to generate databases and statistical information that it then markets to other sources and the scientific community in general, even though the test results are meaningless.

In the summer of 2016, a federal appeals panel of three judges affirmed a lower court decision saying the lawsuit had to be settled privately in arbitration, rather than publicly and in court. Writing the opinion, Judge Sandra Ikuta pointed to the fact that, in order to use the test, customers had to agree to

23andMe's terms of service—which contained a provision stipulating that disputes had to be settled out of court.[3]

In the wake of the FDA's decision in 2013 to put a halt to the company's health testing, the rate of new customer sign-ups dropped in half. Faced with a potentially devastating loss of business, 23andMe pivoted to the business of DNA-based ancestry reports (plus Neanderthal Percentage Breakdowns).[*] In the words of 23andMe's senior director of research Joanna Mountain, "We started out with focus on health—and ancestry testing came along for the ride." This pivot was possible because, apparently, in the eyes of the regulators, information about possible Croatian ancestry was less explosive than being told you were a carrier for Tay-Sachs disease. And so this became a strategy to stay in the business of DNA without worrying that inaccuracy might somehow lead to someone's untimely demise. And it worked. By late 2015, the company had more than a million users, double what it had at the time of the FDA's kibosh.[4]

If 23andMe had come to ancestry services in circuitous fashion, the even more unlikely story was that of AncestryDNA, a genealogical search service run by industry heavyweight Ancestry: a for-profit company whose founders were members of the Church of Jesus Christ of Latter-day Saints. Many of the

---

[*] By October 2015, the company was once again allowed to offer customers reports on carrier genes, albeit for fewer diseases, and with less comprehensive information. Customers can opt to have their genetic and health information used for medical studies; according to *The New York Times*, pharmaceutical companies pay 23andMe to use this data in drug development. In May 2015, the company announced it would begin developing drug therapies itself. (It remains in the ancestry business.)

largest online genealogical databases are connected to the church, though it's a fact that is not exactly promoted by the Mormons. For example, FamilySearch.org, another Web-based genealogical networking and research site, is a project of the LDS church. While the church doesn't hide this fact, it doesn't exactly trumpet it, either: At the very bottom of the home page, in *tiiiiinnnnny* letters, is written the following:

© 2016 by Intellectual Reserve, Inc. All rights reserved. A service provided by The Church of Jesus Christ of Latter-day Saints

You could be forgiven for not having any idea that the website had anything to do with Joseph Smith. Ancestry—makers of one of the three leading DNA tests—is likely to become a publicly traded company again after being taken private, but it retains certain loose associations with the LDS church: Two of its former heads were Mormon, its corporate headquarters are in Lehi, Utah, and the church and the website announced in 2014 that LDS Family History Centers worldwide grant members of the public free access to Ancestry's formidable digital archives.* What's more, the same year, it was announced that members of the LDS church are also granted free subscriptions to the Ancestry.com worldwide site (as well as FamilySearch .org partner websites)—there's even a special registration page for LDS members. Which is all to say: pretty nice deal, if you're Mormon or find yourself hanging out at Mormon community centers.

---

* The church's Family History Centers are open to the public.

Why, exactly, do Mormons keep coming up in the context of genealogy?

Mostly because the church has decreed that the dead can be posthumously baptized into the faith, as a way of strengthening and expanding God's eternal family—which creates a need for a scientific way to trace and discover long-lost (and oftentimes deceased) relatives. Today, the Church of Jesus Christ of Latter-day Saints is to genealogy what the NFL is to American sports: unquestioningly the most powerful and profitable enterprise, with the most resources and the biggest audience. Mormon-run ancestry and family tree services have achieved dominance and extraordinary profitability on their own merits (the church registry itself has more than two billion names that have been traced) but also because the questionable stuff— the religiously specific stuff—is largely kept behind the scenes. Except (like with the NFL) when controversy splits the whole thing wide open.

In the case of the Mormon church, the most controversial practice to infect its ancestry wing is the practice of posthumous baptisms known as temple ordinances: baptizing the souls of deceased people using living stand-ins. If you weren't Mormon, the practice of posthumous baptisms first became widely known in 1995, when evidence came to light that the LDS church had performed temple ordinances on as many as 380,000 Jewish Holocaust victims[5]—as well as prominent non-Mormons, including Pope John Paul II and Gandhi*—and later entered those names into the church database.[6] Effectively, if

---

* You had to give it to the Church of Jesus Christ of Latter-day Saints, if only for the pluck!

privately, the Mormons were calling the head of the Catholic church one of their own.

Faced with an onslaught of *ohhellno* from the Vatican to Temple Beth Zion,[7] the church vowed to stop the most egregious posthumous baptisms, if not the practice itself. In fact, they couldn't really police the database, which, as of 2007, had two billion names in it. And so in 2012, perhaps it wasn't all that surprising when *The Boston Globe* reported that, in addition to Anne Frank, slain *Wall Street Journal* reporter Daniel Pearl was among the Jewish folks that the Mormons were (still) claiming for their own. The church explained that errant members had been acting on their own accord to give the deceased "access to salvation," however belatedly.[8]

The outcry from non-Mormon religious groups was that this was a distressing practice and shouldn't be continued. Men and women who worshipped and lived as Jews and Buddhists and Catholics and so forth might not have been thrilled to find themselves, decades later, entries on the Mormon rolls. According to the LDS website, the ordinances are important because they prepare the blessed to "live forever with Heavenly Father and our families after this life." Not only that, but the ordinances apparently prepared blessed souls with "spiritual power and direction during mortality."

FamilySearch.org—which declares on its website that its "resources are helping Church members find more ancestors needing temple ordinances"—offers a basic guide to those looking to perform temple ordinances on their deceased ancestors:

1. Find the ancestors who (still) need temple ordinances.
   (This can be done online at the website; a special section

on "temple opportunities" informs family members whether any ancestors still need ordinances. If the direct lines seem "done"—which is to say, already posthumously baptized into the LDS church—the website encourages searching for "cousins.")

2. Once ancestors still needing ordinances have been identified, users can print out ordinance cards with the relevant ancestors' names to take to the temple for baptism. Printing on standard white office paper is acceptable.

3. Bring the cards to the temple, where a church official or otherwise qualified elder can perform the rite.

It is all a fairly orderly process, apparently. But families like Pearl's took issue with the memory of their son's Judaism being somehow compromised (if not actually degraded). "For the record," his parents told *The Boston Globe*, "Danny did not choose to be baptized, nor did his family consent to this uncalled-for ritual."[9]

And yet, in the here and now, as I contemplated the services on offer at Ancestry, and the projected costs and benefits of temple ordinance, I came to the ultimate conclusion that I was actually totally fine with it. On the most fundamental level, at least the Mormons cared. I—who had been running around in seed-bead necklaces, enthusiastically ticking off the hapa box, with little effort put into finding out who was responsible for my admissions-friendly futureface—who was I to be outraged that someone was claiming Henry Wagner for his or her own? Up until this journey began, I couldn't have told you what year my great-grandfather was born in, or how many children he'd fathered. To be indignant about a secret Mormon baptism somewhere in Puerto Rico or Tucson seemed peevish: At least *they* knew his birthdate.

Admittedly, it was easier for me to skip lightly over the issue of faith, given my own motley religious upbringing. Which led me to a secondary determination, one that had nothing to do with my own shortcomings and transparent self-loathing: If someone from another faith wanted to take a stab at saving my soul from eternal purgatory, who was I to complain? I had taken a pretty mediocre insurance policy out against the hell-fires of damnation.* Was I going to reject free secondary coverage? Probably not.

As it concerned my family, I contemplated the possibility that if I began using the Ancestry platform, partaking of its DNA tests and registering for its online archives, U Myint Kaung—who spent his twilight years in a monastery on a hill, renouncing the earthly pleasures of the material world in a bid to become a more enlightened Buddhist and ready his soul for its next reincarnation—might someday end up listed as a member of the Church of Latter-day Saints, his name included in the Mormon registry rolls, which were locked away behind the fourteen-ton doors of the Granite Mountain Records Vault, which was built into the Wasatch Range twenty miles outside of Salt Lake City. Henry Wagner, a paradigm of Catholic virtue (at least when he arrived in America), might find himself in an alien congregation, far away from the shadow of the IC Church.

I guess if I'd have asked the more religious elements in my family—both alive and dead—they might caution that the

---

* After all, I could barely recall the names of all twelve disciples.

weight of my decision could be considered fairly enormous. But I found such (theoretical) protest mostly absurd. (Wasn't the circumscription of any religion potentially absurd? Unfortunately, none of us would find out until it was much too late.) I decided that U Myint Kaung would have been tickled. Maybe my sense of humor was inherited from him; the DNA test wouldn't confirm that, but I hazarded an optimistic guess in the affirmative. Henry Wagner, possibly more than anyone, might understand the arbitrary nature of worship: Sometimes you were born into devoted faith; other times you had to find that devotion later on in life. And as far as my own religion, knowing that it was highly likely that Alex Wagner's name would end up behind Mormon granite—well, I was just happy someone was claiming me for their own.

Family Tree DNA was making the most intriguing promises to the public, and therefore had to be examined. And since 23andMe—at the time—wasn't offering questionable information on Wicked Diseases, I would play no part in contributing to any unseen database, nor would I be faced with unwanted and possibly life-shattering genetic health results.

So I decided to do all three tests: Family Tree DNA, 23andMe, *and* AncestryDNA. There was no harm in blanketing the field, in overnighting as much saliva and cheek-swabbed cellular DNA as possible to as many processing centers that would take it. I would risk Mormonizing my Catholic and Buddhist ancestors and would get in bed with what might just be a modern-day eugenics movement and find yet another way to open the Pandora's box of my own blood. What could go wrong?

———//———

CHAPTER ELEVEN

———//———

I was certainly afflicted with the narcissism of self-testing, eager for data about *me me me* that would separate my indubitably unique DNA from that of the hoi polloi. Was it too harsh to presume that DNA-based ancestry testing was an exercise in self-involvement? Sure, *some* people (like my enlightened professor friend Maya) were taking the test to see how interconnected we were as a species, scientific affirmation of the hidden bonds that linked us to one another. And yet in less charitable hours, I contemplated that the makers of these tests were capitalizing on an illness that was increasingly symptomatic of this modern age—something that was precisely the opposite of Maya's lofty quest: the quest to turn inward rather than outward; to look for differences between us rather than similarities. To find, ultimately and irrefutably, the thing that separated you from the rest of humanity, as if you could somehow exempt yourself from its degradations and humiliations. This had long been an existential quest; now we simply had technology to abet our search.

All of the tests I purchased cost between one hundred and three hundred dollars per kit. If you limited your testing to one person and one test, you might be able to call it a deal: a cool Benjamin to find out you were secretly Italian? You couldn't afford not to! But once you were hooked on the addictive practice of ancestry testing, chances were that you'd probably want to get your mother and father involved—just, you know, to *get a little more information.* And if that information was weird or juicy or in some way controversial, you'd probably buy a few more tests for your uncle in Chiang Mai, Thailand, or your cousin in La Crosse, Wisconsin.

One hundred dollars became five hundred dollars; three hundred dollars became fifteen hundred dollars. People were giving the DNA kits out as Christmas presents, birthday presents, anniversary gifts. It seemed odd (to me, at least) that Santa Claus would leave the truth about one's ancestral heritage under the Christmas tree, or that an unwitting husband might prove his wife's false paternity as a ten-year anniversary gift, but the more I talked to friends and family about what I was doing, the keener their interest. It was like having a fairly accurate Ouija board: Everyone wanted to play. By the end of this project, I'd easily spent well over two thousand dollars on an array of DNA-based ancestry kits, most for this project, some handed out as gifts. This was a lucrative game, all the more impressive since most consumers were usually entirely in the dark about the actual technology they were purchasing. Mostly they took the test and waited, hoping for news that would scientifically affirm—or transform—who they were and where they came from.

Each service's full-color website garlands the kits with

amazing science talk, and a heady rush attends the arrival of these futuristic-seeming gizmos. Some of the kits rely on spit samples for the needed genetic material, saliva that's collected using a small vial with a spit guard. This is awkward. Other tests use the DNA from a cheek swab, which is administered via a small, doll-sized toothbrush. Both devices are unlike anything you might ever normally come across, and because of this, everything feels very *Gattaca*.

I started out by testing myself. After all, my DNA would have genetic information about both Henry Wagner and U Myint Kaung, whereas my parents' would show only discreet European or Asian bloodlines (or so I imagined). Still, it would be necessary to test them, too: to obtain the fullest picture of our family lineage, you wanted the biggest data set. The more people tested, the better the picture. And the older they are, the farther back the genetic information.

Over the course of two afternoons, I swabbed my cheeks with the Thumbelina-sized toothbrush for the good men and women at Family Tree DNA. This was not as easy as it would seem, mostly because you must wait one hour after you eat or drink anything, and I am apparently a very thirsty and hungry person who consumes something liquid or solid approximately every forty-seven minutes. In the end, I had to set a timer to remind myself not to put food or drink in my mouth.

Once that was complete, I dropped the swabbed toothbrush head into a small vial of preserving liquid, registered my kit online, and packed the sample away in a padded envelope destined for the Lone Star State, where it would be analyzed in what I could only imagine was a gleaming lab populated by white-coated genius geneticists.

A few words about enlisting my parents in the project: It had been some time since I asked them for anything substantive, and certainly anything vaguely complicated or complicating. Even as a child, I'd never asked for much, and as far as I can recall, they weren't particularly hands-on as it concerned my upbringing. (Note: This isn't just a retrospective, therapy-induced accusation.) My mother bragged that she had never had to wake me up for class or bother me about schoolwork (although this became a source of mild shame when she found herself in a circle of kvetching peers), and my father was often gone for work, a phantom who came home late and yelled on the phone about polling data in southwestern Ohio. They roused themselves briefly to object to my choice of college, but then lapsed back into whatever the opposite of helicopter parenting is.

I was on my own when it came to my professional life—only after I'd accepted a job offer did my parents find out I was even interested in the particular field. ("You're covering the White House now?" they'd say, in delighted surprise. "You're going to be hosting a TV show? That's great!" as if I were telling them that I had planned a vacation to Belize or had finally started meditating.) I had certainly never made any work-related requests of them.

In fact, the requests I made these days tended toward asking them to take better care of *themselves*—to go see the cardiologist (my mother) or the physician (my father)—or the occasional fact check on a detail as it concerned the family recipe for chicken with tangerine peels (Mom) or the 1972 Iowa caucus (Dad). Inviting them to take part in anything more high-stakes and unusual was like offering a hot-air balloon ride to a cat:

The prospect was both mystifying and fearsome, and I hoped it wouldn't end in disaster.

My mother was, as she is wont to be, slightly baffled by the whole process—she typically avoided anything smacking of the Internet or unfamiliar scientific processes. But she was game. She approached my grandmother about donating some of her saliva for a 23andMe test, and reported back that our favorite nonagenarian was "very enthused!"

"I thought she would say, 'Oh what a bother,'" my mother recalled. "She hates things she's not expecting. But I explained that we were going to analyze her spit for genetic material and it would tell us what her heritage was."

My grandmother was nothing if not extremely interested in herself and so dutifully sat on the couch to expectorate her sample.

"She didn't have much saliva!" said my mother, by way of a warning. (It was enough.)

As it concerned my father, I think he was somewhat skeptical about why he was being asked to do this. He'd given me a thorough catalogue of his childhood memories and knew that I'd spoken to his sisters and my cousins to fill in the missing pieces. He knew I'd gone as far as his grandfather's birthplace of Esch-sur-Alzette, and he was likely annoyed (or hurt) that I hadn't asked him to come with me, though as far as I was concerned, a father-daughter excursion was never in the cards. I'd had limited time and wanted to get the work done—not to get caught up in what I knew would be multiple meandering and possibly totally inconclusive reminiscences about our past. Not to mention, my father had an annoying habit of adopting (his version of) the local accent, in a pathetic and ill-advised bid to "fit in." Once, when we were in Paris, someone actually answered his French-accented English in actual French—and then he was really up shit's proverbial creek.

Perhaps it was my own paranoid projection, but I worried that he could smell the bouquet of Mogen David wine in the air, and knew that I might be searching for some sort of illicit truth about our family, rather than chronicling our extraordinary story of triumph and faith.

"I'm so interested in what we'll find!" he emailed me, unconvincingly, upon receipt of the zippy multicolored 23andMe test kit. "When will we get results?"

I surreptitiously registered my email address for his results, in case the tests came back showing him to be indeed 24.7 percent Ashkenazi Jewish . . . or something otherwise significantly unexpected. As open-minded as I knew my father to be in his political leanings, the narrative about where he'd come from—and the ethnic traditions he'd inherited—were central to his concept of self, and he was increasingly reliant on this narrative as he got older. He felt kinship with all of Washington's Irish Catholic pols—especially ones from the Midwest—a union that was sociocultural as much as professional.

Though I, too, was technically part of this stock, I was never a part of this circle, owing in large part to my age and gender and weirdly independent childhood; this conclave was the province of older, white men. He had regular beers and burgers with them, he made note of the ones who worshipped at Holy Trinity church in Georgetown, and he often shook their hands on Sunday after mass, before they launched into talk of Congress or the White House or whatever was animating the world of politics. To cancel (or threaten) this membership in this flock using genetic data that showed him to be of other blood would have created a schism that I was not at all excited to broker. If some anonymous geneticists in Silicon Valley determined an ethnicity counter to his expectations, I figured I'd need to walk him through the results . . . and then spend some time battling it out with him to convince him they were, in fact, accurate.

I felt a healthy amount of trepidation about all that was at stake, but, unsurprisingly, I decided to ignore it and instead went forward, hoping for the best—like a teenage homecoming queen descending to the basement in act two of a slasher flick.

Ever since the start of this harebrained odyssey, I had been looking for community. With scientific precision, DNA could ensure me of my place in a sprawling, continuing narrative; confirm my role in this cast of characters; and declare, finally, that I belonged somewhere, even if it wasn't a country or a city on terra firma. The double helix might reveal that I had people in Indonesia, Iran, or Tibet; or maybe "home" was just Burma and Luxembourg and always had been. No matter the result, I would find myself in a long, unbreakable chain. I could know that I was not an astronaut without a base station: There was life in the universe. I longed to finally receive a message, like a static-riddled dispatch from Mission Control beamed across oceans of time and space: You Are Not Alone.

CHAPTER TWELVE

—— # ——

Several weeks after taking the tests, the emails started coming in to inform me that the results were waiting for my perusal. "Learn more about you!" the inbox message enticed, and, oh, did I want to learn more about me! But first there was my mother and her results.

23andMe found she was:

55.2 percent Southeast Asian
14.9 percent Chinese
11.3 percent Broadly South Asian
8.8 percent Broadly East Asian
5.4 percent Mongolian
3.4 percent Broadly East Asian and Native American
1 percent Unassigned
less than .1 percent European

My grandmother, according to 23andMe, was:

46.9 percent Southeast Asian

13.3 percent Chinese

10.8 percent Mongolian

10.2 percent Broadly East Asian

8.8 percent Broadly South Asian

5.8 percent Broadly East Asian and Native American

2.9 percent Unassigned (!)

1.2 percent Korean

.1 percent European

and less than .1 percent Sub-Saharan African

Both of the women had a very hefty amount of unexpected Asian DNA: a strong amount of Chinese DNA, and a sizable amount of Mongolian DNA. When I told my mother that my grandmother appeared to be 1.2 percent Korean, she giggled and said, "Well, that explains why she likes to fight so much!" (I guess you can say things like this when your nonagenarian mother is hard of hearing.)

But the assessment that both she and my grandmother had a considerable amount of Chinese blood was an interesting turn of events, because while my grandmother still held a certain animus toward the Indians, my mother was absolutely petrified of the Chinese. As she would have it, the Chinese, and particularly today's Chinese, were *the* existential threat facing the denizens of Planet Earth. Not just in terms of China's increasing economic power, but for its support of genocidal regimes around the world, its rampant infringement on intellectual property, its questionable record on the environment, and its treatment of its own people—including the systematic suppression of free speech and other democratic ideals.

There was a factually grounded debate to be had on this issue, and one in which my mother was not necessarily on the losing side. But perhaps because of her myriad concerns about China, she had a nearly impossible time acknowledging anything positive the Chinese did for the globe: their contributions to modernity (paper, fireworks, gunpowder), their long and storied intellectual history (Lao-tzu, Mao Tse-tung), their food (which, in truth, she loved above all else, and food was more sacred than perhaps anything in our house), their current role in propping up a healthy amount of the American economy through trade, and their own powerful, increasingly world-turning economy. If there were ever any compliments for the modern people of China, they were issued begrudgingly.

Instead, my mother constantly looked for—and flagged for me—articles that shed unfavorable light on the Chinese (such as a *New York Times* report on the annual dog-meat festival in Yulin), as if she were waging a one-woman info war on the country. Her distaste was a specific thing—one rooted, yes, in intellectual concern, but also in obvious bigotry directed toward an entire nation.

When I emailed her about this alleged and significant portion of Chinese DNA, my mother had an explanation, or, rather, an assertion followed by a hypothesis.

Yes, ok that must account for the cantankerous part of me. Even so, I am wary of Chinese people from China, especially the moneyed and govt-associated ones. Did you see the article in the NYT today about shell companies building and buying hyper-luxury homes in LA? Am sure there is a lot of Chinese money in there, too.

In a note both self-effacing and self-absolving, my mother had immediately zeroed in on the fact that the Chinese DNA clearly was responsible for the most reprehensible parts of her *and* drew a line of demarcation between the Chinese "from China" (which she wasn't) and, presumably, the Chinese "not from China" (which she apparently was, at least in some small percentage). The not-so-subtle subtext was that those Chinese "from China" were decidedly worse. As if to prove my point, my mother somehow managed to turn the focus to yet another *New York Times* piece that possibly implicated the Chinese in yet another nefarious scheme.

When I pushed her about the other parts of the DNA report, she said she took less of an issue with the Mongolian blood because she found that "romantic," and by this I could only imagine that Genghis Khan on horseback riding across a windswept plain appeared to connote some kind of "romance" in my mother's mind. She was thrilled with the (less than) .1 percent European DNA result, in part because of its cosmopolitan connotations, but mostly because she had long held a fixation with Italian culture, and here was proof (however slim) that perhaps this obsession was genetic destiny.

I understood the results differently. The European (possibly Italian) DNA, originating from a nation nearly on the other side of the globe, suggested Burma's unusual and forgotten history—a time when European merchants could be found in the markets of Ava and Amarapura alike. This random strand of DNA pointed to something bigger: Burma's place on trade routes and the bygone commingling of Syrians and Greeks and Chinese and Kazaks.

That some of this history had shown up in my mother's and

grandmother's results gave me, a contemporary child of Burma, a badge to wear—as if to declare, "See how much we once were?" It was like science was offering a historical correction, or at the very least an asterisk on the headlines of despair and distress that were all anyone wrote about Burma these days. It reminded me that our impoverished nation was, truly, once a place of cosmopolitanism and cultural exchange. I thought of the Syrians who remembered the statuary of Palmyra, the Citadel of Aleppo and mosques of Homs—before all of it was reduced to ashes and dust. (For people from places of misery, remembering the ancient past is an act of renewal.)

I was energized by this result, but I was also . . . a little forlorn, self-diagnosed with a mild case of historical FOMO: Why couldn't I have been there to experience any of this? What had it been like? And why did I have to be the one who came of age in the Internet era and the rise of a ruling military junta? I imagined the cross-pollination on the streets of Amarapura, the linguistic derring-do required to broker exchanges in Italian and Burmese.

I thought of the first Mongols entering Burma, and my mind immediately conjured the wind-whipped Khans from the plains (yes, this was romantic). I imagined the early Chinese commingling with the Burmans, mixing to the degree that one day they became each other, with only a border to separate them. What a rich history there was in our veins—all that past and all those peoples, all that blood from centuries ago. And what a task it was to manipulate that very same lineage and make it something else, to live in direct opposition to Luxembourg's stuffy and self-righteous motto: We Will Remain What We Are. With each successive generation, we were becoming something radically, perhaps even unrecognizably, different.

And then there was the issue of the "unassigned" DNA. What, exactly, was that? On the 23andMe website, the company offered its version of a disclaimer:

This report can tell you:
- The location and amount of your DNA that is similar to DNA from other people with known ancestry.
- How your ancestry was likely inherited from your biological parents (if at least one of them is linked to your profile).

This report cannot tell you:
- The precise origins of all of your ancestors. The results presented here are estimates, which may change over time as our algorithm improves.
- Ancestry estimates for populations for which we do not have sufficient data.

Those were useful caveats, even if they were kind of unclear. ".1 percent European" seemed like a pretty exact "estimate," after all. What was the margin of error? And what "populations" did the company not have data on? (What the hell did they mean by "populations," anyway?) With doubt slowly creeping in, I began to wonder how the tests compared to one another.

My father had taken the test—and I looked at his results to see what science had to say about him.

23andMe found he was:

48.2 percent British and Irish

25 percent French and German

18.2 percent Broadly Northwestern European

4.0 percent Broadly Southern European

1.6 percent Scandinavian

1.2 percent Broadly European

1.1 percent Italian

.7 percent Balkan

Overall that was 100 percent European.

There was nothing in there about Eastern European blood that might suggest Ashkenazi Jewish or Sephardic Jewish DNA, or any Jewish DNA whatsoever. Indeed, there was nothing left to hang the Jewish Theory on, save for Henry Wagner's reported taste in Mogen David wine—and that seemed more than shaky; it seemed desperate. To a large degree, I'd made my peace with this result but still it stung like a lost splinter, too deep to excise.

The nearly two percentage points allotted (collectively) to Italian and Balkan ancestry again made my mother giggle when I told her. "Well, that explains why he likes to fight so much!" she offered. My mother had a lot of opinions about a lot of ethnic groups, which she would probably attribute to her broad reading habits and extensive travels, and which I chalked up to a proclivity toward ethnic tribalism and an innate haughtiness. My father's Scandinavian DNA was somewhat surprising—but then again, my mother had been fractionally European. DNA was expanding our world—even if that expansion was only a few hundred miles north, to Sweden or Norway or Finland.

But if I was being honest, my father's test was mostly a nothingburger. There was so much "Broadly This" and "Broadly That" in the breakdown, it made me wonder how accurately the lab technicians at 23andMe were truly able to pinpoint the DNA that made my father whoever he was. Convinced that spending more money on more ancestry tests would lead me infallibly to the most interesting conclusions, I asked my father to take two more tests: Family Tree DNA's Family Finder and AncestryDNA's test. Because I still hadn't given him the results of his first 23andMe test at this point, he was almost defensive.

"You know, Alex, I never got the results of that last one," he told me over the phone, more than slightly annoyed. "Why do I have to do this again?" I brushed his concerns aside by turning the topic of conversation over to the post-season misery of the Washington Nationals. A few weeks later, I headed down to D.C. to convince him to take the two subsequent tests, this time under the guise of "proving how silly this whole process really is!"

"Dad," I said, "that first test found you to be 1.6 percent Scandinavian! Can you imagine?" I chuckled, haltingly. "Why don't you take some other tests, just so we can see what other absurd results we get back!"

Secretly—and in violation of what I believed to be "scholarly neutrality"—I was praying that AncestryDNA and/or Family Tree DNA would return something interesting or at least unexpected in his DNA—and render all this money well spent. My father relented. He swabbed his cheek and spit some more, then dutifully left the samples on my old front porch to be collected by the mailman.

When I finally got the email alert that the results were ready, AncestryDNA assessed him to be:

43 percent Western European

29 percent Irish

13 percent British

6 percent Scandinavian

6 percent Italian/Greek

3 percent from the Iberian Peninsula

Again, there was no evidence of any Jewish or Eastern European DNA.

I was disappointed. My father's genetic narrative was fairly anodyne. I realize now that I had wanted his test results to reflect the discoveries I'd made through all my research work; I wanted scientific evidence that we were more complicated, more unusual, more crooked, than my family mythology suggested. But I didn't have it.

I remembered my first lessons as a genetic detective: Look for the cracks, pull on the snags, follow the leads. I began to look for anomalies that might suggest error, or (even better) ineptitude, and therefore give me something worthwhile to pursue. There wasn't much to hang my proverbial hat on, except for this mysterious Scandinavian DNA. It was popping up again—and this test found even more of it. I flagged it for later; I'd get to the root of the matter, once I determined what exactly the matter was.

The best and last hope for science to redeem my increasingly harebrained idea was my father's Family Tree DNA's results:

98 percent European (!)

2 percent "trace" DNA

That broke down to:

50 percent Western and Central Europe
35 percent British
10 percent Scandinavian
3 percent Southeastern European

As far as that "trace" DNA went? Family Tree specified that it was likely from Finland . . . although it might just be, as the website stated, "background noise." Before I unpacked that hazy estimation, I stopped first to consider the fact that my father was apparently 10 percent *Scandinavian*. This was considerably more Scandi blood than either of the other tests had shown—so much more, in fact, that it was clear someone had to be wrong. And then there was the 3 percent Southeastern European blood—might this suggest Jewish blood, after all? Maybe this was the test I'd been waiting for. I held tight to my American Express, convinced against all reason that if I put down just a few hundred dollars more on another, fancier test, fate would deliver me the thing I craved. (I could now understand the mindset of Powerball obsessives who'd drive to middle Jersey just to buy a ticket from the convenience mart where the last winner had bought his. It was an obsession, perhaps. Or maybe I was being thorough?)

Family Tree DNA offered an extra-credit, super-specific test of the male Y chromosome line that would return the ancestral origins of my father's paternal line, and could be conducted on existing samples—that is, without having to ask him for yet another spit test. I forked over a couple hundred dollars and went for it, pulling the lever on the DNA slot machine like a Vegas newlywed plowed on White Russians.

The results were so scientific that it was nearly impossible to decipher; there was mention of haplogroups and SNPs and charts with "marker values," none of which I could make heads or tails of. But I did gather that my father had two exact ancestral matches on his Y chromosome: ones from Germany and the United Kingdom.

Once I'd gotten someone on the phone to help me understand these very clinical results, I learned that, apparently, my father was less related—but had similar ancestry—to men in Western Europe, including Belgium, Denmark, France, Ireland, Italy, the Netherlands, Scotland, and Spain. They could offer no specificity on all that Scandinavian blood, which I vowed to take up later (and did). Ultimately, here was more Western European DNA that didn't really signal anything as far as a narrative-smashing revelation. Despite the percentage of Eastern European DNA in the earlier test, no Jewish DNA matches were returned (something this test could actually scan for with some precision). Unequivocally, it seemed, Carl Wagner had no Jewish DNA on his father's side. The genetic profile of my paternal line spoke nothing of a complicated or confused narrative. We were what we had always said we were: white, Christian Europeans.

What did the collective lab results have to say about my own saliva and cheek cells? To be fair, I had probably been most interested in what the test results said about my mother's and father's genetics—their DNA went back further in time, and could therefore (potentially) unearth more interesting discoveries. And yet the narcissism of the project was a siren song: Maybe, just maybe, something dramatic would be revealed. Some bloodline that had escaped detection in previous generations—and this would be the genetic triumph I'd been searching for.

When it came to me, ole futureface, 23andMe told me I was:

37.5 percent Southeast Asian

22.1 percent French and German

21.2 percent British and Irish

5.7 percent Broadly Northwestern European

5.4 percent Broadly South Asian

4.7 percent Chinese

1.3 percent Broadly East Asian and Native American

.9 percent Broadly Southern European

.4 percent Broadly East Asian

.5 percent Unassigned (!)

.3 percent Broadly European

.1 percent Balkan

and less than .1 percent Central and South African

While AncestryDNA determined that I was:

29 percent East Asian

14 percent Scandinavian

13 percent British

10 percent Central Asian

9 percent South Asian

8 percent Irish

5 percent Polynesian

4 percent Western European

3 percent Italian/Greek

2 percent from the Iberian Peninsula

1 percent Melanesian

Plus a few traces of North African, Eastern European, and
Northwest Russian/Finnish

And Family Tree DNA's Family Finder test estimated that I
was:

32 percent Southeast Asian

13 percent British

11 percent South Central Asian

10 percent Scandinavian

8 percent Iberia

8 percent West and Central Europe

7 percent Southeast Europe

4 percent Finland

3 percent Northeast Asia

2 percent Siberia

Plus more "trace" percentages from Oceania and East
Europe

Unlike my mother and grandmother, I showed no specific
Mongolian DNA. One test showed me to have a hefty dose of
Irish (8 percent), while one another found that I had nearly the
same amount of DNA from the Iberian peninsula. One test said
I was 5 percent Polynesian ("Aloha, hapa!"), but the other two
found no Polynesian anything. Beyond the broad breakdown of
"Asian" DNA to "European" DNA, it was a toss-up. There were

wild variations in these smaller percentages and completely different assessments as to what my genetic makeup was, exactly.

And then there was the mysterious "Unassigned" or "Trace" category—which appeared on my DNA results, as well as my mother's and grandmother's. This was apparently the Ziggy Stardust of DNA: You were an extraterrestrial creature from the genetic version of Mars. This DNA was *unlike most of what they'd observed before*, akin to a rare cactus or triple-winged bird—or it was suspiciously dubbed *background noise*. It also appeared to be the opposite of the whole point of this exercise—and I suspected the underlying reason was that the test makers hadn't yet developed a sufficient answer key.

The discrepancies and super categories and unknowns rang a few alarm bells. It looked like each company might want to put the "unassigned" disclaimer on more than one of its categories. Clearly something was amiss if I was being told I was nearly a tenth Irish and a twentieth Polynesian and maybe a little bit Native American and also . . . none of these things at all.

Which brings me to the lingering Scandinavian question: AncestryDNA asserted I was nearly 14 percent Scandinavian (and why not? I had always had a particular taste for brown bread and socialized healthcare), while Family Tree DNA determined that I was 10 percent Scandinavian and 4 percent Finnish. But this was also, weirdly, nearly as much Northern European DNA as my father had, if not slightly more—which seemed questionable at best, given the fact that my mother had approximately 0 percent Scandinavian or Finnish blood. And

then there was 23andMe, which concluded I had no Scandinavian or Finnish DNA whatsoever. What was going on here?

Presuming the companies stood by their results,* how did
they manage the angry or confused customers who didn't
believe—or didn't want to believe—what the vial of spit or
swab of cheek was telling them? Surely I was not the first person in history to receive an ancestry report and find the results
less than convincing. Was there some sort of crackerjack counseling team at the ready to soothe the descendant of an Argen-
tinian elder who was being told his blood was really Norwegian
Irish? A hotline to call when a report spelled out not Scottish
DNA, but southern Italian from Napoli?

As it turns out, there was.

A few calls and emails got me a contact at 23andMe who
worked in corporate communications. After an upbeat if mostly
inconclusive phone call with Joanna Mountain, the company's
senior director of research—who at one point declared, "It's all
about discovery, and discovery is a plus!"—I was connected to
two customer support representatives who dealt specifically
with ancestry concerns, the very soldiers on the front lines of
any DNA identity crisis for whom I had been looking.

---

* Even with my limited knowledge of corporate America, I was pretty sure
this would be the case.

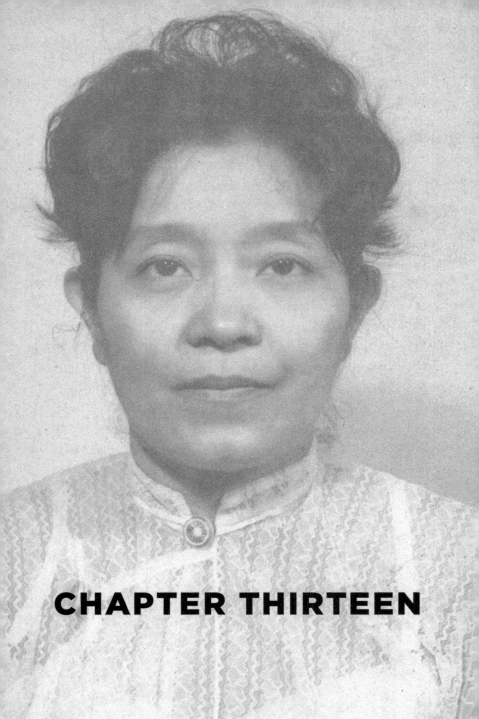

CHAPTER THIRTEEN

———— // ————

Because 23andMe is a product of Silicon Valley, everyone who works for the company appears morally uncompromised and in excellent health. I know this because I visited the place for a few precious minutes during the course of my search for the truth. It is a place with free frozen yogurt *all day long* and snacks that are high in omega-3s; there is a gym where all the employees lift weights together and cheer one another on to lift even more weight together; where the roof deck is outfitted with brightly colored plastic chaise longues in which employees sit and watch the sun set over the California mountains. It is a relentlessly optimistic place, a sharp contrast with some of the fairly serious and complicated questions that arise as a consequence of their services on offer.

When I got on the horn with the two support representatives who'd been delegated to speak with me, Cameron Kruse and Shawna Averbeck, both tamped down the suggestion that the calls they fielded were of any particularly controversial nature. They were well versed with this specific brand of professional reassurance—and explained that "empathy role-playing" was part of their training, though not all of it. "You pick up empathy nuances," said Kruse, "but being straightforward is key."

"Usually when people come to us, they're still in shock and disbelief," Averbeck explained. "So what we do is just try to answer their questions."

"We're there to be part of the process," Kruse added.

According to them both, there are stages of acceptance that people experience when a DNA test comes back with unexpected results. At first, the science is usually questioned—and, according to Kruse, "we explain that we're very confident in the data we return. If someone gets Ashkenazi results, we can fully explain how."

(I *didn't* get Ashkenazi results and wanted to know how this could be, but I'd save that for later.)

Once the customer has accepted the validity of his or her ancestry results, user-generated forums (basically genetic chat rooms) are the next step in the process of coming to terms with their new selves. "Talking about options and possibilities with other peers—that's a really important second step," said Averbeck.

Both representatives conceded that the testing process can make people feel vulnerable and "opened up to the core" but maintained an upbeat assessment about the ultimate result. "As people accept their results and how valid they are—and as they get genetic perspective—they become proud," Kruse declared.

Surely, some discoveries were easier to accept as "plusses," either incidental to a family's story, or more readily donned as symbols of pride. But what about results that challenged generations of accepted history? Assuming the results were accurate, learning something irrevocably life-altering about one's people seemed like it would take more than a chat room to come to terms with, and instead would require a certain deftness and decency—as much as empathy. According to the two I spoke with, the handful of employees in this specialized line of customer counseling were selected based on their personalities: "If they're empathetic or curious, or if they like puzzles, then they would probably be great," according to Averbeck.

"We do puzzle work behind the scenes," she said. "It helps target the response."

Puzzles? I wondered. Were the counselors doing crosswords in between calls?

"We work behind the scenes to help understand [someone's results]," Kruse clarified, "but we don't typically tell customers what we determine, because we aren't positive. It's tempting to tell them, but there are repercussions to all that. There are consequences."

"Consequences" sounded ominous. This was the first time the cheery emissaries from 23andMe had offered a suggestion of the perils inherent in their work—unspecified "consequences" traumatic enough that the counselors and puzzle solvers at the company opted not to reveal them to unsuspecting customers.

"You have to know your role," concluded Kruse. "And 23andMe prepares us really well for that."

How confident were these counselors in their results? Kruse said that in his line of work, ancestry concerns "ran the gamut," but he said calls about Native American genetics are common and sometimes necessitate certain sleuthing.

"Someone might be confident that they have Native American ancestry—and then the genetic test doesn't reflect that," he explained. "Maybe there were tales in their family history about Native American ancestors, and then [those tales] turned out not to be true."

Kruse was confident that whatever data 23andMe was using behind the scenes to determine this kind of ancestry was the right stuff: "We have a good Native American reference population," he assured me. "If there's a Native American in there, it should be reflected." (As long, a company representative later stipulated, as the Native American was not "very far back" in the generations.)

But what, exactly, was a "Native American reference population"? I kept hearing about these so-called "populations," and while I didn't expect that each of these companies had actual Native Americans in the lab helping to analyze spit samples, I also had no idea what this meant practically. In fact, I had absolutely no idea how any of this worked.

What I did gather from this optimistic and efficient phone call—before I hung up the phone, marveling at my ignorance—was that whomever these Native Americans were . . . 23andMe believed they were definitely getting the correct data from them. I suppose that it wasn't surprising that an emissary with a bellyful of frozen yogurt and omega-3 fatty acids, a man with access to a winning California sunset every night, would be so confident—as if determining whether there was "a Native American in there" was akin to making sure there was a tomato in your BLT: Pick up the bun, lift the lettuce, look for the tomato, and it's either in there or not. Simple as that, dude.

Obviously, it wasn't that simple.

With the BLT metaphor stuck firmly in my head, I realized I had absolutely no idea what the bacon, the lettuce, or the tomato represented in this particular field of study, or where these sizable and presumably very accurate populations of Navajo, Iroquois, and Sioux tribespeople were being housed. Though my saliva and cheek cells had been priority airmailed to California and Utah and Texas, I had not the faintest clue what these companies were looking for or how they interpreted their results. Basically, I knew nothing. I'd blindly assumed science would work it all out and give me the answer, and that the answer would remain uncontested because, hey, what the fuck, it was science. And I believed in climate change.

I began trying to unravel what exactly was going on by starting with the type of tests themselves.

There were multiple references to "Y chromosome" and "mitochondrial DNA" testing on all the ancestry websites. I had made my father take one of those Y chromosome tests. I remembered from biology class that men had X and Y chromosomes, and women had two X chromosomes.* So men and women both carry X chromosomes (even though men, unlike women, don't pass the X chromosomes on to their children), so it turns out that male ancestry is mostly tested via the Y chromosome—which passes down genetic traits from father to son, ad infinitum.

Women, including genetic detectives like myself, are tested

---

* Okay, I mostly remembered from biology class but still looked it up on the Internet.

using mitochondrial DNA—which reveals genetic traits passed down from mother to daughter in the same way that Y chromosomes reveal genetic clues inherited along the paternal line. (For the record, mothers also pass their mitochondrial DNA to their sons, but those sons can't, in turn, pass it to their children. It travels with moms only!)[1]

In other words, the primary—and most reliable—DNA tests (Y chromosome and mitochondrial DNA) reveal details about either your father's father's line (if you're a man) or your mother's mother's line (if you're a woman). By all accounts, these kinds of tests provide conclusive evidence if you need an answer on something such as paternity or maternal health, or, in my case, your father's father's father's potentially Jewish DNA.

But if you want something more comprehensive, like, say, ancestry through the generations, there are significant blind spots if you use only these two tests. A mitochondrial DNA test will give me reliable information on my mother's mother and her mother and her mother before that. But the further back in generations you go, the bigger an issue this becomes. Not only will this test leave out all the fathers and grandfathers from back in the day, it will also leave out any information about the mothers of all those fathers and grandfathers, as well as the fathers and grandfathers of all those mothers.

I had to draw out a chart to confirm just how many ancestors this would exempt, and as it turns out, that number doubles with every generation. By the time you got to my great-great-grandparents (the parents of Henry Wagner and U Myint Kaung and Daw Thet Kywe) a mitochondrial DNA test would return information on only one out of sixteen of them.

Like so:

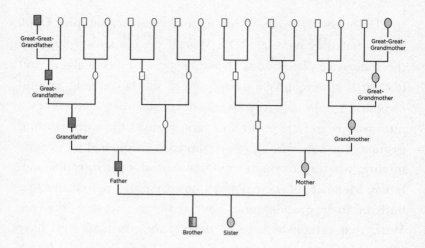

So this was a problem.

Scientists recognize this flaw and, in recent years, have developed what's known as autosomal testing, and here's where the story gets real interesting. (This is where the BLT becomes a lot more like a triple-layer hoagie.) Autosomal testing essentially scans the genetic material found on chromosomes one through twenty-two. (The X-Y stuff is what happens on the twenty-third chromosome.) There's a ton of DNA material inherited from both parents on these chromosomes, so the process effectively searches for what are known as genetic "markers" of certain ethnic groups.

If your DNA shows *certain* markers appearing with *certain* frequency, then it suggests your people may have belonged to *certain* ancestral populations. But all that conditional gobbledygook signals just how contested those markers and frequencies and sample groups actually are. As with anything having to do with ethnicity and biology, autosomal markers are subject to vicious debate.

This is how it works: Each testing company samples DNA from what they consider "Old World" populations. These are the "reference populations" I had been so confused about, and it's not that actual Winnebago are at the lab, sitting around comparing their spit to yours. Instead, scientists and community groups and for-profit companies travel the world to find groups of people who have been mostly untouched by genetic mixing, whether through economic, social, or geographic isolation. Members of these populations usually have to prove that both of their grandparents have uniform ancestry markers. With that established, these people are considered to have DNA that is therefore relatively *pure.*[*] When the scientists, or doctors, or whoever is doing the cheek swabbing and spit testing and blood sampling gather the DNA from what they consider to be a sufficient number of individuals from an *unsullied* (easy now, I'm using that term ironically) group, it forms what's known as a "reference population" for a specific ancestral group. It is, in this respect, a virtual population.

Geneticists scan the reference populations to determine if there are unique DNA markers in each group—and these are known as ancestry-informative markers, or AIMs. These reference populations—basically large(ish) DNA databases—are often then purchased by the big testing companies, including 23andMe, AncestryDNA, and Family Tree DNA. This is what

---

[*] There's a whole second book I could write on this practice, which would probably be the correct venue to expand on the controversy regarding the gathering of this ostensibly "pure" DNA. In certain instances in the past, those being sampled did not actually give consent to have their DNA used in this way.

that disclaimer on the 23andMe website was referring to with its caveat:

> This report CANNOT tell you ancestry estimates for populations for which we do not have sufficient data.

Which raises the question: Okay, which populations have "sufficient data"? As it turns out, mostly geneticists have amassed general reference populations for the regions of the world circa 1492, when the Old World met the New—which is to say, when there were distinct groups of humans who had not yet theoretically intermarried or interbred. There are reference populations for European, African, Asian, and Native American blood.

When people like myself want to find out who their ancestors were, our autosomal DNA is scanned for those AIMs. Depending on what AIMs come up, scientists make a call about your ancestry.

Which is to say: If 22 percent of my autosomal DNA shows the AIMs that correspond to the reference population for Northern European, then, by that math—I'm 22 percent Northern European.

As you can imagine, there are *a lot* of complications with this process.

First off: There's the problem with the yardsticks themselves—the DNA in the reference populations. Who's to say what "pure" means? The very concept of someone— anyone—having homogenous blood seems both arbitrary and impossible. At what point in history was blood considered "pure"—before East Asian blood mixed with Portuguese blood? Or before East Asian blood mixed with other, different East Asian blood? The year 1492 is *one* line you could draw between the Old World and the New, but there are plenty of other moments in history that came before and after that when a seemingly homogenous population mixed with another, and the DNA of a people was forever changed. The British colonized Burma in the mid-1800s, but the Pyu of Yunnan entered lower Burma in 200 B.C., and the Mon of Indochina arrived around A.D. 1000. At what point was Burmese blood considered "unmixed" and exempt of outside influence? The determination was subjective and largely dependent on what sort of time frame you were looking at: hundreds of years ago . . . or thousands of years ago. Or millennia.

And then there was the issue of the map: Some DNA was classified using political borders (for example, Irish DNA) while other DNA was defined using regional assignments (for example, South Asian DNA). As it concerned the latter, what countries made up South Asian versus Southeast Asian DNA? As it concerned the former, classification was wholly dependent on the borders you drew—and borders were pretty subjective things in the nineteenth and twentieth centuries (thanks, imperial powers!). A white paper written several years ago by several leading evolutionary geneticists noted:

Many estimations of genetic ancestry are designed to distinguish contributions from reference populations that live in particular geographic regions (e.g., West Africa, Europe, East Asia, and the Americas) that were prominent in *colonial-era population movements*. This creates a bias that might lead us to define ancestry in reference to particular sociopolitical groups. Moreover, our knowledge of diversity, and hence the genetic contributions to ancestry, of populations in many other parts of the world (e.g., East Africa, South Asia, Arabian Peninsula, and Southeast Asia) is *limited.*[2]

Colonialism! It was inescapable in the definition of a people. These scientists rightfully cautioned that we were still classifying our ancestors using the arbitrary lines drawn in the sand by imperial powers. But the British and French knew little to nothing about the genetic contributions of the Mon and the Pyu—hell, they had named the country "Burma" after the Bamah and, in so doing, basically delegitimized the other 135 ethnic groups inside the country's borders. Employing their estimations for a contemporary understanding of descendants from the region seemed both questionable and unreliable, even if it was inevitable. I was offended for my Burmese people who would have their lives measured against a British yardstick (once again) or whose biological contributions might not even register, due to colonial whimsy or oversight or prejudice (or all three).

As it concerned the questionable metric of 100 percent purity and subsequent fractionalization, even if you could pinpoint some mutually agreed upon moment in time, before which all DNA everywhere was homogenous and afterward was heterogeneous—there was the very practical question of how to find people who still had that DNA. To find men and women who had lived in geographic isolation for such an extended period of time seemed rather difficult, especially these days. In the age of FedEx and TripAdvisor, with all of our blessed commercial and ethnic commingling, who could truly claim to carry genetic markers that precisely matched the genetic markers carried by the Yoruba in the year 1442? Probably no one.

I called up Dr. Michael Bamshad, professor of pediatrics and adjunct professor of genome sciences at the University of Washington and a leading authority on evolutionary genetics. I wanted to better understand the idea of reference populations—because the whole thing seemed pretty seriously shaky.

"For accuracy in a reference population," Bamshad explained, "you need a gold standard. And it's not clear that there is a gold standard."

This was problematic. How many people were in these reference populations? Were the reference populations for the Bamah as sizable as the ones for, say, the Irish? Because the DNA testing companies often relied on reference populations from outside groups, you had to imagine that the market demand for consumer tests on the part of Irish Americans was greater than the demand from, say, the Burmese. Especially because Burma had languished in poverty and an Internet blackout for most of the early twenty-first century, and the Burmese were (generally) not easily able to drop three hundred bucks for a genetics test that you had to order online. If there wasn't a lot of demand coming from Rangoon, then my guess is that the testing companies wouldn't be going out of their way to find and purchase Bamah reference populations.

On its website, 23andMe at one point detailed the information about its DNA database as follows: "We compiled a set of 10,418 people with known ancestry, from within 23andMe and from public sources." (In case you were wondering, the company notes, "This a big jump over the 210 individuals that powered our original Ancestry Painting feature.") Most of the reference data sets, according to the company, come from its consumer database: DNA submitted by people who have purchased the kits. The rest come from public data sets, including the Human Genome Diversity Project, HapMap, and the 1000 Genomes project. So 23andMe wasn't relying on purchased DNA—it was relying on public databases . . . and on DNA from its users.

But if a bulk of its reference data was coming from consumers, wouldn't that inevitably mean an excess of DNA from affluent, educated Americans who could afford to drop a hundred bucks on a lark—which is to say, mostly white folks?

I got on the phone with 23andMe's senior director of research, Joanna Mountain, and asked her whether the diversity of the data sets was a concern. "That's something we think about a lot," Mountain said, and explained that the company was working with geneticists elsewhere in the world—in places including Sierra Leone, Congo, and Angola—as part of their "focused efforts to expand the diversity." But these "special collections" of data weren't being used, at present—they were still in the collection phase, according to Mountain. And she didn't have a time line for when they might be available. "We're trying to use them in the future," she said.

With this in mind, I wondered how big (or small) the reference populations happened to be for each region in my ancestry breakdown. For my broadly 44 percent "East Asian and Native American" heritage—which comprised Native American (Colombian, Karitiana, Maya, Pima, Surui), East Asian, Japanese,

Korean (South Korean), Yakut, Mongolian (Daur, Hezhen, Mongolian, Oroqen, Tu, Xibo), Chinese (Chinese, Han, Hong Kongese, Taiwanese), and Southeast Asian (Burmese, Cambodian, Indonesian, Lao, Malaysian, Filipino, Thai, Vietnamese) blood—23andMe was using 808 samples from its consumers and 560 from public databases, for a total of 1,368 samples overall.

For my less than .1 percent Sub-Saharan African heritage— West African (Bantu, Cameroonian, Ghanaian, Ivorian, Liberian, Luhya, Mandinka, Nigerian, Sierra Leonean, Yoruba), East African (Eritrean, Ethiopian, Maasai, Somali), Central and South African (Biaka Pygmies, Mbuti Pygmies, San)—the company was using 228 samples from consumer DNA and 393 from public databases, for a total of 621 samples overall.

I asked her how much data was "enough data" to obtain an accurate result, and Mountain offered, "It's not that we say, 'We need a minimum of this.' We look at the data we have and say, 'How granular can we get?'" In a subsequent email, her colleague Andy Kill clarified: "We look at our data and say, 'What can we tell you?,' so we're confident in all of the reference populations we have and the accuracy of the results based on those populations."

In cases where the reference populations are smaller, for example, the "South Asian" population, Kill wrote, "That forces us to be more general in the result." He later added, "In cases where we can't pinpoint a certain country, we will up-level that assignment to a region." This is why the company labeled those segments of my DNA "Broadly South Asian," rather than citing specific countries.

On that note, I asked Mountain how the company defined

"countries"—given the fact that a place like Burma, and its borders, had changed mightily over the years. She offered a cryptic "It's not today, but it is not that far back in time." She added, later, that this meant "before mass intercontinental travel."

In the months after I spoke to Mountain, 23andMe began offering its users an Ancestry Timeline, which tells you the time period in which you theoretically inherited that French DNA (for me, sometime between 1860 and 1920) or that Chinese DNA (between 1770 and 1860). But that doesn't take into consideration the fact that China in the late eighteenth century looked different on the map from what it does today—it just means that one of my relatives in that time period gave me what we now consider to be "Chinese DNA."

AncestryDNA, meanwhile, informs users that its "reference panel (version 2.0)"* contains 3,000 DNA samples from people in 26 global regions, depending on a fraction of the data that 23andMe is using. Given that there are fifty million people in Burma alone—the fact that AncestryDNA has only three thousand samples spanning less than a seventh of the globe seemed . . . not all that comprehensive.

For the region of "South Asia" (India, Pakistan, Nepal, Bhutan, Bangladesh, Sri Lanka, and Burma), AncestryDNA has 161 reference samples on file.

For "East Asia" (including Russia, China, North Korea, South Korea, Mongolia, Burma, Japan, Taiwan, Philippines, Indonesia, Thailand, Laos, Cambodia, Vietnam, Singapore, Brunei, and Palau), the company has 645 samples.

For Eastern Europe, it has 646. (Just to ballpark the ratio

---

* Woe be to any suckers who used version 1.0.

here: If you include just Ukraine, Poland, Romania, the Czech Republic, Hungary, Belarus, Bulgaria, Slovakia, and Moldova, then the population of the region would be somewhere around 150 million people.)

I got on the phone with Cathy Ball, Ancestry's chief scientific officer, and again asked what she thought was a "good" amount of data for an accurate reference population. Ball gave me kind of a nonanswer:

"You will never get any scientist to say, *I don't need more data*," she said.

But when I asked her whether certain populations would have more comprehensive reference material because of market demand (the Irish versus the Burmese, in my case), Ball was remarkably forthright.

"Absolutely," she responded. "We ask ourselves, 'What would be informative to most Americans? What, in theory, would be useful?' Western Africa, Europe—those people are places where we concentrate on. England, Ireland, Scotland. Part of it is opportunity. Some places we don't have—and it's basically practicalities. Maybe [samples] weren't collected there and we don't have a ton of customers building family trees [from those places].

"Then there are places like China," she continued, "where you have multiple ethnicities, and it's gonna be pretty hard to know who's Han Chinese and who's from another ethnic group. We don't claim to be specialists, but we try our best.

"And then there are places like Egypt," said Ball, "where people have been going back and forth for years, and what does it mean to be Egyptian? It's messy but it's also interesting."

Indeed, it was interesting, and it was certainly messy. Ball addressed all the concerns I'd had about the accuracy of these tests and confirmed that there were reasons to be concerned. There wasn't going to be great reference data for more "exotic" ancestry (like mine), and the existing DNA material was often collected and classified according to questionable parameters (social, political, and ethnic divisions were not exactly standards that everyone agreed upon).

What I was learning in these conversations was that if you were a white person from Europe, you might very well get a more accurate result than, say, if you were a brown person from anywhere else in the world, especially countries with not a lot of purchasing power. (What else was new?)

As a case in point: Ancestry had 272 samples on file for Scandinavia (a region comprised of less than 27 million people), but only 161 samples on file for "South Asia" (a region comprised of 1.75 billion people).

Given these statistics, it seemed hard to believe that any of these companies would have enough material—or the right method by which to analyze it—to accurately reflect the DNA that might have been carried by my Burmese ancestors in the mid-1800s, and by "hard," I meant "damn near impossible." This information certainly went a long way in explaining why my mother and grandmother were being assessed with such strong Chinese and Mongolian roots: Those were big parts of the world, and presumably there was more reference data for them. I wouldn't have been surprised if we were some of the very first Burmese people to even take this test!

I appreciated the fact that sociocultural borders and genetic purity were never going to be agreed upon, and that each company's DNA database was a work in progress. But the fact that there wasn't at least some sort of limitation imposed upon these ancestry results—something beyond the vaguely worded caveats and "confidence indexes," a more distinct signal that the regions and time frames were somewhat fungible and arbitrary—seemed disingenuous at best.

I reached out to the consumer hotline at Family Tree DNA to sniff out a little more on these ancestry breakdowns and, after several days of calling and being put on hold, was put in touch with the company's founder and CEO—a charmingly cantankerous entrepreneur named Bennett Greenspan.

"The problem is that the consumer wants a *yes* or *no*," said Greenspan. "They want a blanket answer: 21 percent Irish and 14 percent English. That's what people want. Science is not that simple."

I understood this to be a partial cop-out: Greenspan acknowledged that the percentages were kind of BS but insisted that customers wouldn't have bought the tests if the results were presented as anything less than definitive. It was the same line of argument that the makers of nacho chips offered whenever anyone asked why their food was stuffed with artificial cheese flavor: Sure, we could take out the extra orange cheese product, but nobody would buy our nacho chips if we did! The real stuff (actual cheese, concession of data limitations) wouldn't sell.

I wanted to know if Greenspan had a theory about why I'd been told that I was alternately nearly 15 percent Scandinavian, with little French or German DNA to speak of . . . and also not specifically Scandinavian at all, but instead one-fifth French-German?

At first, Greenspan suggested that one of the tests (not his!) might be overcorrecting for Scandinavian DNA because of its underlying database. He referred to it as "the Sorenson repository"—a set of DNA acquired when the company bought the Sorenson Molecular Genealogy Foundation DNA collection. According to one expert I spoke with, a company that used a collection like this could overemphasize the Scandinavian in its customers.

My Internet sleuthing confirmed that in 2012, Ancestry—which had been primarily an online network for traditional, records-based genealogy—wanted to get into the lucrative business of DNA-based ancestry testing. To do so, the company needed some data from reference populations, and so it acquired the Sorenson Molecular Genealogy Foundation—a genetic research foundation with (surprise!) ties to the Mormon Church.

The lab's founder was billionaire Mormon businessman James LeVoy Sorenson—a self-made mogul whose wealth, according to *Forbes*,[3] came from a variety of products ranging from disposable surgical masks to real estate to blood filtration equipment to Mormon lingerie ("Elegance of Modesty" was the product tagline) to heart monitors and video compression technology. When he died in 2008, he was Utah's richest man.[4]

Sorenson spent much of his life fascinated by medical "gizmos," which reportedly got him into the world of DNA science. In 1999, he created the Sorenson Molecular Genealogy Foundation, assisted by a Brigham Young professor named Dr. Scott Woodward. Many of Sorenson's samples were collected at church-sponsored events, with the lofty goal of "sharing genetic data to show how the similarities we possess are greater than our differences."* In a 2004 interview, he declared: "We are all sons and daughters of God. By understanding how closely related they are, people will treat one another differently. Once the database is complete, it will become a gold mine of information."[5]

His son echoed these sentiments, affirming to the *Deseret News* after his father died, "He had a great love for people and a great altruistic desire for peace, particularly in the latter part of his life. The whole DNA project and his foundation and the money that's been spent there was really motivated by helping people to see how they're related, and, through that, gain a greater sense of belonging or kinship and get people thinking a little bit more about each other."

As further proof of these intentions, Sorenson also founded the Sorenson Unity Center and the Sorenson Multi-Cultural Center. And yet, profit was never exactly absent from the billionaire's mind: In 2001, Sorenson created Sorenson Genomics, a company that offered its customers paternity tests and ancestry tests—even then, DNA tests were an exploding, multimillion-dollar market. In 2006, Sorenson Forensics was created to provide "forensic DNA casework services for federal, state, and local crime laboratories and assisting Officers of the Court in individual criminal cases." In addition to having created a database to theoretically bring the world closer together in perfect harmony, Sorenson was officially in the lucrative business of DNA testing.

---

* Obviously, I cringed when I read this, because my goal at the start of this project was mostly—no, *actually*—the same. If I'd known then what I know now!

When Ancestry purchased the Sorenson Molecular Ge-
neaology data, Sorenson's collection of DNA samples became
the property of AncestryDNA.[*][6] Many of these samples, collected at church affairs, were from Mormon worshippers, and
they in turn may have had Scandinavian heritage (according to
a 2009 Pew study, 86 percent of Mormons in the United States
are white).[7] If Sorenson had a particularly large collection of
Scandinavian DNA, then, based on logic, AncestryDNA would
therefore seem more likely to return Scandinavian results for
its customers, like me and my father.

But Greenspan's own Family Tree DNA test had returned
similar results—in fact it had shown my father to be 10 percent
Scandinavian, while I was allegedly *also* 10 percent Scandinavian. Was this the fault of his database, too? Greenspan was
(naturally) more defensive of what his team had determined
about my DNA.

"There is some concordance between ourselves and [oth-
ers]," he offered. "And if you think of your history, those people
in Scandinavia came over from places like Poland, Belgium, the
Netherlands, and Luxembourg. We're seeing that in your DNA.

"All of us are kind of a cornucopia of the DNA from the last
couple thousand years."

So we were just a cornucopia. Simple as that, dude. Except

---

[*]   The two groups were criticized when Ancestry provided DNA samples from
its Sorenson collection to the Idaho Falls Police Department, which was looking to make a DNA match for a 1996 murder. Despite the fact that certain Sorenson data was classified as "protected," Ancestry complied with the
government's subpoena and gave law enforcement access to the DNA collection without donor consent. The subsequent lead drawn from a partial DNA
match was later found to be a dead end.

for the fact that my father had only *6 percent* Scandinavian DNA, according to Ancestry's test, and I—according to the very same test—had 14 percent Scandinavian DNA! How was it possible that I—somehow—had more Scandinavian DNA than my father? It was pretty clear that my mother was not Scandinavian, unless she had really forgotten a significant portion of her family history.

On this, Greenspan agreed.

"I'm gonna say—and I'm trying to figure out a way to put it nicely—that it's error. It's just noise. It would indicate . . . trying to *overfit* something."

The explanation that being a fifth Scandinavian was "just noise" was a fairly significant concern—and by "significant" I mean it seemed to be actually more of a holy-shit moment. It was one thing to be inexact in the art of percentages; it was another when a company was suggesting to a customer that, essentially, her grandfather or grandmother was from Sweden.

"Yeah," said Greenspan, "you could have been hanging up your lederhosen for . . . some sort of Scandinavian clothing."

Neither one of us could name a Scandinavian article of clothing, which might have posed more of a concern *had I actually been Scandinavian.*

I was fairly incredulous that this sort of ancestral oopsie was (inevitably) happening to thousands of other people all over the place, men and women who were presumably rethinking their Christmas holiday to include a Saint Lucia celebration in midwinter, young girls with braids running around the living room with candles in wreaths on their head and whatnot. (Beyond the potentially misguided cultural identification, it was a fire hazard.)

I asked Ball about this: Was it possible that certain tests had told me I was Scandinavian rather than French-German because they just happened to have a ton of Scandinavian DNA on hand? Or was it something else?

"Not to throw Northern Europeans under the bus," Ball began, "but the farther you get away from Africa, the less genetic variation you're gonna see. It also makes it harder to tell between one population and its neighbor. Especially if they insist on marching their armies back and forth and sharing their genes with one another."

Apparently, this Scandinavian Problem was not limited to just my DNA results: Online amateur genealogists had blogged about their own questionable Scandinavian results.[8] One explanation was that the British Isles were more of a "melting pot" than previously understood, including sizable populations of Scandinavians who migrated west. If you had Brits in your bloodline, then their DNA might thus be read as "Scandinavian." Which highlighted the problem I'd had with these classifications all along: At what point did British blood become "British" and at what point was it "Scandinavian"? And, to Ball's point, wasn't almost all European blood in particular the result of historical mixing? Those damn warring European countries and their intermarriages! Separating that DNA was arbitrary and confusing.

About this, at least, there seemed to be some agreement. Joanna Mountain from 23andMe was up-front about the problem. "At times we've over-polled certain ancestries," she said. "You're always trying to refine, each company is always trying to improve up on its [results]—and that's because each company is in a different stage of refinement. It just as easily could have been [23andMe] that came up with that result." (She noted, of course, "that companies differ in their reference population data and the algorithms used to make ancestry assignments.")

I couldn't help but think that if some of these companies were making significantly inaccurate assumptions about my European heritage, to what lengths were they over their skis in areas of the globe where the reference data was even less developed? It made me wonder again about my mother's and grandmother's "Mongolian" DNA.

Ball explained one reason why Mongolia often showed up in ancestry reports.

"In China," she said, "it's illegal to collect DNA and take it out of the country, which limits our ability to do those kinds of collections."

Mongolia, Ball explained, "is close to China, so it's geographically as close as you can get to China without breaking Chinese laws."

In other words, my Burmese DNA *might* have registered as Mostly Chinese (because there was no Burmese DNA on hand), but instead of Mostly Chinese, some of it registered as Somewhat Mongolian (because it was really hard to get Chinese DNA out of China).

So I was a descendant of Genghis Khan because of market forces and political realities. And I was Scandinavian because of market forces and political realities. It was far-fetched enough that I found it somewhat funny, even though other people with less of a questionably loose handle on their heritage might be (rightfully) pissed if they were returned similarly faulty results.

Not surprisingly, as it concerned the even smaller and less

significant ancestry percentages—my father's .7 percent Balkan bloodline, as reported by 23andMe, for example—certain experts were completely dismissive.

"All of those things tend to be stretches," said one expert, who wished to remain anonymous. The companies that offered fractional breakdowns were doing so, this expert said, mostly "for commercial reasons."

And if a company couldn't come up with one of these alleged and intriguing "really accurate results"—.1 percent Italian, for example—it would be at a market disadvantage, but it might also be considerably more truthful. Winnowing DNA slices to tenths of a percent—or even single percentages—seemed like a fairly exact science, and from what I was seeing, the whole process was supremely inexact.

"Some interpretations are more reasonable than others," Dr. Bamshad conceded. According to his experience, yes, certain companies were making claims "that population geneticists would raise an eyebrow toward. They create narratives," he said, "and their basis in reality is sometimes fairly modest."

That seemed like a polite way of acknowledging that some of these ancestry profiles tripped into the realm of the fantastic and possibly absurd. That indeed, you could unwittingly hang up your lederhosen for . . . something Scandinavian; that you might forsake your longyi for . . . a Mongolian item of clothing.

But Professor Jeffrey Long, professor of evolutionary anthropology at the University of New Mexico, was sanguine about the whole endeavor. I asked him whether people should believe any of the results they got.

"It depends on the level of precision you want," he told me. "In the broad strokes, people would probably see fairly reasonable results, but oftentimes people aren't interested in the broad strokes. People want to know if they are from a particular locality of the world." People did indeed—even if it didn't matter whether they were actually from that part of the world.

Having spoken to scientists and experts and associated persons, I came to the conclusion that the landscape of consumer-focused DNA ancestry testing was a lot like the Wild West: Full of optimism and ambition and broken dreams, populated by groups of some charlatans and pioneers and inventors and evangelists. Much like the shop owners who offered miracle powders and gold-divining tools to adventurous settlers on the frontier, these genetic testing companies offered the curious customer a chance to (literally) Validate Uncertain Relationships! Confirm Family Lore! And Gain a Genealogical Leg Up! Most charitably, this was just the dog-eat-dog world of commerce, part of our ongoing American hustle. This was the way we did things, and sometimes (many times), we offered promises that we couldn't keep.

And yet if this was part of the reality of capitalism and the hustle, wasn't the flip side of this—also part of the American hustle—the reality of regulations and transparency? Of lawsuits and fine print? Dr. Bamshad explained that he and some colleagues were trying to establish a way to make the information on reference populations "publicly available and transparent." Some guidelines were needed—standards, you might call them—establishing how researchers and companies were performing these tests, and how genetic genealogists were determining the ways in which the data should be analyzed and interpreted.

Not everyone necessarily agreed.

Professor Long said that "the amount of reference data is astronomically better" now than it was in the early years of consumer genetic testing. "And some of the companies have very large reference populations themselves. I'm not sure it would be possible to make a compendium of all the reference data available."

If it was too much to hope for more specific disclosure on company data, what about a window onto the interpretation of the results themselves? After all, the reading of results in an autosomal test was not uncontested science. Not only were the classifications in large part vestiges of colonial conquest, there were also apparently backroom puzzle solvers deciphering the results. And then there was the reality that this testing scanned only a limited piece of one's genome—given how much material there was on chromosomes one through twenty-two.

The American Society of Human Genetics says:

> Because the genome is finite, only a small fraction of ancestors are represented by each given genomic segment in an individual, and every ancestor does not necessarily pass on his or her DNA at any given genomic segment to a descendant, so *one can only ever have limited information on the origins of a given individual's ancestors* [emphasis mine].[9]

Wasn't it incumbent upon these companies to, you know, better explain that the results could be, occasionally, wildly wrong? Only a very small part of the genome was scanned, and those limited results were compared against limited reference data, which was then assessed according to certain laboratory preferences. Which were, by their very nature, limited.

This was the arms race of the ancestry market: When one company was able to offer its customers surprising or even shocking genetic information, the pressure was on for all of its competitors to do the same. With "results that make people say, 'I thought I was German, but I'm Scottish!' that's all people want to hear," according to Greenspan.

Here we were again blaming the nacho-chip-chomping bubble butts for their insatiable lust for extra nacho cheese product: Ya can't take it away from them! "Unfortunately, we live in a world where people read less," Greenspan said. "Everything is distilled into a ten-second sound bite. That's not what people need; that's what people *want*. Sometimes you need to know a little or a lot more to understand the answer."

Yeah yeah yeah, I said—I was tired of blaming myself for all the snack chips I had known, and, anyway, shouldn't there be something, somewhere, that stipulated to the unsuspecting cheek swabber: WARNING: DO NOT START EXTOLLING VIRTUES OF IKEA BECAUSE OF APPARENT SWEDISH DNA?

"I think all the companies try to get those asterisks across," said the unnamed expert. "How well we do on that front, I don't know, given that you have people on television like [Henry Louis] 'Skip' Gates, who loves the percentage test and hawks the percentage test . . . and delivers it with the moral authority of a person on the TV. It becomes challenging when a member of the public does that. Sometimes it works well; sometimes it doesn't."

In other words: Sometimes you were Scandinavian, and sometimes you were Mongolian, and all of the time (at least where these tests were concerned), you were gonna have to accept the results. Simple as that, dude.

And yet, I confess: For the six days that I believed myself to be partially Scandinavian, I began cultivating a taste for equanimity and butter cookies, mentally ticking off my taller-than-average height as a vestige of my Nordic ancestry. I thought about my Mongolian blood and explained away my lust for fur-lined clothing as a genetically determined sartorial predilection. I felt—fleetingly—a sense of *pride*. That satisfying peace that comes with conclusion, as if I could finally say, Yes, world, this is who I am, a modern-day amalgamation of Scandinavian and Mongolian genes, tossed into a blender and thrown halfway around the world.

But in the end, these percentages, these flossy statistics, were just a ruse. They were gold-colored nuggets glinting at the bottom of a riverbed, shiny nothings that lured people like me to unknown frontiers by promising one thing and delivering another. Ancestry results played on our most basic desire to know ourselves, to belong to something innately. And then they exploited that desire by delivering something possibly real, possibly diluted with half-truths and educated guesses.

In the back of my mind, I knew the question of identity and heritage was more complicated and deserving of ethical treatment than perhaps some of these scientists (and myself) might have considered. And so I decided to contact the éminence grise of skeptical sociologists—a leading critic of consumer-based ancestry testing—Troy Duster, professor of sociology at UC Berkeley, who said immediately, "Autosomal AIMs are nutty and complicated, and that's where the transparency becomes the central issue. These markers are based on proprietary entrepreneurial developers who don't wanna give away their secrets.

"If you can't replicate that test," he explained, "if you can't show your strategy ... then you're asking for a kind of faith on the part of the consumer."

In Duster's opinion, that was a lot to ask.

But he, too, hit on the tension inherent in the whole practice of commercial genetics: Companies want to maintain a market advantage. They want to do things in a cost-effective manner, to scale, and as much on their own terms as possible. This was Greenspan's point: Consumers want the most accurate results —but they also want some sense of reward, a feeling they've learned something that they didn't know before, that the investment was worth it. Those competing interests can end in questionable results, and, sometimes, inaccurate ones.

Was it fair to feel indignant about the status quo, the fact that most eager consumers were in the dark about just how much the companies themselves were in the dark?

I raised this issue with Dr. Long.

"Well," he said, "would you ask for the recipe from the chef if you enjoyed your meal?"

I thought that seemed an inapt metaphor—after all, I took penne arrabiata seriously, but not as seriously as I took, say, my heritage. Dr. Long persisted.

Testing your DNA was like a fun-house excursion, he said: "What if I went to a crystal ball reader and she told me my sister was not my sister.... What would I think? Maybe a reading of your DNA is no more accurate than a crystal ball."

That was a revelation.

"There may not be that much more to the science than crystal ball reading," Long repeated. "When it comes to a direct-to-consumer test, I would tell people not to give much more credence to it than recreation."

CHAPTER FOURTEEN

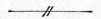

The tribe is not strictly speaking a genetic population. It is at once a social, legal, and biological formation, with those respective parameters shifting in relation to one another.

—Kim TallBear[1]

So the DNA tests were compromised, and by "compromised" I mean "possibly inaccurate to the point of uselessness." And yet, millions of people were taking them. And millions of people, inevitably, had a more nuanced and complex picture of their roots, even if that picture was a wavy-gravy, Magic Eye version of the truth. I tried to sort out what this meant as far as my original question: Who am I and where do I belong? Was there a solution to the existential loneliness that had followed me around like a shadow all these years, one that might answer the primal call for identity and community?

The search to discover my heritage had ended up fracturing my understanding of my people. I was not the natural inheritor to some forgotten society, but, rather, I had been grandfathered in to a million splinter groups: the hustling Luxembourgers, the nationalists of Burma. Each group had a subgroup, and each subgroup was so particular that it blew up the whole idea of ancestral community: I was not the expression of some intangible Southeastern Asian/Western European id; I was the offspring of a very specific group of (very complicated) people.

In fact, I was coming to the sinking realization that my hope that *discovering my identity* would provide refuge and belonging was itself a trap—it was a con just like the DNA ancestry tests were a ruse, designed to lure in the questioning with zealous promises. Because if you looked closely enough at where you've come from—as part of the quest to determine "identity"—you'd inevitably find failures and exceptions, the truth of which would destroy the myth that you could find some peaceable, faraway kingdom of elders that would confirm your belonging to something greater than just little, old, weak-kneed . . . you. You'd find mixed blood, not the pure hemoglobin of princes. You'd find that you were a little bit of a lot of things, a person drawn from many different people of many different persuasions. There was resolution in that, but it was still damn lonely.

Maybe there was some solace to be had in simply understanding this. I thought about James Sorenson's lofty dreams of peace: "By understanding how closely related they are, people will treat one another differently." If the knowledge that we are all humanly amalgamations from around the world could, in fact, help tamp down the vitriol and hate that was increasingly defining us, if it could undermine the Us versus Them dichotomy in our present national debate or slow the spew of demagoguery, then it might actually be worth it. The faulty results and the questionable science, the arbitrary classifications and significant blind spots. The legitimization of colonial boundaries, the massive oversimplification of ethnic identity. Could this kind of science bring us closer to a more perfect union, act as a weight on the moral arc of the universe to bend it ever so slightly further in the direction of justice, and put us on a more direct path to becoming whole?

When I looked at a map of the world—found on each company's website—highlighting the countries where my DNA could be found, I was awash in pride.

I had no claim to Australia, Greenland, the Middle East, most of East and West Africa, or Russia—but other than those places, the *entire world* was highlighted, blasted into full color by my DNA. This was visual confirmation about ole futureface —numbers that reflected a certain global reach: I was quite literally a citizen of the world! Here, in my occasionally broken-down body and increasingly creaky bones, was a veritable mini United Nations of genetic material. Never mind the truthiness of the science behind it; I had third-party assessment showing my universality, my mutability—and that seemed a reason for hope. So much has been made about our borders, how effectively we might close them off and secure the entry points to "protect" our national identity. But here was a body that bled across the world—from sea to shining sea. My map was a refutation of xenophobia, a double-down bet on the world as a sprawling place of commingling and communication, rather than a series of tightly drawn political boundaries and passport checkpoints.

But, in this hopeful embrace of Pangaeatic heritage, was I the rule or the exception? Would most people see it this way? Certainly, a good deal of the country was open to pluralism and mixing. But not all of it. Specifically: Would America's white majority rejoice at the brownness, the unassigned nature of this American heritage? A sizable group of white Americans, after all, had made their opinions known in recent years—and they had spoken resoundingly in favor of protectionism and tribalism, rejecting the gray areas of multiculturalism for the sharp relief of black and white, and demanding walls and policies to separate us, not unite us. They would be no fans of what my map portended. This America felt fear when it came to cultures mixing—a fear that was centuries old—and the shrinking of the world had not done anything to allay it.

With this history in mind, the fractioning of personhood, readily available thanks to my various test results, seemed a ghostly reminder of antebellum one-drop rules and racial phrenology, when blackness or Jewishness was something to be measured and marginalized (and destroyed, not celebrated).

Professor Duana Fullwiley at Stanford, who specializes in medical anthropology, was one of the most prominent voices urging caution in the burgeoning practice of DNA-based ancestry testing. I asked her whether—in a well-intentioned, progressively minded quest to eradicate cultural differences by revealing complex ancestry (a project considered by both Mr. Sorenson and myself!)—we might be, in fact, inadvertently reinforcing the idea that we were all genetically different from one another.

Professor Fullwiley was diplomatic.

"Well," she said, "it *could* work out that way . . . but I think oftentimes people glom on to two or three specific [parts of their heritage], and these come to represent someone's whole identity. And the methods of these technologies feed that behavior, rather than showing people how fluid identity might be. Instead of inciting people to be more curious about the world, now there are only one or two things they might be focused on."

She added: "I don't see [DNA–based ancestry testing] as deconstructing race, as some people do.

"In general," she continued, "we're still thinking of very basic racial options in very basic racial terms. The actual concept of race is fortified by these technologies. I feel that the tool of ancestry testing, as it's constructed—organized and collected data by continent—reiterates our way of seeing race in simplistic terms."

Many (if not most) scientists and geneticists concur that the classification of "race"—as such—has no basis in scientific reality. In 2000, leaders of the Human Genome Project announced that the human genome contained no real racial differences and that we are all just one race—"the human race."[2] These scientists concluded that human beings share "99.9 percent of their genes, such that researchers cannot point to clear, qualitative genetic breaks between one population and another."[3]

And yet, the practice of this DNA detective work emphasized the opposite. They were all about finding difference in our genes: Fundamentally, these were businesses whose entire model was selling the idea that we were each genetically determined to be different. I was, for example, 50 percent European and 37 percent East Asian. As these breakdowns told us, we all had distinct ancestral lines, separate and unique from each other, as determined by a DNA-based test. And where there's difference—no matter how neutral or meaningless—there is an arbitrage opportunity to turn that difference into someone's favor or fortune.

"The tools we have today that parse ancestry in terms of percentages play into the idea that there are pure racial types," Fullwiley told me. People who took the DNA tests had their genetic material classified according to reference populations on various continents—but oftentimes, Fullwiley said, the people in those same reference groups didn't even understand themselves to be classified as such. In other words, the so-called true Siberians and Melanesians weren't necessarily characterizing themselves as Siberians or Melanesians—they were assigned into those categories by someone else.

I recalled an article I'd read earlier by a group of leading sociologists wary about genetics and their impact on how we Americans imagine ourselves.

"Websites of many companies state that race is not genetically determined," the sociologists said, "but the tests nevertheless promote the popular understanding that race is rooted in one's DNA—rather than being an artifact of sampling strategies, contrasting geographical extremes, and the imposition of qualitative boundaries on human variation."[4]

By drawing the questionable line between someone's makeup and "genetic science," consumers might be led to the iffy conclusion that race was based in science—even though that science was a product of subjective determinations and constants that had more to do with sociopolitical realities (including the whims of various and sundry British lords) than they necessarily had to do with any natural genetic separations.

"Because race has such profound social, political, and economic consequences," these sociologists concluded, "we should be wary of allowing the concept to be redefined in a way that obscures its historical roots and disconnects it from its cultural and socioeconomic context."[5]

But when I asked evolutionary genetics scholar Dr. Bamshad about how DNA-based ancestry testing was informing—

or perpetrating—misguided ideas about "race," the professor agreed that race was "not a very good tool for classifying populations," but did not consider race entirely irrelevant.

"Race is one of many ways to define populations," he said. "Any definition of a population is relatively gray, because you have to make an arbitrary definition of where to draw the line. There are hundreds of definitions of race. But race captures some biological information: It's one of many identities that a person has. [We see] genetic ancestry and popular notions of race—as well as other parts of identities—as overlapping with one another. They overlap to different extents in different people."

As Bamshad proved, just how precisely race matters (or even exists) differs wildly, depending on who you're talking to. According to a study conducted by Bamshad and others, geneticists and anthropologists have divided opinions on this.[6] When asked their opinion of the statement "Races don't exist," 61 percent of geneticists disagreed, while 59 percent of anthropologists agreed.

When responding to the statement "Race is biologically meaningless," only 42 percent of geneticists agreed with it, while 71 percent of anthropologists did.

Bamshad concluded, "Do common notions of race used in the United States capture some information about your biological and genetic identity? Absolutely. In the overwhelming majority of people, that is absolutely true. The better question is: Is that information meaningful? If so, in what context, and in what way?"

For me, it boiled down to one question: Was this stuff moving us closer together or farther apart?

I asked Professor Long, the man who put as much stock in DNA-based ancestry testing as he did in crystal ball reading.

"Unfortunately," he said, "I think it's moving us toward more division. And this is something that bothers me about the field. As an evolutionary biologist, I have to think of unity and diversity simultaneously."

When you looked at ancestry tests, Long said, "You're looking at the top ten feet of the tree, rather than the whole tree. All my genes are African—but they were given to me by Europeans. That's how I like to think about it: Genetic ancestry has been transferred, but there's no point at which it starts."

I liked this concept: the idea that, in the beginning, we were all the same; we just took different routes to get to our modern selves. Some people took the Andes, others trekked across sub-Saharan Africa, and still others walked an overland route across the frozen Bering Strait.

But conceiving of heritage and ancestry in such a fashion required a certain deftness. It did not come with a big, multicolored map that announced you were a citizen of the world, and it basically, ultimately, put all of us *Homo sapiens* in the Unassigned category. It was not a particularly easy discipline to practice because we had been taught to desire singularity and specificity, to champion the special things that set us apart, to ask, "What's your blood?" rather than assuming that our blood was, in fact, really all the same. Long's way of thinking and understanding our place in the world would not do that. In fact it would do the opposite.

Ancestry tracing was a greedy sport: People who did it wanted as much information and as many statistics as possible. Relinquishing one's claim to a specific heritage was especially difficult in the deeply personal and political divide over identity. Moreover, it didn't take into account the radically different realities experienced by people who looked different from one another, even if they were genetically the same. (You'd have a hard time convincing a young black man that he was scientifically identical to a young white man, given the presumably opposing set of realities facing each.)

For his part, the ancestry-testing critic Professor Duster was resolute: Ancestry maps—like the one I had gazed on with pride—had irrevocably negative outcomes.

Duster recalled the work of Professor Jennifer Lee at the University of California, Irvine. "What she's shown is how, even though we're all mixed in this way and that, when you have an Asian and white mixture, you still get a binary world. You don't have people saying, 'We're mixed!' People identify with one or the other. Asian-white students may get categorized as hapa, but when it comes down to their actual activities, look at the patterns in terms of dating and marriage—and it is dramatic."

I thought about this as it concerned myself, a hapa of Asian-white parentage (never mind the percentage). And it was mostly true: Growing up, I had identified with white culture (*Saved by the Bell; Garfield*) more than Asian culture (Thingyan celebrations, durian fruits). I married a (really very great) white guy. I credited this to the fact that I was raised in a very white quadrant of northwest Washington, D.C., and was—in my classes and on my sports teams and in my professional adult life—mostly surrounded by white people.

I was still proud of and excited by my Burmese heritage. In fact, I understood it to be a mark of honor, the thing that made me futureface, the thing that set me apart from . . . all those white people. And, by the way, if I could have gained entry into a Burmese peer group that wasn't largely composed of bullying twelve-year-old boys throwing water at me in the chilly weeks of early April, I like to think I would have. Maybe I would even have married one.

As I defensively reasoned through all of this with myself, I felt a creeping sense of apprehension, because, well, I hadn't really ever looked for that group of friends, nor had I dated that phantom Burmese suitor. I hadn't poked at that other half of me—the Asian side—until something approaching guilt had set in. Maybe that was genuinely the result of circumstance, maybe it was due to a lack of curiosity, maybe it was laziness.

Or maybe it was because it was, in truth, a lot easier to be white than Asian where I was growing up, surrounded by the people I was surrounded with, working with the people I came to work with. They were all white! And part of being ambitious about succeeding in their world meant fitting in. And fitting in meant embracing the dominant culture, which was . . . white culture—not someone else's.

Being able to throw the signs and read the cues of Caucasia made it easier to scale and conquer the world of Ivy League universities and American media, to approach the top echelons of what we think of as success in this country. I wanted this, badly, even if it was ultimately an unsatisfying fit. But you couldn't be safely ensconced in that world while you were still part of another—that's not how membership worked. Whiteness, even in the twenty-first century, remained a fairly singular thing, one that did not meaningfully embrace hyphenated co-branding: It was all or nothing. So I put aside my Burmeseness and my skin color and its potential pool of suitors. That was just the truth.

Maybe Duster and Lee were right: Nobody really existed simultaneously in multiple racial worlds, no matter what their ancestry results said. Belonging was still a binary proposition, if not a permanent one. And fractional breakdowns of ancestry might not bring us together any more than hyphenated ethnic designations made society more accepting—people still picked and chose who they were (and who they wanted to be with), even if the offerings themselves happened to be more diverse. I was a case in point.

Instead, it seemed that the most affirming way to bring us closer to one another in this time of American fracture, to repel the tide of tribalism that happened to be cresting over the United States, was to hold fast to perhaps the only useful truth that had been revealed in all this ancestral investigation: We are all from the same place. We took different paths to get here, we made different choices along the way, we checked off different boxes when it came time to decide on language or governance or cuisine or values. And as much as those divergent choices have drawn us apart, placed us lately in different parts of the globe or on opposite sides of the line, the beginning remains immutable, constant, reassuring. It is a reminder that ultimately, we are all in this together—still.

We are, furthermore, bound for constant motion—this is the course of *Homo sapiens* on Planet Earth. In particular, this is what knits Americans together: the fact that a great deal of genetic motion has come to a rest, fairly recently, in this place, on this land.

And that's what my world map of DNA made clear: Alexandra Swe Wagner was (yes) born lately into somewhat fraudulent stock, filled with men and women of compromised morals, but if you delved further back in time, if you looked at what the map was really telling you, it was that I was a product of people who lived and died far away from the country I now called home.

The lesson was not about how my people had assimilated into American culture, or their immigrant derring-do; it was another thing entirely. The map revealed that my—our—circle of human existence inexorably widens, and will continue to widen with the passage of time. These genes will not be American forever. Take a look at the Wagner ancestry map in several generations hence, and I'll bet you the locus of action will be in another part of the globe entirely. And this, at last, is the whole point: We come from the same place, and despite our separations over generations, we are ultimately headed back together—in ever-widening circles of travel and marriage and childbirth and time. Genetically speaking: We are one.

Specifically speaking, as it pertained to the reason I had first embarked on this transcontinental odyssey, this historical/archival/genealogical voyage, this Vegas-style genetic testing bender: The entire concept of "my people" didn't actually exist. There was no such thing. And a community of all was ultimately a community of none.

So, what was the story that I could tell about myself, to myself, to explain who I was?

The story I would tell was unvarnished: I was part of a community in upheaval and ecstasy. My people weren't dead; they were very much living. They were grappling with change and uncertainty, and looking to do what seemed the most right, as far as they could determine.

There were no genes between us: We didn't share bloodlines or DNA or even geography. Instead, they were the men and women who struggled in similar ways, and held fast to the same ideals, and sought good answers to heavy problems. I realized, after all of my research was done, after looking so hopefully to the past, that the present was the only community I would and could ever know. Now—the struggles of the present, the hope it offered for the future, the examination it demanded of the past—this was the constraint that created a community.

I have recognized these people—my people—fleetingly. They were the ones digging in their pockets for loose change to give the kid playing the buckets on the subway platform, the ones who complained about the fact that the neighborhood had changed too much since they'd last lived there, the ones who remembered that the guy upstairs lived alone and, because it's the holidays, shouldn't we check on him?

My people were the ones who liked the sound of old horn samples and occasionally listened to records at cochlea-threatening volume. They were at Madison Square Garden in September 2016 when Kanye West appeared to float in the air: dancing below him, a churning mass of teenagers and twenty-somethings in skinny jeans and bomber jackets—the differentials of their black and brown and white skin erased in the amber glow of the Martian lights. They, just like me, really wanted the tour merch (sea-green baseball caps!) and they waited in line, just like me, to pay too much to an artist who we all knew was an asshole but damn did he make good music (and damn did those sea-green baseball caps look good that fall).

My people were the ones going to the church and the synagogue and the mosque and the monastery, not because they were being forced to or because it was expected, but because the bedrock principles of these faiths—mercy and kindness and goodwill—were things that not only appealed to them, but that they wished to cultivate more formally and forcefully in their own lives, however belatedly.

These days, my people are the ones looking at the paper— whether archly conservative or bleeding-heart progressive— furrowing their brows at the headlines, turning up the radio for the story about healthcare or immigration, hitting SEND on an email with Important Political Information or Otherwise Necessary News About the Forgotten Among Us. They are scared, some of the time, about what lies ahead—but they still believe that if they try hard enough, they might fix it, might steer a more righteous course.

All those years back, I thought I was alone—the only noise in the world was the sound of a shuffling deck of cards. Oh, but there was life, down the street and up the block, in other rooms, other cities—though I hadn't found it yet, hadn't bought the plane ticket or opened the guidebooks. (I was too young!)

I'd find it not in Rangoon or Esch, in places my family had long since moved on from, among people who were no longer ours. My blood was not coursing in these lost cities. Instead, it was gushing through New York, where the rats still ran on the subway tracks at lunchtime and the halal truck was already steaming at ten-thirty in the morning. And in Mumbai, where the construction was constant and the excitement unalloyed about what was to come in its place—where the optimism of expectations was nearly too demanding. And in Detroit, where one way of life had come to a crushing, grinding halt, and in its place something new was emerging—something that was not without its own cracks and fissures but had, undeniably, the tremors of optimism. These were big, sprawling, terrifying metropolises that very nearly ate you up, but in the process of avoiding failure and self-destruction you found the things that made it worth trying to survive to begin with.

My people were the hordes—masses who fell asleep on the subway because they were working too hard or maybe were too drunk, who honked incessantly and inappropriately because, dammit, *Don't block the box!* In taxicabs. In crowds. Swarming, moving, chaotic throngs of people who were white and black and brown and soon-to-become brown and just-lately brown. (We were all once brown and will again be brown before the end, after all.) All these people, pushing toward one another but also toward something else—something unseen but still bigger, better, and undeniably ours.

I had been looking in all the wrong places for the string that connected us—in family lore and foreign cities and dusty files and sampled spit. I had asked dead men and dead women for the answers to my questions, but of course they couldn't give them to me, couldn't tell me who I was and where I belonged. The people who knew (even without knowing they knew) were alive. They'd been with me from the beginning.

EPILOGUE: A WORD ABOUT LIVING (AND DYING)

———— // ————

"Alex," my father would say, "we are born alone and we will die alone," and I would roll my eyes in semi-mock tedium when he said this. But when he did die, unexpectedly, it was indeed alone. Perhaps the only expected part of his sudden death was the fact that it was so singularly lonesome, a fulfillment of the prophecy he'd intoned to me so many times before. This was how he was always going to go out, after all. His last moments were spent by himself inside the house where we'd lived as a family—until divorce and college and adulthood made it so there was no real family unit left to speak of.

The mailman found him (a fact that I thought he would relish from the hereafter with comic irony), a foot soldier of the same corps his own father belonged to. As far as my father had come—as many miles as he'd put between himself and small-town America, and its rhythms and customs—it was a representative of that world, where things were delivered by hand and neighbors knocked on doors regularly, who ushered him out. As depressing as this was, I think it would have made him happy.

In the days after he died, there were phone calls and emails, too many white flowers, a few handwritten notes and text messages, all expressing a certain amount of shock and sadness, but also regret. "We hadn't seen each other in so long!" one said. "I always wondered how he was doing," wrote another. "We'd always ask each other—have you seen Carl?"

It was clear that so many people my father had known for the definitive years of his life—which is to say, his life when he lived it largest and most fully—had become, however inadvertently, estranged. My father was proud and angry and could hold a grudge. Even the best of his friends would remark on the combustible nature of their friendship—"No risk, no reward!" was essentially their calculation—and he had, especially in his later years, allowed his various frustrations and indignations to isolate him.

There were people he saw in passing, of course: neighbors with whom he shared gardening tips or dry cleaners with whom he engaged in casual political talk, a handful of people he'd meet for a drink or for lunch. But his community—the ones who remembered his fight on the floor of the Democratic National Convention in 1980, or could recall the hotshot organizer from the McGovern campaign—the men and women who had defined his world, who knew him intimately, and who had understood his passions and compulsions and grievances and inspirations? They had, in many ways, receded into the background.

My father became a purveyor of wistful nostalgia about glories past, content to reminisce about who he'd been, rather than repair the relationships that had made him the man he understood himself to be. He was preoccupied with a halcyon construction of What Was, not pushing forward in the present by navigating the necessary ups and downs of love and sadness, disappointment and success. While this may have been an easier way to live, it was also a lot lonelier.

In the days after his death, I thought about this as my lesson: His life had become a homily, a narrative untethered to the here and now. He, like so many others, had forsaken the messiness of flesh and blood for something more addictive but decidedly less real, the myth of who we once were. As it concerned the winding, circuitous path I'd been on for all these days and months, trying to understand who my people were (and where to find them), his death marked an endpoint: not simply to his life, but to the honey-hued family narrative about Iowa corncobs and stickball at sunset, the frozen Mississippi in winter and the decency of the lone black dry cleaner in town.

This was the end of the fable about our people in the heartland. In its place would be something more truthful and less satisfying, a family history that was equal parts comedy and tragedy. I could tell my son about his grandfather (and his great-grandfather!), about what made them interesting and compelling and sometimes terrible, what mistakes they'd made along the way. What was gained and what was lost, where we had come from—specifically—and who had been there before—honestly. What we earned and what we were given. Here was a chance to open a new chapter, this time with the truth. And to live in the world—as difficult and complex and heartbreaking as it is—and not in the past.

As it concerned the other side of my family tree—the

branches that began on the opposite side of the world—I had started out this fantastic adventure by speaking with the oldest person I knew, our matriarch, my mother's mother, Mya Mya Gyi, the Emerald. I was reminded, by virtue of her increasing age, of the brevity of life, the transience of our time on the planet. She was in her late nineties when we began speaking, and it was a race against time to get as much information from her as possible.

With my father, I'd felt (incorrectly, as it turns out) like time was on my side—he had years ahead of him, or so I thought. But with my grandmother, I could feel the sands slipping through the hourglass, the seconds melting away on the clock. Sometimes I even panicked. Who else would have the information she had? Who would remember the things she did about our family? About Burma? Where else could I find a yardstick by which to measure, in all my twenty-first-century earnestness, the bigotries and unresolved conflicts of our family, a standard bearer through which to divine our evolution? Time was running out, and there was so much more to know! It was stressful.

But then, equally so, each time we spoke, I was struck by how much you could pack into a life. That if you were ambitious, somewhat thoughtless, and most certainly brave, your time here would seem very long indeed. (How high the highs of a life well lived, how deep the lows of unresolved mistakes!) She'd seen so much of this world, met so many people; all the diamonds and curries and bowls of piping hot chicken noodle soup she'd had since her very first one in Augusta, Maine, during that first winter in America. She—unlike my father—lived in worlds and worlds and worlds, ones that kept unfolding with each stage of her life. What a seemingly unstoppable thing it was, this kind of existence.

Near the end of my research, she fell sick, abruptly. This had happened before, following a rogue mushroom consumed after an ill-advised foraging trip around northwest Washington (and a subsequent omelet made with said mushroom). But she had survived that, and well, shit, she'd survived so much that she would certainly survive this bullshit phantom illness. Because of course she would.

But no, this time she did not. She grew very weak and stopped opening her eyes to us, and no amount of chicken broth—piping hot or not—would pass her lips. The last thing she said on this planet was not to me, or to my heartbroken, dutiful mother who stood in worried vigil for nearly three weeks. The Emerald was rarely in the mood for emotional generosity or consolation, after all, something we all secretly knew.

It was to my husband, who had stopped in her room late one afternoon, and happened to be wearing a brand-new watch. He appeared in the doorway, and, sensing his presence, she opened her eyes and said, "Good to see you!" as if it were teatime and she wasn't on her deathbed. He came closer to her and, without looking down, she said to him—the last thing Mya Mya the Emerald would ever say—"Nice watch."

It was, as far as last words go, completely in sync with my grandmother's generally insouciant and materialistic existence. It was a statement from the same girl who had, nearly a century before, extorted a Dodge motorcar from her father. She still coveted pretty things, unaware of the turmoil around her. It was cruel, too, in the way that she was and had always been. (Could she not have said it was good to see my mother, or at least acknowledged her daughter's existence before she passed from her own?) It was selfish. It was, undoubtedly, hilarious. (Especially to my husband. She had always had a way with men.)

It was also beside the point. This was what I realized only after the fact, when this whole project was completed: She wasn't thinking of last rites or leaving us with some Epic Final Thought, because for her, there was no last of anything. There was no reliance on dim memories: There was only the making of new ones. And all of this, her Buddhism taught, would continue—until nirvana had been reached.

I wasn't a devout Buddhist, but I, too, had come to the realization that our story—which was necessarily her story—continued. My grandmother didn't need to say something profound that day, because it wasn't, actually, the final word on anything. She may have been done on this earthly world, but her children and her children's children (and their children!) were still alive. She wouldn't know where we'd end up or how the story would change, what twists and turns might await her family—but she wasn't worried.

It was up to us.

ACKNOWLEDGMENTS

———//———

Thank you to:

First and foremost, Chris Jackson, who worked with me on this project for many too many years, and who made a confusing jumble of thoughts into an actual book with purpose. The thing you are holding in your hand would not exist without him (I really mean this).

Eli Horowitz, for being patient and thoughtful, as he always is, and for helping me channel the necessary Muse of Mystery required to write a book of this sort.

Cousin Geoff Aung, for indulging the harebrained spirit of this endeavor and helping with all manner of Burma research and obscure Burma political history.

Cousin Karl Wagner, for planting the seed of curiosity and helping to make it grow.

My mother, Swe Thant, for answering too many questions and having an extraordinary generosity of spirit when it came to the ambitions of this book.

And thank you to my husband, Sam Kass, who is my lighthouse—and without whom I would be lost. What luck that I get to live this life with you.

NOTES

CHAPTER ONE

1. "The New Face of America," *Time*, special issue, November 18, 1993, cover, content.time.com/time/magazine/0,9263,7601931118,00.html.

CHAPTER TWO

1. Yoni Appelbaum, "The 11th Plague? Why People Drink Sweet Wine at Passover," *The Atlantic*, April 14, 2011.
2. Gregory Rodriguez, "How Genealogy Became Almost as Popular as Porn," *Time*, May 29, 2014, time.com/133811/how-genealogy-became-almost-as -popular-as-porn.

CHAPTER FOUR

1. Adrian Levy and Cathy Scott-Clark, "Between Hell and the Stone of Heaven," *The Observer*, November 10, 2001, www.theguardian.com/theobserver/2001/ nov/11/features.magazine37.
2. Laura Mallonee, "Startling Photos Capture Myanmar's $31 Billion Jade Mining Industry," *Wired*, May 17, 2017.
3. Sean Turnell, "Cooperative Credit in British Burma" (IDEAS Working Paper Series from RePEc, 2005), 5.
4. S. D. Sharma, ed., *Rice: Origin, Antiquity, and History* (Enfield, N.H.: Science Publishers, 2010), 459.
5. U Khin Win, *A Century of Rice Improvement in Burma*, International Rice Research Institute (Los Banos, Philippines, 1991).

6. John F. Cady, *A History of Modern Burma* (Ithaca: Cornell University Press, 1958), 72–73.

7. Bureau of International Labor Affairs, "Child Labor and Forced Labor Reports: Burma," 2016, www.dol.gov/agencies/ilab/resources/reports/child -labor/burma.

8. Ibid.

9. Turnell, "Cooperative Credit in British Burma."

10. Ibid.

11. Ibid., 15.

12. Ibid., 17.

13. Ibid., 19.

14. Government of Burma, *Report of the Land and Agriculture Committee, Part III: Agricultural Finance; Colonisation; Land Purchase* (Rangoon: Superintendent of Government Printing, 1938), 90.

15. Government of Burma, *Report of the Burma Provincial Banking Enquiry Committee, 1929–30: Volume I* (Rangoon: Superintendent of Government Printing, 1930), 176.

16. Nalini Ranjan Chakravarti, *The Indian Minority in Burma* (London: Oxford University Press for the Institute of Race Relations, 1971), 28.

17. Ibid., 8.

18. Mahatma Ghandi, "Young India" (1929), in *Young India 1919–1931*, vol. XI, ed. M. K. Gandhi (Ahmedabad, India: Navajivan Publishing House, 1981).

19. Chakravarti, *The Indian Minority in Burma*, 47.

20. Ibid., 48.

21. Hans-Bernd Zöllner, ed., Myanmar Literature Project, Working Paper No. 10:12, "Material on Thein Pe: Indo-Burman Conflict," www.phil.uni-passau .de/fileadmin/dokumente/lehrstuehle/korff/pdf/research/mlp12.pdf.

22. Donald M. Seekins, *State and Society in Modern Rangoon* (London: Routledge, 2011), 44.

23. Zöllner, "Material on Thein Pe: Indo-Burman Conflict," 133.

24. John F. Cady, *A History of Modern Burma*, 305.

25. Zöllner, "Material on Thein Pe: Indo-Burman Conflict."

26. Donald Eugene Smith, *Religion and Politics in Burma* (Princeton: Princeton University Press, 1965), 109–10. Also see Michael Adas, *The Burma Delta: Economic Development and Social Change on an Asian Rice Frontier, 1852–1941* (Madison: University of Wisconsin Press, 2011), 206.

27. Chakravarti, *The Indian Minority in Burma*, 158.

28. Ibid.

29. Zöllner, "Material on Thein Pe: Indo-Burman Conflict."

30. Kate Hodal, "Buddhist Monk Uses Racism and Rumors to Spread Hatred in

Burma," *The Guardian,* April 18, 2013, www.theguardian.com/world/2013/apr/18/buddhist-monk-spreads-hatred-burma.

31. Krishnadev Calamur, "The Misunderstood Roots of Burma's Rohingya Crisis," *The Atlantic,* www.theatlantic.com/international/archive/2017/09/rohingyas-burma/540513.

32. "UN Human Rights Chief Points to 'Textbook Example of Ethnic Cleansing' in Myanmar," UN News Centre, September 11, 2017, www.un.org/apps/news/story.asp?NewsID=57490#.WcvzChNSzXQ.

33. Max Bearak, "One Month On, a Bleak New Reality Emerges for 436,000 Rohingya Refugees," *Washington Post,* September 25, 2017.

34. Zöllner, "Material on Thein Pe: Indo-Burman Conflict."

35. Poppy McPherson, "Aung San Suu Kyi Says Myanmar Does Not Fear Scrutiny Over Rohingya Crisis," *The Guardian,* September 19, 2017, www.theguardian.com/world/2017/sep/19/aung-san-suu-kyi-myanmar-rohingya-crisis-concerned.

36. Rebecca Wright, Katie Hunt, and Joshua Berlinger, "Aung San Suu Kyi Breaks Silence on Rohingya, Sparks Storm of Criticism," CNN, September 19, 2017, www.cnn.com/2017/09/18/asia/aung-san-suu-kyi-speech-rohingya/index.html.

CHAPTER SIX

1. Benjamin Gue, *The History of Iowa* (New York: Century History, 1903).

2. Wikipedia, s.v. "Treaty of Prairie du Chien," last modified May 9, 2017, 19:19, en.wikipedia.org/wiki/Treaty_of_Prairie_du_Chien.

3. Wikipedia, s.v. "Third Treaty of Prairie du Chien," en.wikipedia.org/wiki/Third_Treaty_of_Prairie_du_Chien.

4. Native American Netroots, "The 1837 Winnebago Treaty," nativeamericannetroots.net/diary/1806.

5. Andrew Jackson, *The Papers of Andrew Jackson: Volume VII, 1829,* ed. Daniel Feller, Harold D. Moser, Laura-Eve Moss, and Thomas Coens (Knoxville: University of Tennessee Press, 2007), 541.

6. Charles J. Kappler, ed., "Indian Affairs: Laws and Treaties," Oklahoma State University Digital Collection, digital.library.okstate.edu/kappler/Vol2/treaties/win0300.htm.

7. A. R. Fulton, *The Red Men of Iowa* (Des Moines: Mills & Co., 1882), 148.

8. "Fort Atkinson and the Winnebago Occupation of Iowa, 1840–1849," University of Iowa Office of the State Archaeologist, archaeology.uiowa.edu/files/archaeology.uiowa.edu/files/FtAtkinson9.pdf.

9. Fulton, *Red Men of Iowa,* 150.

10. Ibid.
11. Todd Arrington, "Exodusters," National Park Service online, www.nps.gov/home/learn/historyculture/exodusters.htm.

CHAPTER SEVEN

1. *Luxembourgers in the New World*, ed. Jean Ensch, Jean-Claude Müller, and Robert E. Owen. Revised edition based on Nicholas Gonner's *Die Luxemburger in der Neuen Welt*, vol. 1 (Esch-sur-Alzette, Luxembourg: Editions-Reliures Schortgen, 1987).
2. Gale, Cengage Learning, "German Immigration," bit.ly/1voEt29.
3. IAGenWeb Project, "Norwegian Immigration into Allamakee Co., Iowa, Article #1," iagenweb.org/allamakee/ImNat/norweg_tx.htm.
4. FamilySearch.org Wiki, "United States Naturalization and Citizenship," familysearch.org/wiki/en/United_States_Naturalization_and_Citizenship.

CHAPTER NINE

1. Myo Mint, *The Politics of Survival in Burma: Diplomacy and Statecraft in the Reign of King Mindon, 1853–1878* (Ithaca: Cornell University Southeast Asia Program, 1987), 210.
2. James Stuart Olson and Robert Shadle, eds., *Historical Dictionary of the British Empire* (Westport, Conn.: Greenwood, 1996), 2:1088.
3. David Joel Steinberg, ed., *In Search of Southeast Asia: A Modern History* (New York: Praeger, 1971).
4. William J. Topich and Keith A. Leitich, *The History of Myanmar* (Santa Barbara, Calif.: Greenwood), 48.
5. Thant Myint-U, *The River of Lost Footsteps: Histories of Burma* (New York: Farrar Straus and Giroux, 2006).

CHAPTER TEN

1. "Warning Letter, Document Number: GEN1300666, Re: Personal Genome Service (PGS)," U.S. Food and Drug Administration, U.S. Department of Health and Human Services, November 22, 2013, www.fda.gov/ICECI/EnforcementActions/WarningLetters/ucm376296.htm.
2. David Dobbs, "The F.D.A. vs. Personal Genetics Testing," *New Yorker*, November 27, 2013, www.newyorker.com/tech/elements/the-f-d-a-vs-personal-genetic-testing.

3. Paul Tassin, "23andMe DNA Testing Kit Class Action Settlement," September 19, 2017, topclassactions.com/lawsuit-settlements/lawsuit-news/820889-23andme-dna-testing-kit-class-action-settlement.

4. Andrew Pollack, "23andMe Will Resume Giving Users Health Data," *The New York Times*, October 21, 2015, www.nytimes.com/2015/10/21/business/23andme-will-resume-giving-users-health-data.html. Also see Anne Wojcicki, "A Note to Our Customers Regarding the FDA," 23andMe blog, February 19, 2015, blog.23andme.com/news/a-note-to-our-customers-regarding-the-fda, and FDA News Release, "FDA Permits Marketing of First Direct-to-Consumer Genetic Carrier Test for Bloom Syndrome," U.S. Food and Drug Administration, February 19, 2015, www.fda.gov/newsevents/newsroom/pressannouncements/ucm435003.htm.

5. Ian Urbina, "Again, Jews Fault Mormons Over Posthumous Baptisms," *The New York Times*, December 21, 2003, www.nytimes.com/2003/12/21/nyregion/again-jews-fault-mormons-over-posthumous-baptisms.html.

6. Tom Heneghan, "Will Pope Benedict Become a Mormon After He Dies?" *Reuters*, February 5, 2007, www.washingtonpost.com/wp-dyn/content/article/2007/02/05/AR2007020500445.html. Also see Howard Berkes, "Mormon Church Limits Access to Controversial Baptism Rules," National Public Radio, March 9, 2012, www.npr.org/sections/thetwoway/2012/03/09/148318491/mormon-church-limits-access-to-controversial-baptism-records.

7. Mark Oppenheimer, "A Twist on Posthumous Baptisms Leaves Jews Miffed at Mormon Rite," *The New York Times*, March 2, 2012, www.nytimes.com/2012/03/03/us/jews-take-issue-with-posthumous-mormon-baptisms-beliefs.html.

8. Michael Levenson, "Mormons Baptized Slain Reporter Daniel Pearl," *Boston Globe*, February 29, 2012, www.bostonglobe.com/news/nation/2012/02/28/mormons-posthumously-baptized-wall-street-journal-reporter-daniel-pearl-who-was-killed-terrorists/7BJlGNn5gHxNvuHoso5eoI/story.html.

9. Ibid.

CHAPTER THIRTEEN

1. Steph Yin, "Why Do We Inherit Mitochondrial DNA Only from Our Mothers?," *New York Times*, June 23, 2016, www.nytimes.com/2016/06/24/science/mitochondrial-dna-mothers.html.

2. Charmaine D. Royal et al., "Inferring Genetic Ancestry: Opportunities, Challenges, and Implications," *American Journal of Human Genetics* 86(5) (2010): 661–73, www.ncbi.nlm.nih.gov/pmc/articles/PMC2869013.

3. Matthew Miller, "Shrewd, Very Shrewd," *Forbes*, March 1, 2004, www.forbes
.com/global/2004/0301/032.html.

4. Joe Bauman and Brice Wallace, "Inventor James L. Sorenson Dies at 86,"
Deseret Morning News, January 21, 2008, www.deseretnews.com/article/
695245817/Inventor-James-L-Sorenson-dies-at-86.html.

5. Matthew Miller, "Shrewd, Very Shrewd."

6. Jim Mustian, "New Orleans Filmmaker Cleared in Cold Case Murder," *The
New Orleans Advocate*, March 13, 2015, www.theadvocate.com/new_orleans/
news/article_1b3a3f96-d574-59e0-9c6a-c3c7c0d2f166.html.

7. Pew Research Center, "A Portrait of Mormons in the U.S.," July 24, 2009,
www.pewforum.org/2009/07/24/a-portrait-of-mormons-in-the-us.

8. CeCeMoore, "My Review of AncestryDNA's Admixture Tool and a Glimpse
into the Future of Genetic Genealogy," June 26, 2012, www.yourgenetic
genealogist.com/2012/06/my-review-of-ancestrydnas-admixture.html.

9. Charmaine D. Royal et al., "Inferring Genetic Ancestry: Opportunities,
Challenges, and Implications."

CHAPTER FOURTEEN

1. Kim Tallbear, *Native American DNA: Tribal Belonging and the False Promise of
Genetic Science* (Minneapolis: University of Minnesota Press, 2013).

2. "Remarks by the President, Prime Minister Tony Blair of England (via sat-
ellite), Dr. Francis Collins, Director of the National Human Genome Research Institute, and Dr. Craig Venter, President and Chief Scientific Officer,
Celera Genomics Corporation, on the Completion of the First Survey of the
Entire Human Genome Project," White House press release, June 26, 2000,
www.genome.gov/10001356/june-2000-white-house-event. Also see Duana
Fullwiley, "The 'Contemporary Synthesis': When Politically Inclusive Genomic Science Relies on Biological Notions of Race," *Isis* 105, no. 4 (December 2014): 803–14, www.journals.uchicago.edu/doi/10.1086/679427.

3. Ruha Benjamin, "A Lab of Their Own: Genomic Sovereignty as Postcolonial
Science Policy," *Policy and Society* 28 (2009): 341–55.

4. Deborah Bolnick et al., "The Science and Business of Genetic Ancestry Testing," *Science*, April 25, 2011, 399–400.

5. Ibid.

6. Jennifer K. Wagner et al., "Attitudes of Genetics Professionals and Anthropologists Toward Race, Ancestry, and Genetics: Results of a National Survey," *American Journal of Physical Anthropology*, November 2016.

PHOTO: © SAM KASS

ALEX WAGNER is a television and print journalist. She lives in New York City with her husband, son, and cat. This is her first book.

Twitter: @alexwagner

To inquire about booking Alex Wagner for a speaking engagement, please contact the Penguin Random House Speakers Bureau at speakers@penguinrandomhouse.com.